Follow My Dust!

A biography of
ARTHUR UPFIELD

By Jessica Hawke

With an introduction by
DETECTIVE INSPECTOR
NAPOLEON BONAPARTE

ETT IMPRINT, SYDNEY

1 The author with Arthur Upfield

ETT IMPRINT
PO Box R1906
Royal Exchange NSW 1225
Australia

This book is copyright. Apart from any fair dealing for the purposes
of private study, research, criticism or review, as permitted under the
Copyright Act, no part may be reproduced by any process without written
permission. Inquiries should be addressed to the publishers.

First published by William Heinemann 1957
This edition published by ETT Imprint, Exile Bay 2015

Copyright © Don Uren, 2015

ISBN 978-1-925416-10-7
ISBN 978-1-875892-92-1 ebook

CONTENTS

	An Introduction	vii
1	The Man to Be	11
2	Off to Gaol	19
3	Signing Rent Books	34
4	Where All are Bastards	52
5	One Spur Dick	71
6	The Red Irishman	97
7	Wandering Millie	113
8	'Wire Five Quid!'	133
9	The Amateur Bull-Fighter	157
10	Hen-House Brew	175
11	It in Satin Pants	207
12	The Debonair Murderer	237
13	A Lamb in the Jungle	254

ILLUSTRATIONS

The author with Arthur Upfield	ii
A monarch iguana	95
A chain of caterpillars	95
A tame kangaroo	96
Wild dog puppies looking for their mother	96
An aboriginal lady	111
Blackfellow's letter-stick	111
A sandhill: the background of *Death of a Swagman*	112
The sandhill has blown across the track since the utility was last this way	112
Upfield at his desk	131
The dray from the rear, where Upfield wrote *The Sands of Windee*	131
The Brooking Range, East Kimberley: the background for *Cake in the Hat Box*	132
The Wolf Creek meteorite crater, described in *Cake in the Hat Box*	132
Upfield at the time he met the original of 'Bony'	233
Upfield with Mr. James L Hole in 1950	234
The rain-shed where Rowles and Ritchie found Ryan and Lloyd	235
John Thomas Smith, *alias* Snowy Rowles	235
The residue of the fires which consumed the body of Carron	236

ARTHUR W. UPFIELD

HIS
EPITAPH TO BE

A boy: every wind blew fair.

A youth: he mutinied.

A young man: he wrecked the ship.

Then he built another.

AN INTRODUCTION

I am able clearly to recall my first meeting with Arthur Upfield. It came about when I was myself embattled with forces tending to push me down to the nomadic existence and mental outlook of my mother's people, for, you should know, my mother was an aborigine and my father was a white Australian. I knew neither parent, and, when a small baby, had been found with my dead mother beneath a sandalwood tree, and was cared for and reared by the Mission Matron. To her I owe a first-class education, and the eradication of an inferiority complex threatened by duality of race.

I had engaged sporadically in police work, and had taken employment as a stockman on a station in the south-west of Queensland, when Arthur Upfield was brought to my hut to work with me. I was not at the hut when Upfield arrived, and I found him baking a brownie and cooking dinner. In the kitchen, we stood either side the table and took stock of each other.

He was of my own age–thirty. He was dressed as any stockman of that time dressed. He was tall, lean, hard. Brown hair grew a little low on his forehead, which was narrow, and the back of his head was broader and higher than the face, indicating a minus concentration and a plus imagination; and, I observed, his ears were fawn-like, denoting quick thinking, and his mouth was mobile and hinted at a sense of humour. About the chin there was a trace of sensuality and arrogance.

His smile of welcome was swift, the smile lighting his hazel eyes, and any reserve I may have had was banished by the outstretched hand and the warmth of its clasp. He spoke rapidly, and when animated was inclined to slur his words. Absence of reserve in him overcame my own, and, when we sat down to his dinner of curry and rice and stewed apricots, I found myself answering a barrage of questions. Should the answer of necessity be prolonged by detail, quite often he would not be listening, so anxious was he to put his next question. Many of his questions were of so personal a nature that I had to evade them until much later when I came to know him better.

As a horseman he passed, but without honours. He had much to learn as a cattleman, but then cattlemen are born, and southern England doesn't produce cattlemen. By white stockmen standards he could read tracks passably well; he could cook above average, and he liked poker, which I never did. What commended him chiefly to me was his thirst for knowledge. He never attempted to impress me, and never betrayed a hint of superiority over me.

Thus within a week I informed him on matters I would not speak of to any of a hundred other men. It was almost a pleasure to tell him that my registered name is Leon Wood. The subject of the aborigines, the totemic structure of their society, the powers of their magic men, their letter-sticks and smoke signals, he returned to time and time again. Having watched together a migration of rabbits, his questioning concerning these rodents, as well as the migration of rats and mice farther north, became almost embarrassing by its persistence.

I was compelled to acknowledge slight bafflement to myself. Here was a man seeking information and obviously assimilating it, and yet the standard of his education was much lower than my own–but not on all points. A probe now and then proved that he knew very little of algebra, nothing of the higher mathematics, very little of Latin, and was entirely ignorant of Greek. He had me on English history, and on the first great voyages.

We were five months together, and his companionship did much to bring about certain decisions I was able to make relative to my own future. Neither of us was at all put out when the station reorganised its manpower, and we left to travel together for a few miles before parting.

Shortly after this, I received a special appointment within the

Queensland Police Department, and years later an assignment took me into western New South Wales, and to my second meeting with Arthur Upfield. He was now working as cook at a place called Wheeler's Well, but when I visited there he had no one for whom to cook, and I wondered how he endured this loneliness, as he seemed happy enough and showed no effect of solitude.

Upfield was now more matured, much less excitable, more aware of responsibility to himself. He hadn't lost the habit of firing questions like bullets, but he had gained the patience to listen fully to the answers. Having followed him into the kitchen, and eventually having opportunity to note its extreme tidiness, I saw at the end of the table, against a wall, a shallow wood box partially filled with foolscap, and this provided such interest that, on my friend leaving the kitchen for a minute, I could not forbear investigation.

And in that box was the solution of several mysteries concerning my friend.

The idiosyncrasies were all explained. The shape of his head should have elucidated them for me long before, for I am no stranger to the teachings of the great Italian, Lombroso. The unusual mixture of humility and arrogance, the unusual combination of patience and impatience, and a contempt for the human herd together with a passion to study the herd's instincts, all indicated the individualist, the rebel, and the sensualist in one. Circumstances could have made this man a great criminal, a great crusader. Inherited attributes are more often than not submerged by unfavourable circumstances, or opportunities wrongly timed.

About a month after I bade farewell to Upfield at Wheeler's Well, I received from him a letter in which he said he was writing a novel of crime detection and that he had decided to build his investigator on me and name him Napoleon Bonaparte. In modern parlance: just like that. Obviously I could not fail to be interested in the career of this fictional character destined to become popular in the Americas, Great Britain and many countries of Europe. I have, of course, read all the chronicles for which I have supplied most of the basic material, but my main interest has been in the evolution of a man who has surmounted obstacles even greater than those with which I have had to contend, and, moreover, has achieved a commendable degree of success without having battered down competitors to do so. No outstandingly successful man in commerce or politics may claim that. From Log Cabin to White House is a much easier road than that followed by Arthur Upfield, and, also, very truly yours,

Napoleon Bonaparte, D.I., Queensland P.D.

CHAPTER ONE

THE MAN TO BE

I

Toward the close of the nineteenth century, Gosport, England, was a fortified town, and a main supply base of the British Navy. Situated on the western side of Portsmouth Harbour, it might be thought that Gosport was merely a suburb of the greater town, when actually the growth and maintenance of British sea power and the threat to England by the Emperor Napoleon Bonaparte contributed to the preservation of Gosport's independence.

To Gosportonians the Navy came first. The very mention of the Senior Service almost caused the hearer to pull his forelock or raise his hat, while the Army, although greatly respected, remained in the background until the Boer War again brought it into prominence. They had a sublime faith in the Navy, their living came from the Navy, they were ever one with the Navy, and God help old Boney if he landed the Grand Army either side of the harbour and tried to storm the chain of forts, and the earthworks connecting them, which protected Gosport.

From the land side, you could enter Gosport only by one of the few bridges spanning the moat, and then through a tunnel in the rampart, or you could cross the harbour from Portsmouth by ferry. Shortly after the Napoleonic threat had faded to St. Helena, there landed from a ferry an Oliver Upfield, to become an assistant in the shop of a draper on the High Street, and eventually to set up in business for himself, choosing rambling premises in a street which had become the main outlet to the new suburb of Forton springing up outside the rampart. The premises were renovated and became a compact structure, having some thirty- odd rooms above the shop.

Oliver Upfield married into the Way family, a member of which subsequently became the Chief Justice for South Australia, and, for a term, Deputy Governor. On the other side of the picture was an Upfield who was in America when the Civil War broke out. He also was a business man, and something of an inventor, for it is recorded that he manufactured a clothes prop which he hawked up and down the country, incidentally collecting military information and making extra profit. He ended his career at the extremity of a rope, and therefore was regarded with some disfavour by those at home.

To Oliver Upfield were born seven children, of whom James was the eldest. He grew to become much like Oliver: shrewd in business and generous to the limits of wisdom. James entered his father's business, eventually became a partner, and ultimately the sole proprietor.

As James's two brothers passed from this business to distant places, so the shop staff increased until there were a dozen or more assistants living in. Old Oliver stood for no nonsense by his sons with his female assistants, and he pressed on James advice which James came to pass on to his sons. Excellent advice, too, for a young man whose father has made himself financially sound, but advice at which Cupid thumbs his nose. There came to join the staff a young girl from Birmingham. Eighteen she was, and, according to pictures of her, truly lovely. James was twenty-six when he married Annie Barmore, and to them were born five sons, the first being the subject of this record.

2

The child was registered and christened William Arthur, but when the shop boys began to ask after little Bill, the aunts and the grandmother had the names reversed, as Arthur was less likely to be degraded. However, temporarily they had forgotten the influence of Charles Dickens and the child came to be called Arker-Willum.

Arker-Willum entered a world composed of Queen Victorias, circuses, jubilees, naval reviews, military bands, and naval and military pickets who appeared to have fluttering eyelids at sight of the nurse-girl in charge of him.

There were several Queen Victorias–three, in fact. There was Grandmother Way and her two unmarried sisters who always dressed like the Queen, even inside the house. Grandfather and grandmother had left the business premises to live in the later-established suburb which was swiftly to extend to the outer residential area named Alverstoke. The sisters owned, above all things, a butchery business, and their treasured and only male assistant was a person named Pafford. Pafford took in the sides of beef and carcasses of mutton, and cut them up. Pafford delivered meat to customers per handcart. Pafford it was who kept his eyes on dogs that entered with their owners.

When visiting Grandmother Way on Sunday afternoons anecdotes about Pafford caused these ladies to laugh softly, and the one about Pafford and the customer's dog served for many weeks. Pafford was exceptionally ugly; the customer was a grand dame who alighted from a brougham and swept into the shop followed by the poodle. She was paying her account when the poodle cocked a leg against the chopping block. Then the dog yelped and fled to the carriage without. Miss Way said sternly, "Pafford! What did you do to that dog?" Pafford replied, innocently, "Nothing, mum. I only looked at him."

These Queen Victorias were to have great influence on Arker-Willum, marriage placing many burdens on his young mother. As a bride she found herself mistress of a multi-roomed house, three domestics and a house boy. She had to order and check supplies to feed the assistants living in, and even in those days, when a cook left on impulse, she had to do most of the cooking, teaching herself to cook with the aid of Mrs. Beeton. The monthly household accounts had to be audited and passed to the office, where the chief cashier would write the cheques. And on every occasion there was a storm of protest by her husband before signing the cheques.

What with all this added to the succession of babies, it is remarkable that at the age of sixty Annie Barmore had not one grey hair. She never had the depth of wisdom possessed by her mother-in-law, but she learned much from the older woman whose advice was: "When your husband raves about bad trade and the terrible cost of living, remember that trade was always bad and living costs always terrible. The good wife bides her time. All the Upfields are rampant lions one minute and docile little lambs the next. And remember, too, that all the Upfields are genuine lambs, and only imitation lions."

The year following William Arthur's appearance, there came Edward, and the year's difference in age was almost unmarked when both could walk. They were taken out in the same pram, and were invited together to children's parties. When a circus came to pitch its tents in the park outside the rampart, they were placed in one of the wide lead-covered window-boxes overlooking the street. Far down the street the first outriders would appear, and then came the gilded thrones and the gilded chariots, all drawn by magnificent horses–the circus of Lord George Sanger.

There was the Diamond Jubilee. All ironclads in the harbour fired salute guns. The *Victory* moored off the Gosport side of the harbour, and all ships, all windows of the houses either side of the harbour were gay with bunting. At night all ships were outlined with lights and into the sky sped rockets. And the children were carried upstairs to the top floor, up the ladder to the skylight, and so to the roof, from which this fairy scene could be viewed.

An open cab would be hired to take the family to the Haslar Wall, to see the old *Victoria and Albert* steaming out from harbour, and on board was the great Queen, who was never seen by the family who waved and cheered across the mile or so of water. Time passed, a long long time, and one evening the boys were taken to a children's party. Like all parties, it was a joyful event, until abruptly a shadow fell and the voices stilled, and all the children were sent home. News had come of the Queen's death, and the awful solemnity of it entered childish minds not yet able to encompass the fact of death.

The two boys attended a school but a short distance from the rail crossing where the branch line entered the naval victualling yard. They saw the soldiers standing at this crossing and watched the engine appear from the great gates to the yard, then the few carriages, and the draped coffin seen through the windows of one.

The passing of that funeral train marked the end of an era for Arker- Willum, for whom era was to follow era throughout life.

3

To relieve pressure on the home front, Arker-Willum went to live with his grandparents and an unmarried aunt.

Their house was spacious, and had a secluded front lawn, a carriage driveway bordered by beech trees, and a rear garden, where around a central lawn were espaliered apple trees. Near the back wall of brick grew a fine russet apple tree, and beyond the wall lay a new world–the green playing fields of the new barracks occupied by the Royal Marines.

Grandfather Upfield, as many of his generation and class, was stern yet generous, and like his peers the motto by which he lived was 'My word is my bond'. He was tall and lean and upright. He wore a white square-cut beard and his grey eyes could be penetrating. When setting out to attend business, or a meeting of the town council, invariably he wore a frock-coat and a tall grey hat.

Grandmother was vivacious, intensely practical, and she possessed the gift of diplomacy which maintained her position as ruler of the family without her husband ever suspecting it.

At this time their youngest daughter was unmarried, and her tasks were to assist the old people, watch over the small nephew and supervise two domestics. She was gay, yet could be tight-mouthed, for in her were all the attributes of her parents. She was a great ally to her mother in managing father.

Without fail the family walked the full mile to the Alverstoke church, passing along the elm-lined road, then taking the high-hedged lane crossing farm land to the outer township of Alverstoke. Crocuses heralded the spring, may trees blossomed and the new leaves were delightful to chew. Finally the blackberries bloomed and the fruit was ever enticing. To the child, Lovers' Lane was always fairyland inhabited by gnomes and elves.

On one occasion as they returned from church, this sylvan world was utterly shattered. Grandfather abruptly began a tirade about the household expenses.

"That milk account!" exploded the old gentleman. "Surely we do not use all that milk?"

"Ratty checked it," replied grandmother. "Beside, we have Arker- Willum with us. He has to have as much milk as possible. You know very well he is chesty, and the doctor . . ."

"All right! All right! We'll pass that. But tell me, how did we come to burn three tons of coal, when Mathews sawed up that storm-blown elm? I don't understand it. It must stop. We have to reduce our spending in conformity with our income."

"I quite agree," gently spoke grandmother. "What did you think of Mr. Watson's reading of the Second Lesson?"

"We will confine ourselves to finance and discuss our spiritual reaction to the new curate at a more appropriate time. We shall certainly have to dispense with Millie." Millie! Why, Millie was the child's favourite of the two domestics. "George will have to be told to work only three days a week. The expenses must be brought down."

"Very well. We'll do all we can," came the soft sweet voice of the woman who obeyed.

So it went on all the way home. A tacit silence engulfed the family throughout dinner. Arker-Willum was warned to be seen but not heard, and to leave not one tiny scrap on his plate.

Following the enormous dinner, grandmother retired to her room, and grandfather stalked to the back garden, where he reclined in a chair in the shade of the great apple tree, draped a silk handkerchief over his face, and relaxed. After the chores were done, the domestics retired to their room, and the aunt chose the scripture stories to be read by the nephew.

About half-past three the house came back to normal. Cook prepared afternoon tea in the semi-basement kitchen, and grandmother appeared and went into conference with the aunt. A folded table was taken out and silently put up beside grandfather. Chairs were brought, the aunt set down the tray of tea-things, and grandmother began to pour. "Wake up, Father. Tea is waiting," she said, and off came the silk handkerchief, and upright sat the martinet. "H'm! Tea! Time has flown, to be sure. What have you been up to, Arker-Willum?"

"Reading about David, Grandpa." "Indeed. Quite a hero, wasn't he?"

"Yes, Grandpa," replied the boy, just a shade doubtful that grandfather's approbation of David was quite one hundred per cent.

Grandfather sighed, sipped his tea, ate a cake. He said: "Astonishing how time flies. It will soon be your birthday again, Arker-Willum. Soon the stormy winds will blow, and what will the robin do then, poor thing? Yes, before we realise it, the summer will have flown. We must take advantage of what remains of fit. We shall go to Scotland this year."

So to Scotland they went for five weeks–trains and carriages, mountains and valleys. Edinburgh and the Highlands. Trips on the lochs. And those terrible ogres, expenses and bad trade, were left behind in the old oak chest.

Arker-Willum was taxed one tea-time with leaving sugar in his teacup. Out came the old cliché: 'Waste not, want not'. Grandfather promised one penny a week if Arker-Willum dispensed with sugar in his tea. That suited the boy, but the aunt protested that sugar was essential. Grandfather agreed, and then pointed out that the tuppence a week pocket money was doubtless spent on sugar in the form of sweets. He had a good ally. Never since that offer did Arker-Willum take sugar in his tea or coffee, and in later years when he volunteered to wash dishes in a world minus domestic help, discovery of wasted sugar in a tea-cup always annoyed him.

CHAPTER TWO

OFF TO GAOL

I

Those early years spent with the grandparents were to exert a lasting influence over the man-to-be. Young Arthur William met his brothers only when at school, which was then Bond's Academy, and situated about a mile nearer the centre of Gosport. School was seldom continuous save during the summer, for there were long periods when the boy was confined to his room with bronchitis.

Home discipline, if not quite so rigid, was decidedly beneficial. School homework to be done without aid, and without rebellion. A time to rise and a time to go off to bed. And there were periods when quietness was imposed should grandfather be unwell, or grandmother confined to her room.

Rules obeyed, life was good. Affection was bestowed generously, and the threatened spoiling by the old people was capably balanced by the forethought of the aunt. The boy received every possible advantage. He was the eldest son of the eldest son, and they dreamed dreams for and of him.

Disraeli was dead. Gladstone was lowered into the crypt of Westminster Abbey. Queen Victoria had passed through Gosport from the Isle of Wight to be received by her mourning subjects in London. The Boer War ended and the troops came home, and all the boys and girls stared and cheered Roberts and Kitchener and Buller, when the latter appeared in the dark green uniform of the King's Royal Rifles to lead the regiment to Holy Trinity Church on Sunday mornings. A new and glorious era was beginning.

There was no room for anti-British feeling, either in Gosport or Portsmouth. The Lloyd Georges of those times never dared to run around these towns. The greatest literary figure was Rudyard Kipling, the most loved was Charles Dickens, and in the home of young Upfield, Ralph Connor was chief favourite.

The march of events was presented to the boy through the pages of the *Illustrated London News*, and for him national figures became persons quite likely to call at the house. Beyond these great people, from Disraeli to General Sir Redvers Buller, were a group of others equally real: Mr. Pickwick, Mrs. Bardell, Mr. Snodgrass, Alice and those extraordinary people she met at the other side of the looking-glass. And beyond even these, in a place where they wore strange clothes, were yet other real people, such as David and Moses, and Matthew and John, and the gentle Christ.

Periodically there came to the house a man who had a round red face, light blue eyes, and a ready smile. He came to visit the aunt, and when they set out on a walk, there was a scene because the boy was not to go with them. There came another aunt from America, and with her husband, who seemed to do little but lie on a sofa and be coaxed off to bed even before the boy's time. Then there was a flurry of activity, when all the men wore top-hats and frock-coats, and all the younger women donned new dresses with leg-of-mutton sleeves. Arthur William's father and mother were both there that day, and his father and uncles tied dozens of old boots to the back axle of the carriage which bore away the gay aunt and the man with the round face and the light blue eyes.

2

For a space Arthur William lived with his parents and brothers, of whom there were now four, and when he again went to live with the grandparents, the man who had so long reclined on the couch had gone, and the aunt wore sombre black, and always a bonnet with long black ribbons.

At first, almost every fine afternoon he accompanied this aunt to the cemetery and watched her kneeling beside the grave and snipping the grass with cutters as she watered it with her tears. It appeared that she had much in common with the cemetery manager–tall and cadaverous body, weak brown eyes, long red nose. Sometimes he cried with her. Sometimes at lunch or at dinner the aunt would abruptly burst into tears, and be chided by the grandmother for lack of control. This behaviour always cast a gloom over the boy, to be dispersed only when he could escape into the garden.

When winter came, there were long periods in bed suffering from bronchitis, and then father would come with toys and books, and, inevitably, copies of the *Illustrated London News*.

During the summer months the boy would lie abed and watch the day depart, and nothing delighted him more, winter or summer, than to watch the clouds, and people them with beings from the books read to him.

It was when he was confined to bed that his grandfather died, after a short illness, and then there were two widows dressed alike. When grandma's sisters, the butchers now retired, called to take tea and talk wittily, there were four Queen Victorias, save that the sisters did not wear black ribbons.

Grandfather's passing hurt. Thereafter, Arthur William would not eat an apple from grandfather's favourite tree. But he climbed all the trees, the back wall overlooking the nursery and the division wall of the next garden, owned by a doctor. The neighbour came to believe that Arthur William was interested in his apples and strawberries, and so espied the box on the flat roof of a summer house abutting this party wall. He noted that the boy climbed the wall to reach the roof and to peer into the box, and sometimes stealthily to remove an article, appear to clean it with his handkerchief and replace it.

Curiosity drove him. Hearing that Arthur William was again confined to bed, he placed a ladder against the wall and reached for the box, an old tin one. Within it he found grandpa's half-topper, together with the handkerchief serving as a duster.

Quite often, headed by their band, the Royal Marines would march by, and sometimes the King's Royal Rifles would pass, and came the time when this regiment included detachments from the Colonies which had come to take part in the Coronation of Edward VII.

In mid-summer, when the apples fell, the boy would gather them and place them with exactitude on the rear lawn; the band, the position of all officers, accurately copied. Following a naval review at Spithead, the apples were made to represent the ships; ten apples in a packed line for each battleship, six for each cruiser, four for a destroyer, two for a torpedo boat. Every ship would be in the correct position according to the boy's observation when taken on a passenger ship to view the fleet.

The last act of this period was dominated by a Christmas tree.

As grandma was confined to her bed, she had a large tree placed in her bedroom, and the entire Christmas Eve was given up to dressing the tree and fruiting it with presents. Then it was covered with a dust-sheet until the following evening, when arrived all the grandsons and the one granddaughter. Arthur William had to be the M.C., but it was a most successful party, and when a week or two later grandma settled to sleep the long sleep she spoke of the children and the tree.

3

The passing of Grandma Upfield brought to a close a period in the life of Arthur Upfield, and began another which in all respects was parallel with the greater changes which swept over Great Britain with the Coronation of Edward VII. It was as though everything, from ships to newspapers, horse-drawn public conveyances to the railways, schools, libraries and shops, all were changed in the few succeeding years.

The high-sided ironclads vanished to give place to warships lower on the water, faster, sleeker, culminating in the naval triumph of the dreadnought. The horse-drawn trams stopped, the roads were torn up, and the rails laid for electric trams. The street lights of incandescent gas gave way to modern electric standards. Powerful engines replaced the puff-and-snort locomotives on the railways. And new ways of shop window dressing were studied by business people, new methods of accountancy, new schemes devised to meet increased competition.

Arthur left the sheltered world of quiet affection, where most things came his way without competition, to enter a world in which his parents were fully occupied with business, and where he had to compete with his brothers. They were Edward, a year younger, Frank, two years younger than Edward, toddler Nelson, born on Trafalgar Day, and John, a small baby.

There was no crowding, not in that enormous house over the business premises. At the rear was an enclosed yard providing excellent playing room, and long vacant stables with a large loft which became the play-place in wet weather. What saved Arthur from jealousy created by competition was that, having had to adventure alone, he now adventured in company.

There was always the harbour. There was the 'Green' more often than not stacked with great logs which provided the planks and masts and spars for yachts and small ships, and close by were the shipyards of Camper & Nicholson, who built the series of Shamrocks, and the 'lofts' where the sails were made. And, when bicycles came, there was Haslar Creek, beyond which was the Naval Hospital and outlying forts, and Stoke's Bay, to which the railway was extended; and Porchester Castle, a vast heap of masonry set on a perfect lawn of many acres.

Arthur did have important advantages over his brothers. He had received the concentrated attention of several women; they had had to compete with business for the attention of their parents. Arthur had lived in a vastly different world, a world where dwelt the heroes of books, the heroes beyond the seas. Because of this, not because he was the eldest, he became the leader in games and mischief. His inventiveness in this direction possibly outweighed his failing of being a bad loser.

The shop was opened at eight-thirty, and remained open until nine in the evening, but on Saturday night it remained open and doing good business at eleven o'clock. It seemed that the only reason for the shops not remaining open after midnight on Christmas Eve had a religious basis; and for the first hour of Christmas the Upfield shop was open only to the assistants, who might then select any present they wished.

Discipline of the boys was more rigid on Sundays. First, Sunday School, after which all the boys and girls would march two by two to the Methodist Chapel off the High Street. Here the parents would join the children in the family pew. Sunday School again in the afternoon, a full two hours. Chapel again in the evening. No games were permitted on Sunday. Of books there were many, and there was always one of the assistants or a domestic willing to read to the younger children.

After chapel, supper. After supper the real get-together in the drawing-room, where father told stories of his early adventures, and replied as best he might to questions such as: "Is it true the Navy's going to build a submarine like the one in *Twenty Thousand Leagues Under the Sea*? How big will it be? How fast will it go?" And: "Mr. W. said that soon they'll be able to telegraph without wires. Is he right?" In those days it was never: "Hey, Dad, what about a drive in the car?" Cars were something of a wonder; catapults could be more easily acquired.

There was a well in the centre of the building, based on a skylight over a portion of the main shop. The boys were playing marbles in the yard when father appeared from the rear door. He wore a small black imperial beard. His eyes were dark, and they could stare or laugh, hold you like the point of a sword, or encompass you with a warming glow.

At this moment his eyes were masked. He held in his hand a glass marble. To Arthur he said:

"You see this marble? Some wretched boy must have fired it up into the air, because it dropped down through the skylight and almost hit a lady customer. Did you fire it with a catapult?"

"No, Dad."

"Well now, would you do something for me?"

"Yes, Dad."

"Take this marble to Inspector Smith at the police station. Tell him I sent you, and tell him how it must have been fired into the air by a boy with a catapult, and would he try to find the culprit."

"All right, Dad."

Wide-eyed concern in the eyes of the brothers. Off went Arthur to the police station, where one had to pass through iron gates in a high stone wall, along a wide stone-paved space bordered by prison cells, the court, the quarters for unmarried constables, the officers' quarters, and the charge office.

Inspector Smith was seated at his desk. He was large and red, and sported a handle-bar moustache. Like the constable at the charge desk known by young Upfield, Inspector Smith was a familiar figure. He sat back and listened to the tale, nodding his head gravely, and uttering noises expressive of horror.

"Bad, young man. Very bad," he said. "We'll have to investigate this affair. My word, that customer in your father's shop could easily have been killed, couldn't she?"

Solemnly Arthur agreed. The interview was going off quite well, until:

"I wonder, now." The inspector stood and held the marble against the light. "This tells me a story." He rummaged in a drawer and produced a magnifying glass with which he gave long attention to the marble. "Looks like you fired this. Did you?"

"No, Inspector," replied Arthur.

"Turn out your pockets on to the desk."

A whistle, marbles, odds and ends. Finally the catapult, a real beauty. "Ah!" breathed the big man, leaning forward to glare at the weapon.

"So you did fire it, didn't you, young feller?"

The stubborn liar: "No, Inspector."

The inspector pounded a bell and a constable appeared. He roared: "Lock him up."

Bawling, the criminal was gripped by an iron vice shaped like a hand, and was conducted to the cells. Bawling, the criminal was locked in, and between yells he heard the slow and ponderous feet march along the corridor. An hour passed, and he still snivelled, and then the lesson was spoiled by a woman. The bolt was shot back and there appeared Mrs. Inspector Smith, as large as her spouse and as red of face.

"You poor mite! I never heard of such a thing! Locking you up like this. You come along with me. Dry your tears. Come along."

A softer hand this time, a hand holding a hand. Out of the cell, along the corridor and into the early evening sunshine, across the police yard and into a private door, and thence to a kitchen where the table was laden with buttery muffins. At the table, the large Inspector Smith in his shirt-sleeves.

He waited until the snivelling ended and the guest was eating. "Just tell me the truth, Arthur. That's all."

"Yes, I shot the ally."

The inspector's eyes widened, his face widened, he was the picture of astonishment.

"Then why ever didn't you say so?"

"Say so!" echoed his wife. "How could he when you frightened the life out of him? Never you mind, Arthur. But listen to me. Never tell fibs. If you do wrong, own up to it."

"Of course," supported the inspector. "By the way, how high did you shoot that marble?"

"Out of sight, Inspector Smith. I'm sorry. I won't..."

He was going to say 'do it again', but the policeman cut in with:

"Good! Don't ever tell lies again. And never fire a shot up into the air. You know, what goes up gotta come down. And never fire without a target. So easy to hurt someone."

The weapon appeared from thin air. "You promise to be very careful in future?"

"Yes, Inspector."

"I mean about telling lies."

"Yes, Inspector."

"Good. Take your cat. and be off home."

They smiled at him, and the grandmother and the blessed aunts came through so that he thanked Mrs. Smith for the tea and muffins before clearing out fast. It was a good lesson, but not to be learned for many a year. What was learned was never to lie unless the cover-up was especially good.

But they were good times, sensible times. . . . The police were able to co-operate with parents and when a policeman took an obstreperous boy home, the father dealt it out, instead of stupidly complaining of assault and battery. The schoolteacher dealt it out as and when required, and if the victim whined at home, the parents added their contribution, instead of raving about poor little Freddie being tortured by a cane in the hand of a fiend.

4

Perhaps no man did more than Alfred Harmsworth to prepare the mind of young Upfield's generation to accept the ever accelerating changes, as well as the preparation for the trials even then looming beyond the North Sea.

Down the street was the shop of the newsagent, a shop which became ever more important during Upfield's steps into the reading age. It was at the time that *Answers* drew attention, and what attention! *Answers*, in its brown cover, sold for tuppence, and it arrived in Gosport late on Monday evenings for sale on Tuesday. On the Monday evening there gathered outside this shop many people waiting for *Answers*, their main interest being the current instalment of 'Money'. This serial was followed by another entitled 'Convict Ninety- Nine'.

Among the crowd were boys who were not interested in *Answers* but in a paper called *The Boys' Friend*, a tuppenny paper printed on green paper, which swiftly came to the fore over the *Boy's Own* and *Chums*. Later, *The Boys' Friend* published three tremendous serials entitled 'Britain Invaded', 'Britain at Bay' and 'Britain's Revenge'. These stories dealt with the invasion by Germany of the British Isles.

Another paper issued by the Harmsworth Press, called *The Boys' Realm*, was printed on pink paper. It was published on Saturdays, and devoted to sports. Later still, a third paper appeared, printed on white and called *The Boys' Herald*. This came out on Thursdays. All matter published in these papers was reasonably well written, straightforward and clean, and hard-pedalled on high adventure in the school, on the playing fields, and over all the then great British Empire.

Illiterate and backward children made a ready effort to read these papers, when learning at the national schools was a trial to be endured.

When the new and free library was built, a goodly proportion of borrowers were boys who sought after the works of Fenn, Henty, Marryat, and later still the science novels of the great new writer, H. G. Wells. And there was a decided revival of Jules Verne. There must have been thousands of young men who might never have met these last-named authors had it not been for the boys' papers published by Alfred Harmsworth. Where the schools failed to create silk purses from sow's ears, he did.

5

Arthur became the leader of five boys, a cell within the family, as the family was a cell within the strong heart of a truly great nation. The boys were made independent by the necessity of their parents' business obligations. If one of the boys was abed sick, Arthur would tell him stories, even relating a story serial fashion, continuing for a week or more. When all was well, there was hide and seek, which developed into something like melodrama.

Now the house was of three storeys, and there were two sets of stairs, and all the upper regions were unlighted, some rooms being used as additional store-rooms, others as workrooms for the milliners, and a few as bedrooms. Those rooms occupied by the assistants were in a wing off one of the staircases.

It was a fine house for hide and seek, it being possible for the hunted to keep ahead of the hunters by constantly moving. The only places barred were the bedrooms occupied by the parents, the staff and the assistants, and, after one experience, the roof, which was gained up steps and through skylights.

By day even the youngest, John, could join in this game. By night John could also join with the hunters, who might carry a hurricane lamp, or, when fortunate, an electric torch. Then came the ultimate of the game.

Only two boys engaged in this phase, the hunted and the hunter. No lights were to be carried. Neither wore footwear. The hunted was given five minutes' start, and he would wait somewhere on those upper floors in pitch darkness and silence. The hunter would then start up one of the two flights of stairs, and his success or failure depended on which of them made a betraying noise.

As time went on, the participants learned the position of every creaking floorboard. They learned how to pass before a window, crawling below it, how to open a creaking door without noise. They learned how to control breathing, how to prevent the rustle clothes, or the soft swish of cloth brushing an obstacle. When complete familiarity with every item of furniture in particular rooms was gained, the boys not participating were first sent up to haul and rearrange the furniture.

Read a good thriller, or study the details of a particularly gruesome murder, and then try this out in a large house.

Stand and wait, and torture your ears to catch a sound when there is no sound other than noises from the street miles away. Move without sound from room to room, dark rooms, vacant rooms, dead rooms, and then shrink inward from a sound which isn't human, or shrink away from a Thing which is blacker than the prevailing darkness. And suddenly feel a hand against your face when you have been playing this game for half an hour and longer. And go away back, and play it when you were nine or ten. Reaction will depend, of course, on your imagination, or lack of it.

6

There was an enemy. His name was Budd. The boys called him Prodigal Budd. He was tall and staid and about seventy. His long white beard and his hair needed washing. He wore a black half-topper and a grimy frock-coat. For amusement, he informed on boys.

Edward was with Arthur and Frank on the top floor when they saw Prodigal Budd standing at the kerb on the far side of the street, leaning gracefully on his stick and watching the traffic. Edward was an expert with a catapult, and with stones.

The boys raced down the stairs and out to the stables, where, on bags, the large store of potatoes was sometimes gone over for rotten ones. This day there was plenty of ammunition. They sped back to the top room, agonised by the thought that Prodigal Budd might have moved on.

Glory be! He was still there.

Brother Frank nominated Edward, but Arthur asserted his

unjust claims. There was almost a fight. Standing before the open window, Arthur measured the range whilst holding a potato so rotten that the fluid within would break out under the slightest violence.

The dastardly missile sailed out over the street. The line of its flight was a thing of beauty, and the certainty grew that Prodigal Budd was for it.

The potato missed by a beautiful fraction the brim of the top-hat, missed by another wondrous fraction the tip of the long red nose, exploded grandly in the dead centre of his white beard. The stuff flew upward, outward, and downward. Prodigal Budd dug it out of his eyes, looked about with genuine astonishment, finally looked upward, to see Arthur almost overbalancing on the window-sill, helpless with laughter. It cost the father two shillings, and the son a severe thrashing.

However, all ended well because it was the only bull's eye Arthur ever scored, save with a rifle. Subsequent triumphs were many, but he paid dearly for them all, with the exception of one glorious episode.

7

At one of the several schools at which Arthur blighted the hopes of his parents, the masters who taught French and history were fast friends, united in a passion for photography. Often they were seen tramping the countryside, loaded with large cameras and equipment.

The history master was tall and severe, but just. He was feared but respected, whereas the French master was hated with a deadly thing. He was sarcastic; he for ever praised the few boys who could assimilate his teaching, and sneered and jibed at those who were dense, including Arthur and the son of the Inspector of the Harbour Police.

As often happened, one Saturday afternoon the two boys were

in a rowing skiff, fishing at the entrance to the harbour of Haslar Ceek, and within a few yards of H.M.S. *Vernon*, the submarine depot ship.

A little way up Haslar Creek were a dozen or so submarines moored to the stone jetty, and there was nothing to prevent anyone from walking on to that jetty. As the boys were fishing, they saw the photographers set up their cameras with the intention of taking pictures of the creek and the ships.

Then around the stem of H.M.S. *Vernon* there swept the police launch in command of the father of Arthur's fishing companion. The launch went astern, and the inspector hailed the boys and wanted to know what luck. Luck had been good and he was given most of the fish as he was due to go off duty, and would be home much before the boy. Then up spoke Arthur:

"I say, Inspector! See those two men along there, with those cameras and things? Looks like they're German spies. Been there a long time, and taking heaps of pictures."

The inspector shaded his eyes, stiffened, ejaculated a nasty word, shouted for 'Go ahead'. Off swept the launch, the two boys alternately watching and grinning at each other. The launch went on past the photographers, who appeared to take no notice of it. Then it abruptly headed for the stone-lined bank, stopped with its bow just touching the bank, and men sprang from it. They ran up to the road, converged on the 'spies', surrounded them. One camera seemed to rise in the air, tripod and all. Then followed what appeared to be an interrogation.

Arthur was now all for rowing the boat to the far side of the *Vernon*, but his friend pointed out that he would have to go home some time, so let trouble, if any, come soon.

The men regained the launch, and the photographers moved off. The launch came down the creek, powerful and fast, sending up quite a wash; it passed the rowing-boat, and when the inspector waved a cheerful *au revoir*, the boys regarded each other with slow smiles of relief. After the removal of plates, exposed and otherwise, and a severe reprimand, the photographers were permitted to leave. It was fully a week later when the inspector casually asked his son if he knew those 'spies' were his schoolmasters.

The son admitting to it, the inspector said:

"Lucky for you and young Upfield that they were taking pictures in a prohibited place."

CHAPTER THREE

SIGNING RENT BOOKS

I

Upfield's last school, with the exception of the 'crammer', was the High School, then a modem innovation of higher degree than the National Schools. The building was airy and exceedingly well equipped. All the masters held degrees, and all wore caps and gowns. The mistresses, for it was a mixed school, also wore caps and gowns. The children who passed to this school encountered an entirely new atmosphere.

For one thing, contact between master and scholar was not as close. Corporal punishment in public, administered by every teacher, was at this school something of a rite, and smacked of refined torture. The delinquent was ordered to report to the headmaster. He had to stand outside the door of the headmaster's study, and as the head often took a class in English Literature the offender might stand outside that door for anything up to an hour, more often than not being joined by fellow criminals.

They would wait and twist and nudge and wait. This waiting was especially trying for boys possessed of imagination. To see the headmaster appear at the end of the corridor, approaching with mortar- board set straight and gown flowing, was to see a figure which in later years was to become known as Dracula.

One master really loved was the science teacher. He was short, sharp-voiced, and a Welshman. He was old-fashioned and human. He gave his class to understand that there were only so many minutes to this period and certain work must be done. The work could be accomplished quickly, and were it so, a supplementary experiment would be permitted. As the supplementary was the manufacture of a new stink, or a new method of creating an explosion, the set work was invariably completed well ahead of time.

The little Welshman never sent a boy to the headmaster for punishment, save for something really serious. He would confront the offender, saying: "So you would delay us! So you would distract our attention!" And with that, his palm across one's cheek would cause it to burn for hours.

The universal opinion was that the greatest bore was English Literature, this being the subject name on the curriculum. The examples of English Literature chosen by the headmaster were taken from Scott, Lamb, Shakespeare, and the boys had, in turn, to stand and read aloud. There was no information imparted about the authors, which might have given a human interest to the study of their works. There sat the headmaster on his dais, aloof, impersonal. He created a gulf across which he never met his pupils, and they could not reach him. Without doubt he was an extremely successful chief executive, yet a junior teacher at a National School could achieve better results. It is safe to say that Scott, Lamb, and even Shakespeare were never read by any boy after leaving that school.

Arthur attended the High School for three years. He entered at Form IV, and he left when in Form IV. During his second and third years he topped the class in History and Geography, and was invariably at the bottom in every other subject. Set him a paper on the Battle of Agincourt, and he would still be writing enthusiastically when the bell went. Check the dates, and more often than not they would be wrong. Ask him a fool question such as: "If a man walks ten miles at ten miles an hour, and has a fit in the third and seventh miles, how long will it take him to walk round Trafalgar Square?" he would occupy the allotted time with noughts and crosses. But all would be well if he had to draw a map and outline Drake's First Voyage.

During this period, when fourteen and fifteen years of age, there grew and was completed a hand-written manuscript of some 400 foolscap pages. It was properly set out in paragraphs and chapters, punctuation was reasonably accurate, and the total wordage worked out at 120,000.

Of course, the subject of the story was fantastic, being a voyage to Mars. The mechanics were crude, the grammar was a maze, and the spelling worse. There wasn't the faintest possibility of its ever being published. But it wasn't a task, it was a joy. It was not compiled, all 120,000 words of it, with anything in the author's mind but the joy of accomplishment, the necessity of giving out generated by the fire within.

Once when he was convalescing from bronchitis, the father walked into his son's room, about eleven at night, and found him writing by candle-light. The doctor visited him and found him writing. The father kindly urged the boy to go to bed; the doctor picked up several sheets, read, looked strangely at the patient before making the usual examination. The brothers knew about the book. They listened to each chapter as completed.

But the schoolmasters knew nothing. One or more of them would have sought for the cause of his contempt for spelling. The little Welshman would have talked to him about that tremendous writing effort, would have read it, and pointed out that to become a real author Arthur would have to tackle spelling seriously. Most of the boys entered the dockyard as artificers. Many joined the Navy, where the demand for intelligence was ever increasing. Some went on to a 'crammer' and sat for the Civil Service. One there was, the son of a poor widow, who eventually became a famous naval architect, and another became a draughtsman in the offices of the famous yacht builders, Camper & Nicholson. Two boys were aces. They topped the entire school. They acquired knowledge with the ease of master minds. They went up like rockets; and at the age of eighteen or nineteen they fell back like sticks. It is the tortoise that arrives.

2

There was an uncle who looked like Mr. Pickwick, or would have done had he shaved regularly. When Uncle Charles strode on to the stage where young Upfield was beginning to strut, the imitation Mr. Pickwick was retired from his business of manufacturing flags, and had developed a great passion for exploring historical places and pubs.

Arthur was deputed to be his guide and general informant. It was assumed that as Arthur's school reports invariably placed him as a student of history he must know everything of historical interest in Portsmouth and Gosport. Still, as Uncle Charles's guardian he learned a great deal of history not mentioned in the books.

The first expedition had, of course, to be to the *Victory*, Nelson's flagship moored off the Gosport shore of the harbour.

To make the voyage it was necessary to engage a wherry, an open boat manned by an old salt, duly licensed and waiting in all weather. An ex-Navy man around eighty years old was introduced to Uncle Charles. He had a remarkable growth of short whiskers reminding one of a baby's bib. He wore a shiny peaked hat, and it was his habit to remove this headgear and run a forearm across the peak as though to polish it.

"Is that boat safe?" asked Uncle Charles, and this was futile, because there were at least twenty boats exactly alike.

"Sir, as safe as the old *Victory* herself," replied the ancient. "Now you just step down into her and sit yourself on this here cushion, and you'll fancy yourself aboard the *Victoria and Albert*."

"Hey there, Jude," shouted a ferry captain. "Don't you forget to bring the top-'at back."

This brought a long tirade from Mr. Jude, who sat resting on the oars and obviously enjoying himself. Uncle Charles produced a note-book, and proceeded to jot down the salient points. It was a purple performance, and when done, the wherry owner calmly lit his pipe, took up the oars and rowed with stately rhythm.

The harbour this day was particularly busy. A battleship was on its way down the Channel, two destroyers were coming up from the entrance, an Isle of Wight steamer was circling from the railway pier. And hither and yon sped the small steam ferries. What with all this and Nelson's mighty flagship looming ever higher over the tiny wherry, it could be expected that Uncle Charles would not think to ask and record the answers to the following questions.

"How old are you?"

"Eighty-one," replied the wherryman.

"You have been a wherryman all your life?"

"Exceptin' those times I served in the Navy, mostly in furrin' 'parts."

"How long have you had this boat?"

"Well now." The mariner rested to spit on one horny palm and then the other. "Well now, it must be nigh on twenty-seven years."

"Then you have done well, remarkably well. Take a nip."

The tide was running out, so that whilst the mariner paused to take a mouthful of whisky from the old silver flask, he had lost two hundred yards. Instead of the journey occupying barely twenty minutes, it took the wherryman almost an hour to reach the *Victory*.

They were received at the top of the gangway by a reservist, who , conducted them down below to the gun decks, and finally to the brass plate in the deck marking where Nelson fell. Uncle Charles removed his hat whilst he read the inscription. Then he wanted to know from which side of the ship had come the bullet from the marksman in the Frenchman's rigging.

The return voyage was made swiftly and without further incident, but when again on land, Uncle Charles insisted that the mariner accompany them to the nearest pub, where the two men imbibed rum straight.

To what purpose Uncle Charles employed his notes never leaked out. The expedition to the Blue Post Inn added much information to the record. Here, of course, Midshipman Easy spent a night or so before boarding his first ship, but Uncle Charles demanded to know just where the famous midshipman slept, and on being told that this fact was not precisely known, he addressed himself severely to mine host. Having sampled several glasses of old ale–almost the colour of port wine, and hiding a dirty camel's kick–he was conducted to the old harbour, in the shadow of which the Earl of Buckingham was assassinated. There being no one to answer his questions, he put them to Arthur.

"Why isn't there a brass plate let into the pavement to mark the exact spot? Merely engraving the particulars high up on the wall of the building, which most probably didn't exist at the time, is yet another horrible example of the mental slough into which the nation has fallen."

He was satisfied by the visit to the George Hotel, in which Admiral Nelson slept his last night on shore, for there still stood the four-poster bed in the exact room. Here Uncle Charles spoke in hushed voice to the chambermaid who conducted them upstairs, and reserved his questions until drinking whisky-and-beer in the saloon bar, when he directed them to the bored landlord. What had become of the bedding? Why had not the blankets, at least, been preserved? What had become of the chamber-pots, which, in those days, were universal adjuncts to a
gentleman's bedroom?

Charles Dickens's house entranced him for two days, and when the time came to introduce him to the dockyard, Arthur solemnly warned him that if he produced his note-book, he would be run out by one of the enormous dockyard policemen–without his hat.

The lower end of the High Street, Old Portsmouth, was then occupied by the establishments of junk dealers, ship chandlers, marine engineers, fusty gentlemen engaged in an extraordinary variety of commerce, and a range of hostelries which in their heyday had been patronised by seafarers, from admirals to midshipmen. Here and there along the east side of the High Street there were openings in the brick and stone frontages guarded by ancient cannons partially sunk into the ground to prevent the passage of wheel traffic. Some of these 'holes in the wall' led to wide courtyards fronted by tall and narrow houses in which the history of twenty decades was written on the very walls. Similar exits from the High Street gave access to the stone walls and wharves of the old harbour, which was busy with small ships when Portsmouth was non-existent and Gosport merely a collection of fishermen's huts, in the day of King Alfred.

Once he penetrated to these places Uncle Charles required a deal of shifting. It never concerned him of whom he asked his eternal questions–a woman whitening her doorstep, a retired pirate, a sailor off a Spanish onion boat, the captain of a sailing craft that had brought tulip bulbs and roses from Holland.

3

Then there was Uncle Sam. Uncle Sam was a solicitor's managing clerk. Like Arthur's mother, he spoke with the soft accent of Birmingham, and if Uncle Charles looked like Mr. Pickwick, Uncle Samuel was the image of Mr. Snodgrass.*

---

* Biographer's note: Questioned on this likeness of his relatives to Dickens's characters, Upfield assured me that Dickens's characters were like them, and that their counterparts could be met with almost any day of the week. He assured me that within forty miles of Gosport, that is, away from the coast, many of the people in the villages spoke what was almost a foreign language, and that to see them going to church and chapel on Sundays was to observe every character ever portrayed by Charles Dickens.

Upfield's Uncle Sam possessed an extraordinary mind, and why he never entered politics and rose to occupy the Woolsack was matter for speculation. Uncle Sam's great interest was literature, the 'literary' kind. He could read the leading article from *The Times*, drop the paper, and voice it word-perfect. He could recite without error Shakespeare's every play. He could quote every proverb from the Bible. And, in conversation, one never could be quite sure of the source of much he habitually inserted as asides.

An author had to be dead at least a hundred years to find favour with Uncle Sam, yet he eagerly requested to be allowed to read the great English novel written by his nephew. On returning it, he wrote: "Continue. Let nothing deter you. Be not sidetracked by the lure of wealth through filthy commerce. Press on and write, write, write. You have a great talent, but, Great God! polish that talent with the abrasive of William Cobbett."

4

Upfield had never heard of William Cobbett, save that he was a renegade of recent times and therefore unworthy of a place in history. Now approaching his sixteenth birthday, he had no views concerning his future and revealed no decided aptitude for a career. It was now that the aunts stepped in with the ambition of the grandparents that Arthur should become a doctor. A doctor! This goal was referred to the headmaster, who doubtless raised his superior brows and called on his own talents to be diplomatic. Frustrated, clinging to the ambition of the eldest son being one up on trade, the father was induced to article the son to a firm of estate agents, auctioneers and surveyors, for three years–and might just as well have thrown his hundred guineas into the harbour.

Thus did Arthur Upfield enter one of the professions.

The firm's offices were on the ground floor of an office building where was the editorial office of the local newspaper, and shortly after he became sixteen Upfield wrote a long letter to the editor on the subject of Tariff Reform. That the letter was edited before publication did not lessen the thrill, and Upfield waited for indignant opposition. No irate *pro bono publico* taking the trouble, Upfield then wrote a strong letter, refuting the claims in his first, in favour of Free Trade. This, after severe editing, was also published.

Only now did Upfield decide what he would like to be–a newspaper reporter. But, said the aunts, there was that fee of a hundred guineas, there was that most respectable business career, a profession. A newspaper reporter! Great Heavens! Mixing with criminals and visiting public-houses and the like! In the career chosen for him he would not have to associate with such low types.

Little did they know, little could they have understood.

Observe the youth! A scrawny figure in his first long-trousered suit. Passably intelligent from the nose up, weak from the nose down. Aged sixteen; a one-hundred-thousand-word novel locked in his desk; not one examination passed; all the world opening like a glorious flower, the history of a great Empire printed on the petals, and the scent carrying the romantic essence of a dozen foreign countries to his questing mind. A youth striving to fly without wings. The first adventure into love in ruins, and the broken melody now the accompaniment to the writing of the second great opus.

His first assignment was the collection of rents, there being many hundreds of properties where rent had to be collected every week. He was inducted into this business by another youth who had served his articles, and the one overriding rule was speed.

It meant knocking on a door, waiting for the tenant to answer, signing the tenant's rent book, giving change, and noting the entry into the firm's rent books. After a few weeks the routine was mastered. The town and suburbs were cut into divisions, and you began at one end and carried on through street after street, into alley after alley, until you reached the other end. By then trousers and coat pockets were loaded heavily with coin, from sovereigns to halfpennies, and no filthy paper.

When calling at a terrace of houses, the collector banged on the first door, went on to the second and the third, and so on, and on his returning to the first the tenant would be waiting with the book and the money. To each tenant a cheery greeting. To some a chiding for falling into arrears, to others the hint of drastic action by the terrible, flint-hearted boss in the office. The rents were from three shillings and sixpence up to ten shillings, the houses ranging from slum dwellings, some filthy with fleas, to others as spick and span as the deck of the *Victory*, up to quite commodious semi-detached houses.

The tenants became the collector's friends—and what a field of psychology they were to the embryonic novelist! Many would anticipate his call, knowing to the minute when his knock would sound at the door.

There was Mrs. Black, whose rent was six shillings and sixpence a week. Her husband was a sailmaker. She worked as a milliner. There were no children, but a bed-ridden mother occupied an upstairs room. The front door would be unlocked. The rent and book would be on the table in the front room.

Arthur would arrive, burst in through the latched front door, calling: "How are you today, Mrs. White? When are you going to stop being lazy and get up?" "Oh, I'm about the same, Mr. Upfield. I hope you are well." A pause at the foot of the stairs to gossip for just a moment, then into the front room to snatch up money and book, make an entry and rush out again calling "Goodbye, Mrs. White, till next Monday. You'll be up by then. No more pretending." Slammed door, and again the long silence for Mrs. White.

Then one Monday it happened. Arthur pushed open the door, called up the stairs, received no reply, rushed into the front room. The table wasn't where it always had been. Resting on two chairs was a coffin with the lid off, and Mrs. White lying amid flowers. The precipitate entry flung Arthur against one of the chairs. The coffin slipped off at that end and the corpse partially slid out.

There was the sound of movement at the rear of the house, and frantically Arthur pulled the body up into the coffin and lifted it to rest on the chair. When he turned from the room, the daughter was in the passage with money and rent book.

"Oh, I am sorry, Mr. Upfield. I hope. . . I hope you didn't get a shock, like."

"I'm all right, Mrs. Black. It was a bit of a shock...I didn't expect...I'm so sorry. I'll miss Mrs. White."

"Thank you, Mr. Upfield. Don't go. Come and have a cup of tea." A man appeared behind her, the sailmaker. He said: "Yes, and with a drop of doings in it, too. Oughta had that door locked. Come on, young feller. I got real Jamaica what only the Navy gets." He saw to it that there was more rum than tea.

Then there was Mrs. Pafford, whose husband had been shopman to the grandmother's sisters in the butchery business. She lived in a house once owned by Arthur's grandfather, still the property of the family, and never had she paid any rent. She was large and white-faced, now old and slightly bent. The house was one of six in an alley, and every Monday afternoon young Upfield duly knocked at the door. Mrs. Pafford would open it, having, of course, examined the caller from behind the front room curtain. That Pafford! He was out of work. Or he had been drunk all the week-end. Or he had fallen and hurt himself and was up at the doctor's. The collector would make a cross in his book, smile and chide Mrs. Pafford for not making the attempt to pay even threepence of the weekly rent of three shillings and threepence. Hopeless for the agents to suggest distraining to the owners.

"Ah, yer pore grandma, Mr. Upfield," Mrs. Pafford would moan. "What a lovely lady! And those pore dears wot ran the butchers! Saints they was an' all. That Pafford cried when they was took. The blackguard won't do no crying when I'm took. Ah. . ."

So it would go on as the collector hurried to the next house. And one day Mrs. Pafford really enjoyed herself.

There was a new clerk to be inducted, and he was taken around and introduced to the tenants. On his arrival at Mrs. Pafford's house it was some time, and only after the third knock, that she opened the door, suspicion plain in her black eyes.

"This is Mr. So-and-So, Mrs. Pafford. He will be calling for the rent in future. Will you please let him see your rent book?"

"See me rent book!" shrilled Mrs. Pafford. "You want to see me rent book, Mr. So-and-So." She lifted high the front of her dress, revealing nothing under it, and said: "There's me rent book, Mr. So-and-So. Sign it."

When a house fell vacant, it was Arthur's duty to make an inventory of necessary repairs and pin a 'To Let' notice in the window. In those days tenants were not killed in the rush, but reasonable care had to be taken that a house wasn't let to ladies of easy virtue. Their money was good and prompt, but owners were averse to having their property named in the press as disorderly houses.

Still, they often got past the chief clerk, and were given the keys. At first when Arthur called for the rent, a demure miss would open the door, proffer the book and money, say "Thank you" with a friendly smile and close the door. But later the smiles were promising and often Arthur would be invited to take out the rent upstairs. He might have been tempted, but maybe he didn't dare.

Shades of the grandparents! And of the aunts!

There were all kinds of houses, from the vermin-infested dwelling to the large residences fronting the harbour or opening to the Square; the latter type having had as tenants admirals, ships' captains, and before them retired pirates, gun-runners, and looters in foreign wars. Many a famous seafarer had rented one of these houses to instal a mistress.

There was a house near Trinity Church where no one stayed long, and when a tenant paid to have his lease terminated and left, Arthur was sent to make a careful list of renovations deemed necessary, with special attention to the drains.

It was a very spacious house, overlooking the church, and even then the neighbourhood was peaceful and old-worldly. W. W. Jacobs put the local characters into his stories. It was of four floors and built in the reign of George I. The wide stone steps to the front door were strong enough to guard a castle, and the iron door-knocker was a leering devil daring you to touch it. Inside, you found yourself in a large hall, with a beautiful mahogany-railed staircase leading to the three upper floors. The sun, on the day that Arthur visited the house, poured wine-coloured radiance upon everything in that hall-staircase and bare floor.

Furniture sales always began at the drawing-room and ended in the kitchen, and Upfield followed this routine. The drawing-room needed re-papering. The ceiling would pass. The window-frames required cleaning and repainting. And so on. From the ground floor up the stairs to the first floor, all very quiet and sun-filled and warm and friendly. A beautiful house, a dream house, to be dream-filled again with the glorious furniture which had passed under the hammer when Arthur was acting as auctioneer's clerk.

As he passed up the stairs to the second floor, a coldness caused Upfield to look back and down. He proceeded, and worked through the second floor and went on to the third floor, and there he stood at a window from which he could see over the harbour entrance and watch the sleek form of a destroyer going to sea.

Quite abruptly the view meant nothing at all. His back felt as though bare flesh was pressed to ice. There was nothing in the room. Only the sunlight slanting through the dust motes and laying a golden pathway on the floor–to the door.

Then brave Horatio, who had stalked his brothers in the dark, bolted down all those flights of stairs and out through the front door, at which he paused only long enough to lock it with the great heavy key.

His employer wanted to know why he hadn't completed the inventory. What were the drains like? The water service? The condition of the kitchen and the cellars and the domestic quarters? It was all extremely silly.

The senior clerk was sent to complete the inventory. He noted the drains and the condition of the domestic quarters. But he didn't stay on the third floor long enough to do anything about the rooms there. It was a job which had to be done, so they returned to the house together. They entered the hall, and then decided to note the repairs necessary to the top floor with the aid of imagination, and the real sunlight on the front steps.

5

During the articleship, young Upfield was supposed to pass three annual examinations: the first year entrance exam to the Auctioneers' Institute; the second to earn the Associateship; and the final to become a Fellow.

The first examination would be on a par with the present-day Intermediate, and to study for this, Arthur had to attend a crammer's school twice a week. The first year, in addition to studying, he wrote his second hundred-thousand-word novel, based on the invasion and conquest of Europe by the Yellow Peril. The Yellow Peril won hands down. Nothing stopped it, but it stopped Arthur passing that examination. He tried again the following year, but during that year he had to write the sequel, wherein the Yellow Peril was flung back, and so he failed again.

It was no effort whatever to study routes from China through Tibet, Samarkand, and on to the Bosphorus, defended by the united navies of Europe. Quite a pleasure.

At seventeen, young Upfield was still supposed to be studying, but he had become aware of girls. At eighteen the girls held top place. Studying was something unpleasant and invariably mentioned only by his father. Even the novel-writing faded into quiescence.

Interest in girls was foreseen by the father of five boys, himself not inexperienced at Arthur's age. He had received sound advice from his father which now he handed out to Arthur as a good fellow, and man to man. He said one night when the others had gone off to bed:

"There is no doubt that you are the greatest fool of the family, in fact the greatest fool of an Upfield I've ever met or heard of. You've cost me a lot of money but I cannot see you ever deriving a penny value from it. Where you are going I don't know, and I'm sure you don't either. Both of us know where you are not going, and that destination isn't success, measured by any kind of stick.

"The point I want to make clear is that should you cut your throat we must not be spattered by the blood. If you will remember three wise sayings, you will save us from much worry, and yourself from disaster and sorrow. One: never play around with girls in your home town; do so in a distant place where you aren't known. Two: never make a promise in writing. Three: if you can seduce a girl before marriage, others may seduce her after marriage."

On another occasion he said:

"I've seen you with the same girl at least six times in the last three months. Remember, what the mother is today, the girl will be twenty years hence."

Upfield's first experience with a woman took place in a horse-drawn cab at Southampton, which is twenty-odd miles from his home town. He was then a trooper in the Hampshire Carabineers Yeomanry, and the walking-out dress consisted of a dark blue tunic with chain epaulettes, and skin-tight trousers with a wide white stripe on the outside and strapped under the insteps. All this was a distinct hindrance to illicit love-making, and the experience in the cab was discouraging. The fact that at this time contraceptives were not adjuncts to handbags and pocket-wallets was conducive to morality. Then there was that primary influence over him exerted by the grandmother and the aunts, which was actually a pointer that women were to have a far greater influence on his life than men.

Great-aunt Lucy lived in a Sussex village and had never married. With a sister she had taken over her father's business, and had accumulated enough money to retire under comfortable circumstances. She was verging on ninety when Arthur spent his first holidays with her, a little Dresden-china woman with bright blue eyes, a wonderful smile, and understanding heart, and always good for a substantial tip at the end of the visit.

Her house was of brick, consisting of two storeys, enshrined with ivy. It stood in about an acre of enclosed garden, and quite near was the well-kept village green, where cricket was played as it ought to be played. A housekeeper-general-nurse, with her husband and a son of Arthur's age, occupied the rear portion of the house.

Great-aunt Lucy did not approve of the newfangled motor-cars. She did not approve of certain relatives. When speaking of either, a slight flush would creep into her beautiful face, as though even to disapprove was un-Christian. Arthur's quick friendship with the housekeeper's son gained her approval, for she loved this boy.

Over lunch, the little china lady would relate anecdotes of her early years, and describe with vivid phrase and twinkling eyes the idiosyncrasies of her relatives. Dinner was always at six o'clock, and at eight there was a rigid routine.

At eight, when the sun was setting and the birds were loud in song, she would call Arthur from his book in the garden, and he, obeying, would find her seated at the table in the morning-room with the family Bible in readiness for the evening reading. Her voice was not unlike the voice of the bird beyond the open window, and, despite his failings, Arthur listened with respect and with interest. Following the reading, he listened to a short homily, also with respect, and when the Bible was reverently closed and placed at the head of the table, Aunt Lucy would say:

"Now, Arthur, our glass of wine."

Arthur would produce the glasses from the cabinet, and the decanter containing cowslip, dandelion, or rhubarb wine, bottled by the little lady twenty or thirty years before. When a new bottle had to be brought from the cellar, Arthur was commanded, with a smile, to keep whistling all the time he was below.

As eight-thirty was announced by the ormolu clock on the mantelshelf and the grandfather clock in the hall–and they always chimed in unison–the great-aunt would rise, and Arthur would offer his arm. Thus they left the room to mount to the landing above, where the housekeeper would be waiting to take the little lady to her room.

On Sundays, morning and evening, Arthur conducted the great-aunt to the chapel close by. Sometimes they went for short walks in the late afternoon. Sometimes a carriage was hired and they would drive into the neighbouring countryside.

But after the ritual of conducting the great-aunt to the first landing, the gossamer chains drifted, and Arthur would join his pal, to race away on bikes, or gather with the lads and lasses under the oak trees bordering the Green.

One morning the housekeeper went into the great-aunt's bedroom with morning tea, and found her kneeling beside the bed. She had died praying.

6

The year that King George V was crowned, Arthur's father decided he had had enough. His other sons, two of whom were now in his business, were agreeable to complying with the elastic rules of the home, but Arthur's behaviour was much less conservative. His father said:

"You are going out to Australia to try farming. I have come to look on Australia as the ideal country for you. It is so far away that you will never save enough money to return."

How right he was!

CHAPTER FOUR

WHERE ARE ALL THE BASTARDS

I

Upfield arrived in Australia towards the close of 1910. It was a period of true prosperity. At country stations in the wheat belts farmers waited to induce the immigrants to work for them, while in the cities there were more jobs than men.

There was no breaking-in period for new arrivals. They had left jobs at office or bench, lolled about a ship's decks for five weeks, then set to work on wheat farms, stooking hay, lumping bagged wheat throughout the daylight hours, back tortured, hands raw. They lived in iron huts which they never saw during the daylight hours, and thus were unconscious of the earth floor, the gaping roof, the glassless window.

The Government agencies in Great Britain had promised them land and financial assistance to purchase plant. The same agencies cried "Look!" and showed pictures of new chums taking their ease outside creeper-covered cottages, backed by tall trees and cool shadows. In actual fact they were presented with a flat land baking in terrific heat, and humpies to crawl into at night which were no better than the smaller humpies to which the dogs were chained.

Some of the immigrants were able to flee back to Paradise. The great majority had to stick it out, sink or swim. That situation was the greatest blessing ever bestowed on young men of any country. To sink or swim! And just at the right age to meet the test.

Upfield was met by a wheat farmer at Pineroo, South Australia. The farmer conveyed him per buckboard to the farm four miles distant. It was then dark. They had dinner of cold mutton and bread and jam, with plenty of hot tea. During the night the farmer entered Upfield's quarters, an upturned 5,000-gallon water tank, the entry cut with tinsnips.

"Come on now! Time to rise and shine! Daylight's not far off and we gotta feed the horses."

"Ah-ooo! What's the time?"

"Just gone three. A bit late. Get moving."

Upfield got moving. He washed from a dirty basin, dressed, packed his suitcase, and walked back to the railway station, reaching it long before daylight. He was back in Adelaide before the sun

Next morning he took the *Adelaide Advertiser* to the shade of a park tree, where he studied the 'Situations Vacant'. The Tramways Trust advertised for conductors. Out! The aunts would not care to hear he was a tram conductor. It appeared that every hotel in the city needed kitchen men–without experience, and cooks–with experience. A kitchen man! Swabbing out floors and things. Out! BOUNDARY RIDERS WANTED FOR NORTHERN STATIONS. Boundary riders! What the devil were they? Northern stations... northern... away in the interior of the country... cowboys... horses and guns. Much better. He would become a boundary rider.

The advertiser, interviewing him, said:

"How long have you been in the country? Only five minutes! Go away."

In the young immigrant's wallet was a letter of introduction to Bagot, Shakes & Lewis, Stock and Station Agents, on King William Street. Back to the grind? No! Back to rent collecting and noting renovations needed by empty houses? Certainly not.

Near-by was an Employment Agency. There Upfield was asked many questions and told to wait. Half an hour later he was called to another office where he was introduced to a Mr. Fearon, an elderly man with a greying beard. Mr. Fearon said:

"So you do not like wheat farming, young man?"

"No, sir." Mr. Fearon's front deserved respect. He was told by the applicant that he could milk cows, having learned this and other chores on an uncle's farm just before leaving England. Yes, he could ride and knew a little about horses, having been in the Hampshire Carabineers Yeomanry.

Mr. Fearon decided favourably, and returned to the head office of the Bank of New South Wales, where he was then the manager, and Upfield proceeded to Mitcham and so to the large mansion surrounded by many acres, and situated at the very feet of the hills.

He was given a comfortable room in what once had been the coachman's quarters. He was fed by the housekeeper, who, with her husband and two daughters, hadn't long been in Australia. He practised on the cows, rode the ponies, repaired the fences with a wire-strainer, and generally led a life with which any normal young man might be content. He read and re-read the poems of Henry Lawson, and received then the impression, which was to remain, that Lawson was a pessimist. He read the adventures of the family of 'On Our Selection' and hoped fervently he would one day meet these characters. Tales of the bushrangers left him cold, for they were merely semi-glorified thugs. *The Bulletin* he read from cover to cover. And he never failed to study the 'Situations Vacant' in the *Advertiser*.

The newspaper proved that still more boundary riders were wanted for northern stations. He met a man searching for cattle in the hills, and for an hour they sat and smoked, one either side the back fence, as Upfield put probing questions about the Interior, thus learning something of boundary riders and seeing a hazy picture of the country. The cattle-hunter used a rangy but powerful horse. He wore tight mole- skin trousers into which was tucked a hard drill shirt. A large-brimmed felt hat made him look romantic and he had spurs that jingled. The one missing item was a gun belt.

"Get around a bit, first," he advised. "Them northern stations are no good unless you know what's what." The drawl was pronounced, the attitude to the immigrant one of kindly tolerance. In fact, Upfield never met with any hostility, and came to see why many newcomers to Australia did meet it. Throughout the years ahead he encountered the 'sinkers' who automatically decried Australia and lauded their native country, giving no credit to Australia on any point. Naturally this angered Australians, and nurtured what amounted to a very widespread dislike of the English.

Upfield failed to see any resemblance between the Old Country and Australia, and, therefore, no grounds for comparison. What did it matter that Westminster Abbey was older than any church in Australia? Or if the entire British Isles could be lost in South Australia?

Upfield found most Australians easy to get along with, generous and sympathetic, and possessed of a sense of humour which, if a little broad, was always quick. The Australian looking for a fight needed only to name an immigrant a 'Pommy Bastard' with a sneer, but far more often than not the term was used to express something akin to affection. There were, of course, black bastards, capitalist bastards, police bastards. In fact, everyone in the country was a bastard!

2

After four months with Mr. Fearon, Upfield decided to try a city job, giving him spare time opportunities of obtaining that job as boundary rider. He answered the call for an hotel kitchen man.

It was at Adelaide's premier hotel that the manager summed him up, decided he wouldn't earn his breakfast as a kitchen man, but might be useful to the chef. Thus Upfield was appointed to the position of fourth cook.

He reported for work at seven in the morning, his first duty as fourth cook being to prepare his own breakfast of whatever he fancied. The third cook would be assisting the second cook with serving breakfast to the waiters, both male and female, in their own room off the kitchen.

The chef would spend his first hour smoking cigarettes and sipping black coffee, while working dreamily on his menus for the day, occasionally emerging to confer with his underlings.

The fourth cook's tasks were many and varied, from checking in the vegetables to serving the sweets from a long bench where the waiters would leave their orders, proceed with used utensils to the scullery, and collect the sweets on their way back to the dining-room.

There was a curvy waitress, full-lipped and known to men as a teaser. At a slack moment she would approach behind the bench and stand close to Upfield, brushing herself against him, and retaliation was inspired when in the cold store he was drawing vegetables for dinner. Selecting a large and lengthy parsnip, he skewered it with string, and suspended the parsnip from his waist and under his apron.

Dinner was in full swing when the teaser came again. Her leg met the parsnip, then her hand wandered. Her head jerked. She stared unseeingly at the fourth cook arranging her tray of sweets, and, opening her mouth to scream, fell backward in a dead faint. Other waitresses pounced on the fallen and carried her away, and service continued without further interruption.

The last diner having been served, the chef put a question similar to that put by one of the butcher-aunts to their shopman–'Pafford, what did you do to that dog?' "Upfield, what did you do to that girl?"

Upfield merely removed his apron.

Frequently the staff would work overtime on a special dinner, these private dinners usually commemorating something or other. There was General X-X. He arranged a dinner to which were invited thirty guests, the menu comprising nine courses including

Iced Coffee Royal. Preparation for this dinner was begun three days before the great night.

The chef called Upfield to his office. It was a remarkable room, for the walls were almost completely covered with framed menus from first-class European hotels, menus prepared by this talented cook and autographed by famous people. He was tall, about fifty-five, with lively dark eyes, beautiful hands, and a foreign lisp which might have been an affectation.

"You would like to create a Coffee Royal?" he asked.

"Of course," replied the fourth cook.

"Then you shall."

He dictated a list of liquors ending with two dozen bottles of beer, and instructed his underling to take it to the head barman and draw same. Beer! Beer in Coffee Royal! Having signed the chit, he glanced up at Upfield and said:

"It is an old saying that too many cooks spoil the broth. I have a better. Appreciation of many cooks is seldom unappreciated."

Upfield was relieved of normal duties and instructed to make ready twelve ice-cream freezers. He was not taught how to prepare the mixture to fill the moulds. He was put to work manhandling those twelve ice-cream freezers, hard work which continued all afternoon and intermittently during the evening.

The special dinner was timed to begin at eight. The chef served, with Upfield in attendance, the remainder of the staff busy with the late diners. It was a revelation to the young man, whose role consisted of handing to the chef various utensils, as the theatre sister might attend upon the surgeon.

Finally out came the moulds, and upon each of twelve silver dishes rested a Cleopatra's Needle. Upfield, watching them depart in the hands of the waiters, wondered if the beer in them would be tasted. When they were returned, they were only about one-third or less consumed.

Upfield tasted. No beer! He was told to convey the Needles to the ice chamber, after they had been removed from the silver dishes so jealously guarded by the head waiter.

The kitchen was cleaned up, then all the staff were invited to the chef's office. There the chef read a complimentary message from General X-X, and from behind his desk hauled the two dozen bottles of beer! He produced savouries. The second cook mentioned the Needles, and Upfield was sent for them.

It was a grand party. The kitchen man slept in the wash-up room, the second cook managed to leave the building, the chef dozed in his chair, Upfield lay at his feet like a loyal hound, and the third cook swore he spent the night going up in one lift and descending in the other.

Upfield was presented with two sound opportunities, either of which any young man with even a modicum of common sense would have grasped. The manager sent for him.

"Alphonse has reported to me that you have the address helpful to a waiter. He is prepared to train you. It would certainly be to your advantage."

Upfield asked for time to consider, was told with a smile that many waiters earned more money than managers. In the kitchen', the chef called him into his office.

"A waiter!" he sneered. "A tailor's dummy! An automaton! You observe me. A great cook. An artist. A genius. You stay with me. I teach you all. Listen carefully. I serve five years with pastry cook, two years with butcher, two years with fishmonger. You serve under me, and in ten years you will be like me–an artist." He waved his hands to the framed menus. Springing to his feet, he ran the fingers of those beautiful hands over Upfield's cranium. "You have it all…imagination…the creative gift. I have watched you. Your judgment when cooking eggs with rasher-bacon is good. You continue here, with me, eh?"

Again Upfield said he would like a little time to consider. And the following afternoon he interviewed the man who advertised for boundary riders for northern stations.

3

The call for boundary riders emanated from Elder Smith & Co., who controlled subsidiary pastoral companies, and the officer who supplied the companies with additional labour was a Mr. Laffer.

Mr. Laffer looked at Upfield with dark eyes beneath severe brows. "I've seen you before, although your name doesn't register. When?" "Just over three months ago."

"Ah! I remember you now. You came to me when you had been in the country only five minutes. Well, three months is only six minutes. Come again in a year's time."

At the same time the following day, Mr. Laffer was again glaring at Upfield.

"I told you yesterday it's no use coming here till you've had experience," he said. "Boundary riding! D'you know what a boundary rider is? He's a man who rides all day on a horse, and drives sheep or rounds up cattle. You ever seen a horse? Yes, yes, you told me you can ride a horse. Can you kill a sheep? Ever killed a sheep? No, I thought not. Get out."

The day after was a Saturday, but on the Monday morning Upfield was once more brought to his notice. On this occasion Mr. Laffer shouted. He did things to the papers on his desk. The next day was the last, and Upfield won. A man can stand only so much.

On leaving the kitchen the next afternoon, Upfield hadn't the courage to bid good-bye to the chef and Alphonse, nor had he the nerve to apply at the office for two day wages. He went to the station at six that evening, and was met by Mr. Laffer, who bought his ticket to Broken Hill and gave him vouchers for the coach fares to Momba Station. Under the agreement the cost of the fares would be deducted from his wages of one pound a week and keep, but if he stayed in this employment for a year, it would be credited.

Mr. Laffer accompanied the prospective boundary rider to the door of the compartment, and stood there as though the new employee might bolt. He said:

"If you continue in your obstinate refusal to take 'no' for an answer, you'll end a millionaire or meet with violence. I suppose you tossed in a good job for this."

Upfield mentioned the hotel work and prospects, and Mr. Laffer almost shouted. "The best hotel in South Australia! A double chance like that! And you toss it overboard." The guard whistled and Mr. Laffer stood back and laughed–the kind of laughter that hasn't any mirth in it. The young adventurer felt uneasy as the train pulled out of Central Station. He need not have done, because the experienced Mr. Laffer was quite wrong.

Through the night Upfield cat-napped and was awake and ready to see the new world at dawning. The train was crossing saltbush flats, and the sun presently rose above distant ranges. They were bare and brown, patched with grey and black, and someone said that once upon a time these ranges were covered with scrub trees and the gullies with gums, and the mines came and devoured the lot.

"Going on to Wilcannia, eh?" exclaimed a rough character. "Oh, to Momba! Parcels Post bloke, eh? Well, you'll have to make for the Southern Cross for breakfast and get the coach there. What d'you think of Australia?"

"This is the first time I've seen it," replied the Pommy Bastard. "Looks good to me."

"Yair, but I mean down Adelaide way."

"That's not Australia, chum. This is it."

"Well, if you think this is it, you'll get plenty up west of Wilcannia. Me, I wouldn't go a yard outa the Hill."

At Broken Hill, Upfield lugged his port and roll of blankets along the hot street to the Southern Cross Hotel, the railway yards to his right, and beyond the railway the line of lode, the mine structures, and the smoking smelters. It was early March, and the dust was thick in the power of the north wind. He wore his only suit, a double-breasted coat set off by a fancy white waistcoat, and the trousers were worn short to display the fancy socks above the smart shoes.

Australia! He was seeing Australia for the first time. It was much more than a land of promise, a land good enough for staid farmers, good enough for security-first adventurers from Home, as well as the native-born. It was a land of dreams, dreams become reality and still a land of dreams. It was no foreign country to this young man. He had come home.

The Southern Cross Hotel had stepped straight from Ralph Connor's *The Sky Pilot*. Riding hacks lined the hitching rails. The sidewalk was of boards. Along the street bronzed men drove paired horses harnessed to buckboards. Other bronzed men leaned against the verandah posts, and these watched Upfield approach, muttered to each other and grinned.

"Where will I find the coach office, please?"

"Just along there, mate."

Upfield presented his voucher to a man in shirt-sleeves and open waistcoat of fancy sky-green. He wore a wide felt hat, and dangled a dead cigar between extraordinarily white teeth.

"Momba, eh!" he drawled. "Now look, mate, the Wilcannia coach leaves at ten sharp from right in the yard. Get some breakfast at the dining-room, and ask for sandwiches to keep you going for the day. How long you been out?"

"Four months."

"What d'you think of Australia?"

"I like it."

"Yair, great country. Bit of advice?"

"All you can give."

"You're going to find it hell for six months. Get through them six months and you'll be right for life. I tell all you Parcel Post blokes the same, and not many of 'em stays."

Breakfast! A real breakfast of hot curry and toast and marmalade, and a teapot holding a quart. And a waitress who laughed and wanted to know what part of England he came from, and who spoke with a Scotch burr. There were no scowlers in Broken Hill, no weedy youths or jaded men. The coach waited in the yard, a Cobb & Co.'s coach minus doors, swung on leather, and a leather strap crossing the space where a door would be, keeping the inside passengers from falling out when asleep. The grooms put five horses to it. The driver checked the mail, signed other dockets, told his passengers to mount–a Catholic priest and young Upfield. He mounted to the box seat and gathered the reins into hands the colour of Australian mahogany. He nodded and grooms sprang away. The horses reared and plunged, the whip cracked, and from the yard rolled the great coach driven by one of the greatest of drivers, Fred Essen.

Essen was a large man, having a square face and twinkling grey eyes.

"Sitting comfortable, Father? That's right. Better put that bag under you, young feller. You'll have corns on your bottom, time we get to Wilcannia. Taking a call, Father? Father Murphy will be glad to see you. Told me to be sure you didn't fall off somewhere."

The priest was young, and there was no mistaking his Irish origin. Essen wanted to know how long he'd been in the country and was told five months. What did the good father think of Australia? Essen wanted to know how long Upfield had been in the country. Everyone wanted to know how long the newcomer had been in Australia, and what the newcomer thought of Australia. These were important questions, as though the entire future of Australia rested on the answers.

Over the hills, the barren hills denuded of all the trees which had gone into pit props and fuel for the boilers and the voracious smelters. Miles and miles to Mount Brown and the first wayside hotel. And then across Stephens Creek and into a world where the earth was table-flat, covered with foot-high saltbush all the way to and beyond the horizon.

The track was a real trail. That hotel at Stephens Creek had been a real wild west saloon at the foothills of the barren lands. Here in this immensity of space so filled with sunlight as to be almost a barrier, Adelaide and the world, and Gosport and all the past, totalled unreality. This was the land Upfield had visualised from the world of the past. He clung to the bucking coach, the young priest between him and the driver, who recited bush ballads, and his eager mind refused to accept reality as real.

Looking back, he saw the great trees bordering Stephens Creek already standing in what Essen called burning water. Gazing forward beyond the backs of the five horses, his eyes followed the telegraph posts skirting the track until they merged to a dark line which topped the horizon as level as that of the ocean. Dun-coloured dots on the saltbush turned into sheep. Brown and speckled blobs became cattle. What at first was a tall mast became a sturdy iron windmill.

People? There were none. Other travellers? There were no travellers other than themselves atop this coach on all this bald world of space over land. Every seventeen miles or so a line of low trees sprang up to mark a shallow creek. Beside the creek a windmill and stockyards and a little iron hut, and here the coach would stop and the horses be changed, and the Cobb & Co.'s horse groom looked just like Two-Gun Harry without his guns.

All day the trail followed the telegraph posts. Then, looking back at noon, Stephens Creek had vanished and the hills beyond lay on the horizon like blue-black sea-girt rocks. The heat-charged air caused the world to shimmer and shake, and about four o'clock the horizon ahead became ragged and there arose hills which gradually became mountains separated by great rivers and inland seas. The sun wested, and the light wind died. The dust rose high behind the great vehicle. The horses plodded, the driver constantly calling to them and sometimes cracking his whip. Slowly the mountains ahead dwindled to hills and the hills grew small, and all the rivers and the inland seas faded out, leaving the new chum to realise how tricked he had been.

The sun had set when they came to the edge of the plain fifty miles from Stephens Creek, and to the Topar Hotel, built by the ghost of the man who had built the saloon at Dead Horse Gulch, down in Texas.

"Stay here an hour for dinner," Essen told his passengers. "Drink up and eat up 'cos we got all night in front of us. I'll see you in the bar."

It was almost dark when the fresh horses were harnessed and the passengers took their seats beside the driver. The children shouted. The licensee shouted. His wife called good-byes. The whip cracked and Fred Essen broke into a song about the stockman who betrayed the squatter's daughter.

Immediately they left the hotel, the country changed from plain to dark and mysterious mulga forest. The sand sang under the iron-shod wheels. The light went from the sky and the question in the minds of the two passengers was how Essen could see the track.

Hours passed, and then a horse neighed. The coach stopped, and in the complete dark a man shouted "Good-night, Fred".

There was movement, and the warm sound of sweating horses shaking their pelts. With not a glimmer of light to aid them, the groom and the driver unharnessed the exhausted horses and hitched in the fresh team.

The priest decided to enter the coach and try for some shut-eye. Essen climbed into his seat, and the next stage was begun.

"So you're going to Momba, eh?" he remarked, after reciting many verses about a bushranger called Thunderbolt. "My, that used to be a great station at one time. Three shearing sheds, and one year they broke all records by shearing a million sheep. The Gov'ment took bits and pieces off it for selection, and now there's only a million acres left and couple of hundred thousand sheep."

A million acres! How much would be a million acres? There was Uncle Jim's farm on Earl Radnor's estate. How many acres was that farm? Six hundred odd, a large farm, too. A million acres!

"Work her into square miles," suggested Fred Essen.

"Square miles! How many acres to a square mile? The once-budding novelist gave it up, and the Cobb & Co.'s driver took it over.

"Let me think. Ah! There's six hundred and forty acres to the square mile. Six hundred and forty into a million goes…wait a bit. Get up there! You loafin' bastards. Cor! What d'you think you're doing?"

The whip cracked like a gun, but the horses had stopped and now merely pranced without hauling.

"Now six hundred and forty going into a million ... Here, you get down and take the whip, and lam into them leaders when I say."

Upfield slipped and fell down from the high box seat, taking the whip with him. Essen magically produced a second whip. The coach was listing badly to the near side, the wheels almost buried to the hubs in sand. The priest slept on.

"When I call to 'em, wallop 'em," commanded Essen. "Now!"

His whip cracked and smacked. Upfield worked hard with his, wrapping the long leather round his legs and tripping backward. The horses reared. The coach remained fast. Another effort was as fruitless. Essen said:

"Better wake the father. Coach might go over on its side."

The priest was awakened and he alighted. Essen said:

"Did I see Mrs. Flanagan giving you two thermos flasks just afore you boarded, Father? Might there be coffee or suchlike in them flasks?"

"Coffee, I think, driver. Is it the right moment?"

"It is, Father. The horses want a rest. The young feller and me want a rest."

The coffee was still cold. The horses rested. The driver and his 'off- sider' rested. That was certainly the right moment. The flasks contained much more than coffee.

"Now we'll see," Fred said, and, whistling to the horses, he merely flicked the whip and they walked the coach from the bog.

The priest re-entered the coach to sleep again. The horses jog-trotted, and the hidden sand sang against the hidden wheels, and the world was hidden beneath the blazing stars.

"Six hundred and forty acres into a million goes..."

"Did you stage that hold-up?" asked the new chum.

"Stage her! Now, now, young feller. That coffee was the dinkum oil, wasn't it? Now about them acres. Lemme have a go. Six hundred and forty into a million goes fifteen hundred and sixty-one times. So Momba is 1,561 square miles."

Upfield was silent for some time, and then remembered the size of Hampshire, his own county. The area of Hampshire is 1,621, less than a hundred square miles larger than a sheep station named Momba. He told Essen this, and the driver said:

"Good for you, lad. You can't beat a good education. My grandfather tells the story when he was alive, about how he was baled up by Thunderbolt, my grandfather being a coach-driver like me." And there ensued a tale which had nothing to do with acreage or mileage.

Unable to see anything but the star-studded canopy covering the world, Upfield continued to cling to the top of that coach, rather than attempt to sleep inside it. The experience was too new to be scorned, and the driver too remarkable a character to be deserted. Some time during the night the sky widened, and the rounded outlines of sleeping hills were silhouetted, and then the wheels sang a different tune, as the coach bumped and scraped over bare rock.

The stories that driver related, as though purposely to keep his passenger awake! The songs he sang, and the song Upfield urged him to repeat! It was about the leader of a city gang of toughs called a 'push' and a person referred to as 'The Bastard from the Bush', and one verse went something like this:

'There's a stranger come among us,' said the Leader of the Push.

'Why, strike me dead, it's Foreign Ned, the Bastard from the Bush.

He's been in every two-up school from Bourke to Wooloomooloo,

He's rode a hack and seduced a black, what more could a Bastard do?

'Would you care to break a window?' said the Leader of the Push.

'I'll knock the ruddy house down,' said the Bastard from the Bush.

Would you knock a man down and kick him?' said the Leader of the Push.

'I'd knock him down and gut him,'said the Bastard from the Bush.

'Would you have a moll to keep you? Would you give up work for good?

'Would you live on prostitution?' 'My ruddy oath, I would.'

4

In the year 1911, Wilcannia was known as The Queen City of the West, and was, indeed, the happiest town on the Darling River. There were nineteen pubs, a dozen stores, banks, and private houses bordering the main street, and still more pubs fronting the 'Reserve' lining the west bank. From Wilcannia ran Cobb & Co.'s coaches to Broken Hill, to Cobar, up to Bourke and down to Wentworth. Smaller buckboards carried the mails and passengers out to White Cliffs, Wanaaring, and other remote settlements. On the river, steamers with barge trailers carried loads of wool down to the Murray and Adelaide, returning with roofing iron and fencing wire, dam-sinking equipment and stores. The place was alive. It was the hub, the heart of a vast area of country unknown to most of the inhabitants of the even then bloated coastal cities of Australia.

Wilcannia served the opal fields of White Cliffs, the gold diggings of Mount Brown, and the vast pastoral properties like Momba. To spend their money at Wilcannia came the workers and the managers, the miners and the prospectors, and on a Saturday night one couldn't move on the sidewalks without being jostled by the crowd. The hitching rails were packed with riding hacks and buckboard teams. A mile or two up- river was the famed brewery;

a mile or two out of town was the famed gaol.

The dawn of the day when Upfield was to see Wilcannia for the first time revealed the lumbering coach crossing low hills, and when the travellers descended again to the flat lands, they halted at another horse-change, where for two shillings the groom's wife provided breakfast of soda bread, grilled chops and lashings of coffee.

The night had been long for Upfield on the box seat with the driver, but by no means uneventful. With sun-up the heat returned, the urge to sleep was strong, yet was defeated by intense interest in this new world. All through the long and drowsy morning the coach lumbered over red-sand tracks cut by the wheels of wagons. They met teams of twenty-six and twenty-eight bullocks hauling the great wagons, and once a camel team of twenty-four hauling a load of wool. The road was endless, the mulga forest was endless too. Sometimes a lean and bearded character appeared from the shade of a better tree to which his horse was haltered, and Essen would hand down a station mailbag and perhaps a parcel or two.

Round about two o'clock the coach topped a low rise and seven miles onward could be seen the line of great red-gums bordering the Darling, and, amid the pepper trees, the shining roofs of Wilcannia. With seven miles to go, the journey from Broken Hill was approximately 120 miles…thirty hours on that coach!

Fred Essen, seemingly as fresh as when he started, had come to the end of his repertoire, and now sang again his masterpiece 'The Bastard from the Bush'. The priest, God bless him, possessed true Irish humour. It was now 'Arthur' and 'Fred' but always 'Your Reverence'. It was the priest who asked the meaning of 'Parcels Post bloke'.

"Well, your Reverence, the city offices of the Pastoral Companies seems to think that the back country wants new blood," explained the driver. "Like Arthur here, they send up young fellers, paying their fares if they stop a year. They get landed at the stations with the mail, sort of."

"Does the new blood upset the old?" pressed the priest.

"No more than you're going to upset Father Murphy," replied Fred. "There's all sorts out in these parts. A lot of 'em were Parcels Post blokes themselves, blokes what I brought out from the Hill years ago.

A lot of old coves, too, often go broke in Adelaide and get themselves sent up again by Parcels Post."

Finally, on to the broad main street. The horses, energised by the promise of water and rest, the whip cracking, people waving to the popular driver, they stopped outside the Post Office.

"See that pub there?" pointed Fred. "You go along and wait for me under the verandah."

Arthur promised to look up the priest when again in Wilcannia, and carried the heavy port and the blanket roll to the shade of the .verandah shadowed by the pepper trees. The coach was driven into the hotel yard, and Fred Essen came out to the sidewalk.

"A drink, a wash, a feed," he cried. "Come on."

Ice-cold beer in the bar. Tepid water in the washroom. A cool dining-room. It was three in the afternoon, but there was no grumbling by the staff, no slapping down of food before the customer by someone feeling insulted by having to work. Fred asked the Parcels Post bloke if he possessed working clothes, advised purchasing anything necessary, and after the meal accompanied the new chum to the coach office, where the voucher was handed in for the next section. Shaking hands and slapping a shoulder, he said he was off to bed.

At six o'clock Upfield boarded a buckboard having a seat behind in addition to the wide driving seat. The body of the vehicle was loaded with mailbags and parcels. He was the only passenger. The driver was taciturn and yet comradely. His destination was Wanaaring, approximately 140 miles up the ,alleged river named the Paroo.

Following a sleepless night on the train and another on the top of a coach, Upfield was now aching for sleep. On this buckboard sleep appeared to be impossible, but the driver was aware of the condition of his passenger. When night came again, he roped him to the seat back, saying:

"Now you can sleep if you want."

But the buckboard was much worse than the coach, in fact it seemed to have no springs whatever. The passenger's head ached; every muscle in his body complained, his eyes were as lead, but his mind still ticked.

Some time—a lifetime—later, the buckboard stopped for the umpteenth time. Upfield could see the dim shape of a building. The driver pointed in another direction and said: "There's the men's quarters." He dumped a mailbag and parcels on a hidden verandah. No one appeared. No light came on. He clambered aboard and drove off into the vacuum.

And Upfield lay down on the dry warm earth, rested his head on the roll of blankets, and slept. Voices roused him. It was day again. Men stood about him. One said:

"Better get up and have some breakfast before the sun burns the whiskers off you."

CHAPTER FIVE

ONE SPUR DICK

I

The manager of Momba was a Mr. Murray, who was dark and inclined to rotundity. His residence was substantial, and attached to it were the domestic quarters, the kitchen, and a dining-room for the hands. Of the men, only half a dozen worked about the homestead, but others were always coming and going from distant parts of the run.

As any city-born Australian, Upfield at first was like a pup fearful of straying from the kennel; the native-born Australian, when new to the outback hasn't anything up on the immigrant. In fact the immigrant is more easily broken in than the native-born, who is too cocksure.

After breakfast the men gathered outside the office, and when the manager appeared, each was given his orders for the day. He called Upfield into his office, where the book-keeper enrolled him, and Mr. Murray addressed him thus:

"I don't know why Laffer will send you people here. I don't want you, but I have to take you. I hope you will have sense enough not to go wandering away in the bush and getting yourself lost, compelling me to organise a search, and then, when we find you dead of thirst, having to write to your people and tell them how you perished. Get back to the quarters now and sleep yourself awake. I'll see you again in the morning."

The first job handed out by Murray was to assist a tinsmith make three ten-thousand-gallon water tanks. The corrugated iron sheets had to be curved, riveted, and finally soldered. It was done in the open, and the tinsmith's greatest worry was the willy-willies that danced madly across the landscape and might collide with a partially constructed tank and wreck it.

This work continued into cool April. The food was reasonable, based on the old formula of Ten-Two-and-a-Quarter. Ten pounds of flour, two of sugar, a quarter of tea, with tomato sauce and unlimited mutton. There were no fresh vegetables and for long periods there would be no potatoes. The weekly wage for an ordinary hand was a pound, but that pound was real money. You could hold a real sovereign in your hand.

The sleeping quarters were like a ship's forecastle: two tiers of bunks, the mattress being a sheep's skin or gum leaves encased within a hessian bag. Somewhere on another planet there were feather mattresses and sheets, easy-chairs and comfortable rooms, there was a shop boy to clean boots, and a maid to make the beds. Here was where you swam or sank. Now you decided to become a man or slink back to a city to work with a stand-over boss, your mind and your eyes on the clock, someone to think for you, and then you squandered your wages and considered yourself lucky to end up with a shilling for beer and fourpence for the new motion-pictures. Here you couldn't spend your wages; they mounted and mounted until you were rich and could go to Wilcannia, or Adelaide, and live like a millionaire for two weeks.

Upfield spent his Sunday afternoons in the empty shearers' quarters, writing to his mother, and to balance somewhat his earlier stupidities is the fact that for the next thirty years he never failed to write home every week. Sunday evenings were spent shooting rabbits, of which there were a million or two within sight of the homestead.

Two miles down the creek were the remains of the Momba Hotel. It had been a wallowing sink of iniquity, ever a cause of annoyance to the management of Momba Station. When the chance came to buy the licence the Company did so and, fortunately perhaps, just before Upfield's arrival the demolition of the building began. He, with an older man, spent a fortnight transporting the materials to the homestead, and after that he was striking for the blacksmith. Once he was sent with the bullock driver and his offsider to fetch wood for the kitchens.

The driver was called 'One Spur Dick' because he was never known to wear more than one spur, and no one could say why he wore it. The offsider rode after the bullocks and brought them to stand docilely against a fence, where One Spur Dick yoked them, paired them to the draw-chain, then drove them to the wagon and hitched them to the single pole shaft.

Away they went, the driver talking quietly, the bullocks making nothing of the empty wagon, the entire twenty-eight of them. It was the first time Upfield had left the homestead, and soon it was out of sight. They veered off the track and entered the mulga forest, where dead firewood lay in countless tons.

To the new chum it was all most confusing, as there were no hills, no other features, nothing but the wide-spaced low trees set on the flat, red, sandy earth; scant shrub, tea-tree bush, and more and more mulgas. Save at noon, Upfield could tell east from west, but in what direction was the homestead, baffled him. He said to the bullock driver:

"If you two were to drop dead right now, how would I find my way back to the homestead?"

One Spur Dick leaned on his long-handled whip and appeared to leer.

"Well now," he drawled. "I always like to hear you new chum bastards asking fool questions. I never mind tellin' you blokes anything. We all gotta learn. Come here. Put your feet in this wheel rut. Got 'em in?"

Upfield planted his feet in the six-inch-wide rut.

"Close your eyes. Got 'em closed? Good. Now you keep 'em closed. Now you walk in the rut, and in about half an hour you'll bash your bloody brains out against the office door."

A startlingly simple lesson, but Australians need not crow from the sidewalk of a busy street.

One Spur's offsider sniggered, and One Spur addressed himself to the offsider in language and vocal volume which made the bullocks strain into a false start.

With the passage of time, a few weeks, Upfield developed his 'bump of location'. First he followed the creek until it branched. Then he followed it down to the site of the old hotel. One Sunday he traced the creek downward for seven miles to where it emptied its flood water over the flats of the alleged river named the Paroo. The creek served as a highway, and it was this highway which revealed the two distinctive types of country–the mulga flats and the river flats, both having their traps baited for the unwary.

The large-scale map in the station office, which the bookkeeper permitted him to study, was most helpful. It provided a mental picture, simplified the major problems of the cardinal points of the compass applicable to the locality. The map showed that the road to Wilcannia, and in reverse to Wanaaring, ran north-south, and that it skirted the Paroo River on its west side. So! If you left that road to the west, the sun was always there to tell which was west and which was east, and you merely returned to the east to reach that road again.

All this was elementary, and was but the first lesson. Away from the road there were no natural phenomena to guide one, and it is a long way from thinking you know which is east and west to believing it, and nothing will prevent the Spirit of the Bush from trying to upset your confidence.

There was the Paroo River to the east, a vast chain of empty depressions linked by dry creeks bordered by box trees, every depression exactly alike, each creek like every other creek. To the west the mulga forests, uniformly flat, uniformly covered with red earth, every tree alike to the uninitiated.

All most inviting to the venturesome, all a certain trap to the unimaginative and the over-confident; especially in summer, when the fierce dry heat can play tricks, too. The aboriginal girl-child is trained by its mother and the boy is taught by the young men of the tribe how to move about with confidence based wholly on the development of the power of observation, a power which becomes instinct.

Upfield learned fast. He was aided much by his early love of maps, and assisted by one or two half-caste stockmen with whom he hunted kangaroos, for they showed him how to read tracks, how to uncover the surface root of a needlewood tree, break a surface root and place a quart-pot under the break, and, by setting fire to the foliage, force the sap down and out through the broken root, thus obtaining anything up to a pint of what would serve as emergency drinking water.

And still Upfield was in the elementary class at the School of the Bush, where the teachers were mere bush workers, the aborigines being the professors.

Mr. Murray was returnin.g to the homestead one cool day in April when Upfield had been an employee for some eight weeks. He drove two mules in a buckboard and, as always, was accompanied by a youthful aborigine riding a pair of additional mules as relief. He was driving along a fence, to be sure that sheep were not caught in the angle. There were no sheep, but from the high seat he saw on the ground strange markings, and shouted to the aborigine to come and examine them.

The aborigine dismounted and dragged his mounts to the place, looked at the markings, and grinned up at the manager. Pointing to foot tracks going and coming, he said:

"Parcel Post feller walk alonga here. Arthur Upfield him stop and make marks telling which way go back to homestead. He stop here and light his pipe. He lean a gun against the fence while he sit down. Then he get up and walk back station way."

The following morning after issuing orders for the day Mr. Murray took Upfield aside. Upfield admitted that he had determined to follow the fence into the mulga. Coming to the angle, he had marked arrows on the ground pointing to the homestead. Yes, he carried a gun. Yes, he had sat and smoked for half an hour. He admitted he remembered the manager's warning. He asked a legitimate question:

"How did the aborigine know who made the marks and left the footprints ?"

"Second nature with 'em," replied the manager. "I didn't ask him, but you must have left one or more burnt matches to prove that you lit up. The ground impression of the gun-butt was another clue. It seems you've taken to this country. Report to One Spur Dick. You are promoted to be mule driver's offsider."

2

One Spur Dick was grey of hair and with a ragged moustache. He was tall and tough, but not particularly heavy. Born in this inland country, he had never been farther than Broken Hill and Cobar. He was a Paroo River man, and was married to a woman who had many children, no two of whom were of the same nationality. He was kindly, generous, simple.

The mule harness was taken from the store, put together and reoiled. All one day driver and offsider fashioned hobble straps from prepared bullock's hide. Came the day when riders filled the yards with mules and among them strolled One Spur Dick loaded with bridles.

All these animals had been out on the wide wild range for two years. They kicked and bared their teeth, so One Spur Dick walked them around the yard until Upfield was dizzy and the mules less stubborn. One Spur cornered and haltered the two shafters, opened a gate and drove them into an empty yard. He haltered the two leaders, one of which was a huge gelding. These four animals were well broken and accustomed to the position in the team. The remaining twenty-six, forming the body of the team, were less tractable, some having to be hauled to the yard railing and left to gain sense or choke to death. The team having been chosen, the mob was returned to the range.

Two days were spent 'quietening' the team by going out for loads of firewood. Then rations were drawn for four weeks, for this first trip was to take wool to Broken Hill, and return with stores. Only twice did the team bolt, but without damage to the great table-top wagon, and when they were stopped, the driver would squat on his heels and tell them what bastards they were, and what he would do to reduce their dignity.

This was all right for Upfield, but as he was wholly useless as an offsider it says much for One Spur Dick, on whom was placed twice the labfour. Upfield could build a fire to boil water for tea. He wasn't too bad with an Irish stew. Baking soda bread in a camp oven is an art requiring practice, but One Spur patiently taught the new chum this, and many other tasks.

The wool was loaded at the out-station on the Darling River, where now was the principal wool-shed on Momba. Mount Murchison was the name of this homestead, but no mountain or hill was anywhere in sight. By now the offsider could kill and skin a sheep, knew how to joint the carcass and how to salt it. The night before they left, Upfield killed and salted two ration sheep, and a third, alive, was tethered to the wagon and would accompany them until needed for meat.

Travel was governed by routine; the scene each day always different. The weather was cool by day and cold by night, the air crystal-clear. Upfield became an efficient offsider:

One Spur Dick stirred when a new day raised its signal to the sky. They breakfasted at dawn, the saddle horse and the sheep munching their chaff at the rear of the wagon.

Ready for the track, One Spur Dick would take up his great bullock whip, whistle shrilly and start the leaders hauling the team straight. And again the mountain of wool would move on.

The designation 'offsider' means precisely that the driver's mate assists him by also driving on the offside. With animals harnessed in pairs, and when there are anything up to fifteen pairs to a team, the over-all length is considerable. It is at the pinches where the offsider is of value, for the team must pull together, and must be kept in a straight line.

Where the Paroo meets the Darling River, it is spanned by a bridge having white rails and a timber roadway which would rumble and moan under the heavily loaded wagon. One Spur decided to take the track over the dry bed of the Paroo, and the track angled down one bank and up the other. To take this crossing was a job for an expert, and One Spur Dick certainly needed an offsider, even a new chum, to keep his team and the wagon on the track.

So the day would pass. When the team had been loosed, camp would be made and dinner prepared, and, after dinner, utensils were cleaned by the offsider, whose final job was to boil or bake meat and bread in the camp ovens. Then came ease beside a leaping camp-fire, and tales to listen to–until One Spur Dick learned that his offsider didn't mind reading to him. He joined in as offsider to the offside, that the reading session could begin earlier. Hard covers and paper-backs were exchanged with the coach grooms at the watering places, and when in Broken Hill One Spur Dick would press a pound on his offsider to buy more.

The day they were to reach the Topar Hotel where the mulga ended and the vast saltbush plain began, firewood was added to the load, for there would be none until the hills were reached, and then it would be scarce. The wind on the open plain was bitter at night, and in daytime it was trying to the nerves, hour after hour of it.

The time came to kill the ration sheep and the offsider picked up the knives and led the animal away. The sheep nuzzled his hands, asking for damper crusts. You can't kill a pet. You cannot slaughter an animal you have watered, fed with chaff and damper crusts. Upfield took the sheep back to the wagon.

"I can't, Dick. You do it."

One Spur snorted, demanded the knives and began a tirade, the main purpose of which was to inform the world that no man was more greatly cursed than the bloody mule driver with a bloody Pommy bastard offsider. He grabbed the sheep by the tethering strap and walked off. The sheep bleated once. He came back to the camp-fire. The knives were still clean.

"Kill that bloody sheep," he shouted. "It's your job. Go on!"

So the sheep wasn't killed, and two days later it was exchanged for another from a drover, an unknown sheep being legitimate meat.

3

Broadly speaking, Arthur Upfield was no different from millions of young men of his generation, with the exception perhaps of a mental attribute which drove him to seek new worlds. Many a young man is vitalised by an ambition to achieve something or to be something, but Upfield himself did not know what or how.

For four months he and One Spur Dick travelled the track between Momba and Broken Hill. The winter was normal, long spells of sparkling cold weather, with a short break of rain causing the crossing creeks to run fast and suddenly. Every day provided a new interest: the Cobb & Co. coaches, two of them, one driven by Fred Essen; other teams to meet with and general information to be exchanged; men at the horse changes and those in charge of the Government dams. And if all spoke a language strange to Upfield, he never doubted he would acquire it. The new stars introduced to him by One Spur, the Standard One lessons on the Bush given him by this simple and likeable man, the life in the open, the experience of walking through a rabbit plague as through a flock of sheep, watching the dancing brolgas, the mystery of dark nights, all challenged his imagination.

There was the event which brought doom to the horse coaches and ultimately completely changed the face of inland Australia.

"What the hell is this coming?" One Spur shouted when they were travelling a cut line through the mulga. Upfield, riding the load, stared at the dust cloud pointed by a black arrow-head.

"Car," he shouted down to the driver. The team was stopped.

"Car!" exploded One Spur. "What's that?"

"Motor-car," replied the offsider.

It was, indeed, a motor-car. An Overland. The first car to travel the track from Broken Hill to Wilcannia. It stopped by the wagon. Two men leered at the teamsters. The tired mules tried to bolt. It was the first car they and One Spur had ever seen. By the end of the First World War all the coaches had vanished and nearly all the great teams had been replaced by the motor-truck. Travelling time between Broken Hilland Wilcannia was cut from thirty hours to six.

At the Stephens Creek crossing, where the sand is coarse and deep, a table-top loaded with wool was bogged to the axles, and the tearm of twenty-eight bullocks was exhausted and battered, as were the teamsters. The driver was another 'Captain Kettle', his offsider a younger edition of One Spur Dick. Added to their troubles was the information that the creek was about to run.

The mule teamsters and the bullockies went into conference. Time was vital. To unload those ungainly bales of wool and push and heave them to the bank would cost time, and the water might come and drown the bullocks before they could haul out the wagon. The mules must cross before the creek flooded, else they would be delayed for days.

One Spur said he had spare swingle trees, and suggested hitching his team ahead of the bullock team. Captain Kettle beamed and suggested a drink. The whisky jar went round. Then the mules were hitched ahead of the bullocks, forming a combined team of fifty-four animals.

Whips were discarded in favour of long-handled shovels. The drivers addressed themselves to their teams, their assistants positioned on the offside. The signal was given, and four men wielded their shovels. The bullocks groaned, the mules heaved. Nothing happened.

"Have to unload," drawled One Spur.

"Not on yer life," roared Captain Kettle. "You unhitch your mokes and we get your wagon past and across. Them bloody bullocks stays with my wagon and hauls her out if they has to stay yoked for a twelvemonth. They can bloody well drown and the wool can float off down the creek, but I'm not unloading and loading up again. There's time for another snozzle."

Two men appeared and walked over the bed to join the defeated teamsters.

"Sorta bogged," drawled a huge man.

"Yep, sorta," snarled Captain Kettle. "Have a drink."

"Looks like you gotta unload," opined the huge man.

Captain Kettle swore.

"Well, we could hitch our camels ahead of the mules," the stranger suggested, adding dryly: "Make or bust."

He brought his camels, thirty of them, a superbly built team. They were hitched to the mules, and so there was a team of eighty-four animals. One Spur shook his head. Captain Kettle grinned, his beard pointing to the sky as he picked up his shovel. The general signal was given, and six men went to work. It was a long, continuous united effort. Abruptly the animals lurched forward, some going down to their knees. The line sagged here and there, became a confused jumble. Then onward, the men shouting to halt them, for now all they dragged was the pole and the front wheels of the wagon, which remained bogged.

The camel drivers produced a bottle of whisky. It lasted one round. The teams were separated. The camels ahead of the mules dragged One Spur's wagon across the creek. The mules ahead of the camels dragged the camel-men's wagon over. Then all hands fell to unloading the bullocky's wagon, rolling the bales up the bank—and still the water hadn't come. They hitched camels and mules to the rear of the now empty wagon, and dragged it to the other side of the creek, and then dragged it back to where the pole and the front wheels and the wool awaited.

Within three days, Captain Kettle and his offsider had repaired their wagon, re-loaded, and were on the move. And still the water hadn't reached the crossing.

Down in the cities it was eight hours' work, eight hours' play, eight hours' sleep. Music halls and picture shows, hot showers and four- course meals. Girls to love and horses to back and bosses to consign to hell. Here men with teams worked from dawn to dark, lived on fare as poor as that given to windjammer sailors. Here men ridiculed the pampered city workers, and the city workers returned compliments to the Bastards from the Bush.

One afternoon One Spur tripped over a root in his eagerness to get at a loafing mule and, looking up, saw Upfield laughing at him. He stopped the team.

"Come down outer that, a-laughin' at me like a looney coot." Upfield obeyed. "Here, you take the whip and the ruddy team. I'll do a bit of riding from now on."

Up he climbed, and Upfield whistled to the team. Nothing happened. He whistled again, and the leaders looked at him and the body mules sneered. He commanded them to 'git-up', and six or seven of them closed their eyes and sagged. One Spur yelled with laughter. Upfield tried again with the long whip, and the mules he touched sprang into the collar, leaving the others to snigger. Ever heard a mule snigger? It's apt to deflate you.

One Spur alternated periods of colourful advice with yells of mirth for the next two hours.

"Now listen, mate. You gotta talk to mules and bullocks. Their talk ain't your fancy pantsy yabber," he said. "Them poor coots don't understand. You listen to me."

He whistled and spoke to them of their ancestry, their relations, and the progeny they would never have, and they went hard into collars, and the wagon rolled on.

Upfield realised he would never become as efficient as One Spur and Captain Kettle. You have to be born in a hammock slung under a wagon to become a real teamster.

As always, when on the homeward journey on the last trip to Broken Hill, they camped outside Wilcannia, camping in the town being prohibited. That night they went to town to meet some friends in one of the pubs, and were informed by the Common Ranger that two mules which had got away on a previous trip were seen recently in a certain area.

The following morning One Spur ordered Upfield to take the saddle horse and hunt for the strays while he harnessed the team. The mules were not in the reported area, and, on returning to camp, Upfield found it deserted. Wagon and team were discovered outside an hotel. One Spur was one hundred and ten per cent drunk. The licensee said:

"Better take the lot outa town. You can't let 'em stay there. Agin the law."

"Why d'you let him get drunk?"

"Hoo! Free country, ain't it? Now look, we'll make a hole in the top of the load and dump One Spur into it, and you drive the ruddy team a bit outa town and camp again."

So the hole was made and two men climbed to the top of the mountain and hauled One Spur up on a rope and dumped him into it. Then they joined half a dozen others waiting for the Pommy to make them laugh.

But the mules were fresh and the Pommy got them into action; the men must have seen the wagon rolling down the street, the mules controlled by the offsider who shouldered the whip-handle and permitted the long whip to trail over the ground behind him, precisely as One Spur always did.

Now Upfield was faced by more than one problem. Out of town was the Town Common and, as with such places, feed on the Common would not satisfy a mugwump. There would be no feed this side of the Paroo Bridge, and, if there had been, there were four mules requiring two men to unharness and hobble. Fortunately the road up the river was hard and the going easy.

Then there was the Paroo Crossing, by the bridge or the track. The track was out for one man. The bridge was there, wide enough. But the bridge rumbled and trembled.

Upfield couldn't make up his mind whether to cross by the bridge or take the angled track. He was still undecided when the leaders came to the bridge.

The team was behaving well. They were within twenty miles of Mount Murchison and their own country. The leaders trod the wooden roadway. Their long ears prodded forward as they looked down at it. Upfield whistled and managed to crack the hip. The team held, went on. As each pair reached the wooden road the rumbling increased. Then at last the wagon was on the bridge, which seemed at that moment to be at least a mile long.

All was well. The wagon rolled dead-centre on the roadway. It was midway over the bridge when the team was stopped by yells from above. There was One Spur Dick peering over the edge of the load, eyes glassily directed downward to the offsider, lower to the bridge railing, down and down to the creek bed eighty-odd feet below the bridge. Such was his condition that after the first yell he lost his voice.

It was a situation not to be discussed there and then.

Upfield did have sense enough to whistle the team into their collars, and the mules had sense enough to haul forward instead of swinging to either side and hurtling the wagon over the bridge. When again on firm and blessed ground, Upfield stopped the team and One Spur proceeded to climb down the mountain load like a defongerated spider.

He tried to speak. He strove to blast his offsider. He threw up his hands in despair and set off at a running lurch back to the pub.

There is only the one solution to the problems pressing hard on the new chum teamster: keep the team moving. There were, of course, no houses, and no travellers to assist, save perhaps the chance horseman or driver of a buckboard. Upfield drove on to the boundary fence of Momba Station, arriving there late in the afternoon. He did damage to one gate post, but reclosed the gate and propped the post drunkenly against it. There were heavy sand-bars to cross, but the team was anxious to be home and responded promptly to a call or crack of the whip.

It was growing dark and, when three miles off Mount Murchison, they were met by Murray driving a buckboard, with an aborigine riding one of the spare mules. He was on his way to Wilcannia, searching for his teamster. Murray made no observation following the offsider's report on the mysterious disappearance. He and the aborigine assisted in unharnessing the team and hobbling each animal. Murray turned to Upfield:

"You camp here tonight with the wagon. I'll bring Dick out in the morning. My God! Where angels fear..."

4

Tom Ellis was a barrel-like man of middle age. He patrolled a section of some eighty miles of Momba's vermin fences, riding a camel and using a pack camel to transport his equipment. Upfield found him camped in his tent on the bank of the river. Ellis was enjoying a couple of days' spell, and Upfield had been given three days' break following the last trip to Broken Hill.

It happened that the rider who patrolled the section next to that cared for by Tom Ellis had asked for his cheque. The job, therefore, was vacant.

"How would I do?" asked Upfield.

"Dunno. Bit new, perhaps. You haven't been so long in the country. Lonely job. Anything happen and you'd perish. You see people only once or so in every month. Still..." and Ellis glanced up from a sand-map at the toughened new chum. "No harm in giving it a fling. You'll have to see Murray."

Upfield tracked down the manager.

"No good, Arthur. No good at all. You're too new. I won't hear of it. Besides, I can see you becoming a teamster yet."

Upfield applied the same tactics as used on Laffer, and if only in later years he had continued to apply this method of gaining something desired, he might have risen to greater heights.

"I told you yesterday, Upfield, you are too new to the country to take on that fence job. Another year: I'd consider it. It's no use talking."

Murray was more obdurate than Laffer, but it is remarkable what water-drops will do. The day came when Murray lost his temper.

"All right, blast it! Have the ruddy job. Take it on. Go and get bushed and perish for water; have your scalp torn off by a camel, or your belly smashed in by a hoof, and lie for days and nights screaming for your mother. The summer's coming on. Get to hell out of my sight, and tell Tom Ellis I want to see him."

"Got to break you in," said Tom Ellis. "Bring your things to my camp."

The breaking-in took a month, and even then neither Tom Ellis nor the manager were happy about it.

5

The vermin or rabbit fences on Momba were, roughly, built to the letter of a giant H. The main homestead was mid-way on the horizontal bar, Upfield's section being from this homestead down to the left foot resting on the river at Mount Murchison, Ellis's section being from the homestead to the river via the right leg. Both sections were something like eighty miles in length.

Each rider had two camels–a bullock and a cow, as these, naturally, agree better than two bullocks or two cows. The bullock, being the stronger, carried the pack loaded with water-drums, pack-bags of rations, tools, tent and stretcher, spare wire.

The cow carried the long iron saddle, the saddle space in front of her hump being occupied by the tucker-box containing eating utensils and current foodstuffs, and that behind the hump providing the seat for the rider.

Camels are as different in temperament from mules as mules are from bullocks, and when it comes to intelligence the camel rates higher than both. The exercise of patience will gain much from a camel. Cruelty will achieve nothing. The camel will wait long for the chance to scalp a man or pound him to a pulp.

There is the story of the man who drove camels in a team. He disliked one particular animal, and singled it out for special attention with the whip. The man left the job and after three years took employment on another station as a fence rider. He did not recognise the team camel he had abused, but the camel, now employed on a fence, remembered him. He was minus his scalp and there were few unbroken bones when he was ultimately found.

Any man who likes cats will like camels, will come to understand them, but camels do not like cats, who are apt to run up a leg to the hump. You have to be firm but reasonable. You must not be fearful and must not arouse fear in them. All this was imparted to the new chum, for the rules applicable to this fence work have been worked out by men whose lives have been exposed to the dangers inherent in solitude. You never knew what the next hour would bring, what waited beyond the next sand dune. You could travel all one day and find nothing to be done to the fence. You could leave a night camp and find within half an hour a job costing a morning of time. The rabbits burrowed under the bedded wire; the emus when trying to walk over it would be caught by the neck or the leg and have to be killed before being removed, or smell to high heaven; the wind would shift a foot of surface soil, leaving the bottom of the netting inches above ground, so permitting passage to rabbits; the creeks would abruptly flood and sweep a hundred yards of fence out of sight.

You see no one, day after day and night after night, for three weeks or a month; and after a few doses of that you find strange things happening. And when, for instance, you realise you are talking to the boss seated on a fence post, when the boss is doubtless a hundred miles distant, take advice and go back to driving mules.

Upfield's camels were comparatively quiet, but, like all camels, they had a mania for making off to the paddock where they were bred. They were like Captain Hatteras, who always walked to the north; when released in hobbles they would invariably turn to their spiritual home. Thus it was wise to let them go early, bring them back to camp at dusk, and tether each to a tree.

Upfield's section passed close to a depression named Meenamurtee Lake, and at the time the channel had brought flood water all the way from the hills about White Cliffs. A limpid sheet of water, covering several hundred acres, was surrounded by ancient box trees, and sand dunes of clean red sand outside the trees.

Once upon a time two Chinamen had used water from a previous filling to grow vegetables for the opal gougers at White Cliffs. They had built a two-roomed hut. And then something happened and one hanged himself from a cross-beam.

The camels stuffed on luscious pig-weed growing on the shores of the lake, and there were countless ducks and swans and water-hens swimming on the water or sporting in the shallows.

On arrival here, Upfield always spent the next day in bathing, cooking, hunting. After days of living amid the mulgas, dark and metallic trees, trees having barely any shade, a forest inhabited by wild things seldom seen, and lying o'nights on a stretcher-bed to defeat the ants, staring at the mocking stars and straining the ear to register sound so that the silence might be defeated, coming to Meenamurtee Lake was like entering into Paradise, especially when the moon rode the sky.

Upfield slept on purpose inside the hut, and in the morning he peered beyond the glassless window to see, within sixty yards, teal and black and Queensland grey duck. Invariably he shot two birds with the one barrel, and often a third with the second, when a million or so birds rose in a great whirring mass. At night, if the moon was up, he waded out into the lake for a hundred yards, and, the water up to his chest, fished with a land line and hooked river perch or cod weighing four or five pounds. And no competition. No one other than himself. A lake born to live only for a year, perhaps two, and all the while birds and the fish undisturbed except by a fence-man now and then and for a day or so.

6

Life was easy, perfect for the young man whose only ambition was to explore this fascinating world so secret from about four million people living on the fringes of a continent.

The summer came, and the heat brought the few varieties of snakes thus far from permanent rivers, and enlivened all the ants, from the inch-and-a-quarter-long bull ants to the little fellows no bigger than cheese mites. There were the crows and their language to interpret. There were the wary bush turkeys, the graceful and utterly delightful brolgas, who loved to dance, and, when on wing, floated under the sky like feathers. There were the perky galahs; the Major Mitchell cockatoos; the huge black cockatoos along the Darling; and the lizards, from the monarch iguanas to the small mountain devils. And, of course, the kangaroos, the emus, the wild dogs. All to engross the mind of a man free of the incubus called Time.

It was no novelty now for Upfield to wake before dawn, breakfast as the day strengthened, and be on the daily stage before sun-up. But on this job the day's stage was done before noon, and the remainder of the day he lazed and read novels, ranging from Lever to Charles Garvice and Nat Gould. Time meant nothing, other than the rising and the setting of the sun, when to countless millions life was governed by the clock. As Barnum used to say: "There's a mug born every minute, mugs who cannot live without a clock, mugs ranging from millionaires to workhouse inmates."

What does an hour, or half a day, matter in the drama of an ant war? Time is not in the arena occupied by two eagles battling with a dingo. What has time to do with learning the language of the crows, studying the psychology of camels, learning to read the Book of the Bush? Time was of the essence when collecting rents. Who is free of this thing called Time? The aborigines are. For a golden hour Upfield was.

Upfield owned a dog, apparently good for nothing but chasing rabbits. She possessed speed enough to catch a rabbit if the rodent was sick or tired or something. The course was open, marked by the fence. On his riding camel, Upfield would watch these fruitless pursuits, shouting encouragement to the dog.

One quiet, hot and drowsy morning the dog discovered a monarch iguana, a fine specimen almost five feet in length superficially drowsy and desiring to be alone. When the dog set it, it raised itself on its short and powerful legs, puffed out its neck, became the picture of belligerency. Its bite is not venomous, but the wound takes a long time to heal. The dog refused to be called off.

The encounter created a dense dust cloud from which the iguana emerged like a brown streak. It raced away along the fence, the dog a few yards behind. There were no near trees; the course was perfect. When a hundred yards distant, the iguana abruptly left the fence and circled wide, putting on a fine performance. The dog kept going, for she was nothing if not tenacious, and although she wasn't losing ground, she wasn't gaining. Eventually the reptile reached the fence again, behind the camels, and, seeing these tall objects, it raced towards them, and up the leg of the rear camel, to perch atop the pack-load.

The result was astonishing to the new chum. The pack-load erupted from the bullock's hump explosively, and while observing these many things flying high from an animal engaged in extraordinary contortions, Upfield himself rose high, to bite the dust.

The day was still hot, quiet and drowsy when Upfield awoke, with a bad headache and many other aches but nothing broken. The scene was littered with all his gear and the saddles. The iguana had vanished, but the dog lay panting and was thoroughly satisfied. The camels also had vanished. Fortunately the water-drums were undamaged, and Upfield followed the bush rule when in a fix, by making a fire and boiling water for tea.

Not yet used to 'open country', still a little fearful of becoming lost when out of sight of the fence which had a homestead at either end of its eighty-odd miles, the new chum attempted to locate the camels, and was indeed lucky to find them less than half a mile away, the cow trapped by her noseline entangled in a bush and the bullock feeding near by, and declining to desert her.

Aspirin not then being available, Upfield suffered severe head and shoulder pain for several hours as he lay on his stretcher in the shade cast by a cabbage tree. He was obeying another rule: when hurt, camp.

Months after this incident, the dog had five pups. They had the general appearance of the kelpie, the breed most suitable for sheep work. At first they nestled in a box atop the pack-load, and the mother ignored the rabbits and kept close to the camel's rear. When able to run about, they were a source of irritation and delay, but there was no impulse to destroy them.

The sheepmen at the homesteads frowned, for here were five potential killers, five dogs that probably would run wild and mate with wild dogs and dingoes, but the day came when they changed their tune. As the sun wested one evening, Upfield was camped with two stockmen–the northern boundary riders–who had rigged a tent on high ground overlooking a surface dam.

The sheep had been in to drink, and Upfield's dog took her pups for a walk. They were quite a sight, the mother and the five sturdy pups. At this time of evening a thousand or two galahs, parrots having grey backs and red breasts, flew in to drink, the birds alighting on the banks of the dam and the surrounding flat land. Presently one of the stockmen said, reverently:

"Look at that flaming dog!"

The dog was stalking the packed birds, the pups close beside her, belly low to ground, and when a pup wandered from her she darted forward and nipped it. Then it became apparent that she wasn't stalking the birds, but working them as a sheep dog works a flock of sheep. With the pups about her, she worked the birds off the depression, up the banks of the dam, without arousing one to fly. And she was teaching the pups!

Even the manager was regretful he wasn't in the rush to buy one of those pups.

Christmas came, Upfield's second Christmas in Australia. His mother had sent him a plum pudding in a cloth and two jars of mince. Christmas dinner consisted of salted boiled mutton, with soda bread and tomato sauce, plum pudding with fruit mince instead of brandy sauce. The plum pudding was, naturally, excellent, neither time nor heat having affected it. It was eaten in the shade of the best shade-tree in the bush, the cabbage tree, and beyond the shade the heat was such that to toss a wax vesta out upon the sun-stricken ground was to see the match ignite within fifteen seconds. Upfield experimented with five matches and counted the seconds.

He suffered the first of very few attacks of homesickness. Oh, to be in England now that Christmas was there! The pantry floored with slate, walled with brick, fitted with racks from which were suspended the puddings in cloth, several turkeys, braces of partridges from the farms owned by relatives, and on the slate bench a whole Stilton cheese, and a whole Yorkshire ham cooked to utter perfection.

In all the subsequent years, Christmas in Australia was never Christmas to Upfield.

Leaping fires, not this stifling sun heat. Hunger for food, not this mere eating to live. Good fellowship, not this isolation. Christmas numbers of *The Strand* and *Pearson's Magazine* to read, not a dog-eared Garvice or a Nat Gould. Smart clothes and well-fitting shoes, not an under-vest and dungaree trousers, worn elastic-sided riding boots. Christmas bells, not the hollow-sounding bells suspended from the necks of camels.

Upfield was yet too new to avoid this attack, but the lingering effects were slightly eased when the following day he halted to make repairs to the gate spanning the road to Wilcannia, and there met a traveller, the first human being he had seen for a couple of weeks.

"Yesterday wasn't Christmas," the traveller said. "Christmas Day was six days back."

But who could be homesick for long in such a country?

Upfield never bothered to pitch a tent unless rain threatened. Late one afternoon thunder-rain darkened the sand and filled the claypans. It was short and heavy, and afterwards, in the wonderfully fresh and clean evening, Upfield built his camp-fire and cooked, and when the first stars appeared, there rose from the ground the Bardee moths, having a wing span as large as your hand, and beautifully marked. They put out the slush-lamp. Finally they put out the fire. They drove Upfield to shelter under a blanket and the dog to crouch with her head under his legs.

This late summer rain preludes the nuptial dance of the termites, those prisoners of the dark, of termite hills and dungeons, ordained to be released to mate in the glory of the sun. After the rain the portals are flung open, and there emerges, like billowing smoke, the stream of life to re-create itself. And in the final, the culminating ecstasy of the dance, the couples fall to the ground, where the ants claim them, and the birds snap them up, and perhaps one female of every million will escape to populate a new nest.

Upfield patrolled his section of the Momba vermin fences for slightly more than twelve months before he was given proof that it isn't good for man to live alone.

He was aware that he had formed the habit of talking aloud to imaginary persons, but the final warning rang a loud bell when he found something odd about his meal table inside the hut at Meenamurtee Lake. During the meal he had argued in favour of beer with a ghostly opponent who preferred 'plonk', and the oddity was that opposite his own place he had set the spare cutlery and a pannikin for the ghost.

Four days later he reached the main homestead, where he asked for his cheque. Not without embarrassment, he related the incident to the manager, who said:

"Time to take a spell, Upfield. Only two antidotes for that type of lunacy. Either go get ajob driving a tram, or go on the booze in Wilcannia."

2. A monarch iguana

3. A chain of caterpillars

4. A tame kangaroo

5. Wild dog puppies looking for their mother

CHAPTER SIX

THE RED IRISHMAN

I

There is no kinship between the English tramp and the Australian sundowner save disinclination to work, and the philosophy which carries a man onward to the mirage of freedom. To seek this freedom a man needs to be venturesome, and needs the quality of the courage of the pilgrim. The city dwellers are no less slaves to convention and taboos than the wild savages of the islands and the aborigines of Australia, and for them it is a comforting thought, amounting to illusion, that they are superior to the sundowner.

The name stems from the custom of supplying rations to any man calling at a station homestead, sufficient to carry him through to the next homestead; for the pastoralist depends much on the itinerant workers and did he not issue rations, these workers would not be on tap in a country where 'farms' comprise a million acres, not a hundred. Thus the sundowner can be expected to arrive at a homestead at the end of a day–at sundown.

In the year 1912 and to a much later date, there were three classes of sundowner, if but the one type. There was, and is, the dyed-in-sand- and-mulga class, mostly old men who follow the rivers and creeks, up and down, year in and year out. They carry a blanket rolled within a calico sheet, a billy-can, and what food they have in a swag slung from the shoulder and resting in the small of the back. Next, and higher in the social hierarchy, is the true swagman. He carries his kit as does the sundowner, but he is either' seeking work or a spell of 'freedom' before taking the next employment. Higher still in the social scale is the bikeman, who lashes to the bicycle a 'skeleton' swag, a modicum of rations and a jam-tin billy-can. The bikemen may be subdivided. The pedaller aims to go somewhere as fast as he can push the pedals. He needs money to send to someone dependent on him, and money implies work. The pusher is the man who loads his machine with a light tent, a couple of blankets, rations, a shot-gun and fishing lines, and perhaps a cat or a pup in a sugar bag. He is more independent of the pastoralist than the pedaller, being free to camp where he wishes and follow dry tracks from which other men on foot shy away.

When Upfield left Momba he had equipped himself with a bike; the machine loaded with swag, rations, gun and pup. The pedals had been removed, and the only exertion necessary was to push and keep the machine upright with one hand; thus he was able to walk in complete freedom from weight. He possessed a pay cheque for ninety-eight pounds, which he cashed in Wilcannia for Bank of England notes and sovereigns, the value today being something like four hundred pounds. He could purchase a pair of boots for seven shillings and sixpence, twill trousers for nine shillings, a pound of real tobacco for four shillings and sixpence. We have, of course, progressed mightily since those days– perhaps!

2

The Darling River having been called The Gutter of Australia, the Murray River, of which it is a tributary, may rightfully be referred to as The Great Australian Drain. The Murray is wide and open, slashed and gashed, shallow and torpid. The Darling is narrow and shaded and private. The Murray is just another river. The Darling is Australian; a unique river in a unique land.

The Darling provides proof that Nature abhors a straight line. Rain falling over southern Queensland is prevented by the coastal mountains from rushing to the Pacific Ocean, and the torrents flow southward to the Murray, eight hundred miles or so at the

Victorian border, and then westward to the Indian Ocean. The distance given is from one point to another, but Nature has so fashioned this river that its course measures something like two thousand miles.

Were it not that Man is governed by the mania of building in straight lines, the stranger to the Darling could be forgiven for thinking that men and machines fashioned the main channel, because throughout its length the banks are meticulously graded and the bed is at a uniform depth, save at the sharper bends. It is a river decorated with ribbons and bows called billabongs, and from source to conjunction with the Murray it is head-dressed by an avenue of red-gums which almost meet to complete a green-gold canopy to shadow the water.

The river, when in flood, forces traffic many miles from the main channel, but flooding is rare and the depth of water ranges from twenty- five feet down to a trickle flowing from bend to bend where deep holes have been gouged and the fish wait. Within the great bends it is easy to become bushed amid the billabongs, and as the ground feed for stock is very poor, it is seldom that stockmen ride into them.

Upfield had received ample warning about these bends, had been absorbed by tales of desperate characters who hid in them and sometimes waylaid the solitary traveller whose disappearance would never be noted. He had been urged not to sleep by a campfire, to boil his billy and eat before dusk, and move on for a mile or two and camp in darkness. The reputation of this river was worse than the reality, but the reality was sufficient to dictate caution.

Save when shearing was in progress, the traveller could always find shelter in the shearing shed, and here would others be camped, precisely as the traveller by car will encounter other road-users at country hotels. Newcomers were deputed to tackle the station book- keeper or the cook for a hand-out. At some sheds were found a dozen and more men, many having lived there for a week or so. At most of these communities one man was voted cook and others would have to provision the larder with fish or ducks, and yet others were deputed to purchase tobacco. The newly arrived traveller was invited to dinner, and afterwards joined the others about the communal fire to discuss subjects ranging from station cooks and station bosses to sprees at the bush pubs. Soon he was *au fait* with the reputation of every cook, boss, publican and policeman up and down the entire length of the river. Of all these, the cooks were the most important.

At one homestead Upfield approached the men's cook at the right moment, when the men had eaten and had departed for their quarters. He was a small, sharp-nosed, watery-eyed martyr to chronic sore feet.

"What j'you want?" he snarled.

"A little flour?" suggested Upfield, holding forward the calico bag. The cook screamed:

"Flour! Why don't you loafing swagmen do some work for a change?" Then *sotto voce*: "Give us your bag."

He returned to the back door with about seven pounds of flour.

Upfield suggested a little sugar.

"Sugar!" he yelled. "Sugar be damned, I'm kept short of sugar. Sugar for swagmen!" Again *sotto voce*: "Give us your bag."

So it went on for tea and meat, two pounds of tea and half a side of mutton, all for the ears of the boss on the high note, and all for the traveller on the low.

There was the cook who never handed out anything until dark, and then the gentlemen of the road would return to the camp loaded with tucker enough to feed a dozen men for three days. And there was the cook who never handed out anything at any time; and he ended up on the outskirts of a river town with his head bashed in.

The great majority of swagmen were blasphemers and yet practised Christianity by obeying the golden rule: love your neighbour. The minority could be easily detected as the scum which followed the shearing gangs, never working at any other period of the year, and always spouting the tenets of the Great Labour Movement. To this type you could lose anything from a billy-can to the clothes you stood up in. Sometimes the station boss came seeking men to work at boundary riding, fencing, one of a dozen other jobs. Often men faded away when they saw a boss coming; sometimes, when times were bad and rations short, they crowded him.

All the bosses were famous throughout the back country.

There was Millionaire Tyson, who was approached by two men for work. He told them to follow him. Leading them to a gate, he ordered one to sit on it and the other to keep opening and closing it. Two hours later he returned, and found they had changed places. They were told to report to the book-keeper for their cheques. There was McCaughey, afterwards Sir Samuel. Upfield asked him for a job, and the Dunlop boss said he could boundary ride from a hut half-way out on the run. The overseer was leaving within the hour, and Upfield was told to leave his bike in the store and his swag on the office steps, and take a chaff-bag to the gardener for vegetables.

The gardener was a Chinaman. He gave Upfield seeding cabbages, worm-eaten carrots, and so forth. Upfield was humping the bag from the garden when McCaughey stopped him.

"Empty them out." The boss glanced at the heap. "Bring the bag." Back in the garden they were met by the Chinese gardener. The boss ignored him. Pointing to a bed of young carrots he said: "Pull some of those." The Chinese danced, washed his hands. "Those cabbages look all right. Rip up half a dozen. Sweet potatoes! Just dug, too. Take half the heap." When Upfield was staggering away with the load, the boss said to the gardener: "Pack up, John. Go for your cheque. I've been paying you to grow vegetables for the men as well as for the house."

And there was the boss who had been an Army man. Every

Sunday morning he paraded before the men's quarters in full regimentals; spurs, sword and all. The men saluted, called him 'sir'. They would have called him 'sire' had he demanded it, for after parade he led all hands to the battlefield of the office verandah, where he handed out rum in half-pint pannikins, up to the brim.

3

All the outback towns were known as 'police-controlled'. The senior officer was, in addition to his police duties, registrar of births and deaths, licensing officer, protector of this and that, including the aborigines, and held at least a dozen other offices. What offices he could not occupy were conducted by the postmaster, and between them they ruled areas up to the size of England. Misdemeanours committed on the runs and tracks were reported by the pastoralists, and as the culprits had to enter a town at some time or other, all the policeman need do was to sit and wait.

The policeman at Pooncarie was a good fellow. At the only hotel was the smallest bar in Australia, in which hung a notice reading: 'Please fight outside. Thuds upset the beer.'

Upfield and his dog entered the town. It was warm and quiet this winter morning, the goats lay in the sunlight, and on the middle of the track slept a large grey cat. On seeing the cat, the dog clawed the ground to gain speed. The cat raced into a house, and when Upfield drew level with the house he could hear the dog barking, glassware crashing, a woman screaming and a man shouting. On an arch over the front gate were the words 'Police Station'.

It was not a time to cogitate on the prospects of this bush town, and Upfield continued to push on towards the only hotel. As the place consisted of but a dozen houses, all widely spaced, he hoped to gain sanctuary inside the bar.

Hope lived to within a dozen feet of the hotel verandah. It died when the dog came and playfully tried to entangle the dead cat in the spokes of the front wheel, and a moment later there fell upon the sundowner the shadow of the law.

The substance was tall, wide, broad.

"This your dog?"

"Yes. Seems to have killed a cat."

"My cat."

"Your cat! Pity."

"Killed him in my kitchen."

"In your kitchen! Do any damage?"

"Somewhat. About a quid's worth. What's to be done about it?"

"Pay the damage. What about a drink while we square it?"

They entered the tiny bar, which couldn't possibly hold more than five customers. Upfield called for drinks and paid the policeman a pound. There followed the usual questions: 'Where you come from? Where you going?' Then the policeman called for drinks and paid with Upfield's pound. When they parted, the pound had disappeared into the till, all of it.

At this time there was a police station at Tilpa, and a pub, ten houses, a store-post-office and a million goats. Upfield was travelling with a man named Charlie. They downed a couple of drinks at the hotel, then Charlie departed for the butcher's shop and Upfield sat on the kerb of the short sidewalk. Almost immediately, a voice at his rear spoke:

"Where you makin' for, mate?"

"To my little wooden hut," replied Upfield without looking round.

"Oh! Where you come from?"

"My little grey home in the west."

"Is that so! And you're headed for your little wooden hut, eh? That's just where you *are* going. Come on."

He wasn't a large man, but...Upfield stood. An enormous hand covered with red hair gripped his wrist and indicated forward move–to the Police Station and into a cell at the bottom of the yard. About fifteen minutes later the door was unlocked and Charlie was introduced, still carrying the parcel of meat.

"What you do?" he asked.

"Nothing. And you?"

"Nothing. Just walking back from the butcher's. You musta done something."

An hour passed before the door opened again and the prisoners were ordered outside. They were conducted to a large office beyond the Police Station. The policeman charged the prisoners with being vagrants and having no visible means of support. The magistrate smiled, asked for no plea, no defence. He said: "Ten days without the option."

The prisoners were returned to the cell.

Two hours passed when once more the door was unlocked and the policeman said:

"Come out and have a wash. Dinner's ready."

The convicts walked out, were shown to a lean-to. The gaoler said: "You're in for ten days. I want the Station painted, see? Better work out in the fresh air, painting, than lying down in a hot cell all day. You paint and paint, and then you have your meals with the family and at five every night you draw two bob each to spend at the pub. At six you come back for dinner, and after you get locked up for the night. Clear?"

Clear enough. The convicts agreed to do the painting. The policeman's wife was a super-super cook. The policeman's daughter was a lovely lassie. Two shillings went a long way in those palmy times. The straw mattresses were not too uncomfortable. The evenings were very pleasant. After dinner Upfield told stories to the policeman's daughter, aged eight, and Charlie was permitted to run the phonograph. At the expiration of the sentence, everyone parted the best of friends.

The Station looked spick in its new paint. The magistrate was the store-keeper. The 'convictions' were not recorded. The

Government got its work done cheaply. The criminals enjoyed a good rest and excellent food. Charlie admitted he had no money; Upfield did have about eighty pounds, but the money wasn't visible, as most of it was hidden between the inner tubes and the covers on the bike wheels.

4

Upfield met adventure every day, and if his legs ached when he made camp at sundown, his spirit was unflagging. Most days he travelled alone, but often another would seek his company for a day or two. He travelled with men who were individualists having only one thing in common–the eternal urge to see over the hills and far away.

There was Dave the Spouter. For two hours he had not spoken and probably hadn't heard a word of the general discussion, which this night had been about the locally famous odd characters like Snivelling Harry, the Storm Bird, and Bikeman Bill. Someone noticed a shooting star, and this set off Dave the Spouter to give an address on the stars. The lecture lasted a full hour, and not a man interjected, but all listened raptly. The given facts and figures could have been wrong, but the telling was entrancing and the theory that the celestial bodies are the specks of a mighty world and that the Earth is composed of speck worlds was offered long before the composition of the atom was made clear to the layman.

The Hangman habitually assessed the weight and proportions of a new arrival, and muttered a number of inches determining the drop. A huge red Irishman–and they are rare enough to remember–had a glorious tenor voice, and was accompanied by a shrimp of a man who played the accordion.

The most astonishing fact about all these tireless wanderers was the low percentage of morons among them.

The red Irishman accompanied Upfield for a hundred miles, the strolling musician having decided to try the opposite way. It would seem that this positive Irishman was really happy only when with a negative, and the one regret of his life was that no one would fight him, and he could not bring himself to openly insult anyone.

"They won't take me on," he complained. "They take a look and fade away. Been years since I had a rattling good go. You see this bush pub we're coming to? Well, you start something and I'll take it off your hands."

"Right," said Upfield.

In the bar were men of a droving outfit, a bullock driver and his offsider. The atmosphere was friendly, the conversation loud and lurid. One of the customers knocked Upfield's glass of beer off the counter, and Upfield demanded replacement. On being ignored, he pressed the demand, and the culprit sneered downward from his height of seemingly ten feet.

Upfield had expected his Irish mate to barge in, but the hero had gone on a journey or was asleep. There was only one hit, and Upfield found himself disentangling several visions against a backdrop of midnight. Then the Irishman was picking him up, and explaining as he carried the injured outside:

"I was round the back," he said. "Never you mind, though."

Depositing the lunatic with the bikes parked on the track-side, he re-entered the hotel and extraordinary things happened. The window was open, but it was a small window and jambed into the frame there appeared a man who blinked and spake not. Another shot out through the doorway and failed to stop until he reached the middle of the track. He rushed back into the bar, and immediately re-emerged as fast as he went in, this time collapsing on the verandah, to be joined by another man impelled by unseen power. More astonishing was the dust issuing between the window-frame and the man jambed into it, out through the doorway, through spaces between corrugated iron sheets nailed to the walls; a red haze against the light of the setting sun.

Upfield was gathering his scattered morale when the Irishman appeared still shouting defiance. He gave a mighty slap to the face of the window-trapped man, sauntered to the track, wiped blood from his mouth and before his second eye closed, took up his bike and walked joyously out of town. The affair taught Upfield to foresee the end before the beginning.

Matt Kerr was passionately fond of making money the easy way. He was about seventy, robust, cheerful. Half his swag was strapped to Upfield's bike, he carrying the remainder. They camped one cold evening outside a small town, made a roaring fire, set fish lines and hoped for the best. The best was excellent—two cod weighing something like fifteen pounds. They ought to have been heavier, but the river was muddy and the fish were starved.

"Yair, thirty pounds the two," said the old man. "At threepence a pound that makes seven and a kick. Bit low. Have to fatten 'em. I'll show you."

He fastened a line to the lower jaw of one, and Upfield was told to swim with the fish to the far side of the river and force a stick between the jaws to keep them wide open. This done, the old man raced away, drawing the fish swiftly through the water, and thus adding several pounds. The treatment was carried out four or five times with each fish, making them look fat and much heavier. As such they were sold to the first hotel.

5

The end of winter found Upfield at Bourke, where he met a man who was soft and fat and very tired. He was known as Paroo Ted, and he put a proposition to Upfield which sounded most attractive. The scheme was to sell the bike and buy a boat.

The machine was sold for four pounds and the boat was purchased for three. It had no name, and surely required none.

It was victualled for one pound, and the crew of two began the voyage down the Darling, destination being Wentworth, fifteen hundred miles to the south per river wind and bend.

The trees forming an endless avenue, came forward to nod a greeting, to whisper *au revoir*. An oar was dipped only to maintain the craft in the middle of the stream. They lay back and watched the clouds in the ribbon of sky, and absorbed the life of this great river, the hunting of fish, the cawing of crows, the raucous cries of the black and the white cockatoos, the galahs, the kookaburras, the wrens and the finches. They made no sound to disturb the drowsy iguanas and the watchful snakes. They talked when they wished, and dreamed as the eternal panorama passed by.

At the stern of the boat was slung a large wire-netted cage into which were passed the fish, so that they could live until sold to a bush pub or homestead, or exchanged for tobacco and rations. At eventide they landed and made a fire, a large one to provide plenty of ash and hot coals, and in this ash-heap buried a fish or a duck, after having sealed it well with river mud. And when they broke open the fire-hardened covering, there was the fish without its skin and the duck minus its feathers, and all the aroma and juices retained.

A loafer's paradise? Yes. But there are no stomach ulcers in a loafer's paradise. Crudely prepared food, maybe. But on such you don't suffer indigestion. Of course you deny yourself the pleasure of feminine company, but then you are untroubled by alimony and kindred causes of ulcers.

Petersen and Bob the Card built their house beside the Darling. At a high cliff where the river turned sharply they dug into the face and fashioned for themselves two small rooms. For nine months of the year they fished and shot and nattered with the passing river traffic, and for three months of the year they worked at the lamb marking or the shearing shed on the local station. They had lived so for fourteen years, the money earned during the three months being sufficient for all their needs, from clothes to tobacco. Bob the Card told everyone who called that it was the only way that the working man could beat the capitalist. It could be a good way for the capitalist to beat the working man.

Now and then energy was abruptly called for, and the boat had to be swiftly rowed to one of the banks and tethered. The warning would come as a long-drawn-out banshee wail, and suddenly around a bend would appear a paddle steamer towing one or more barges. The channel being narrow, for small boats it meant getting out of the way or being run down, and even then the small boat travellers must take action to prevent swamping.

On quiet days, when the river lay like a snake in convulsions, the sounds of a homestead occasioned by dogs, chooks, pumping engines, could come from less than half a mile distant, and such were the twists of the channel that an hour might pass before the homestead buildings would be seen from the river, and someone there would wave. As the summer advanced, the boat was moored in the tree shade during the hot hours, and when the moon was high and filling the voyage would continue along a silvered pavement clothed in black by the shadows.

Tilpa slowly slid by, but Upfield did not go ashore in case the policeman wanted to have the Station painted. He couldn't see the bridge across the Paroo above which One Spur Dick had looked into a terrifying pit, but shortly afterwards Wilcannia came and offered landing wharves.

They passed the wool-scouring plants, those days the scouring being done in the water-yards of the river, and the camps of aborigines who stared silently at them from the bank, their children swimming out to surround the boat. Menindee stopped when they went ashore to buy rations.

And so on to Wentworth, where was another large gaol, many hotels and several suspicious policemen. Paroo Ted decided to continue the voyage into the Murray River, but Upfield thought that to run the risk of ulcers for a period might be good for his soul or something.

He bought another bike, removed the pedals and set out for Broken Hill. His legs were weak from having loafed in a boat for two months.

6. An aboriginal lady

7. Blackfellow's letter-stick

8 A sandhill: the background of *Death of a Swagman*

9. The sandhill has blown across the track since the utility was last this way

CHAPTER SEVEN

WANDERING MILLIE

I

Upfield was twenty years old when he set out from Wentworth for Broken Hill, by now wise enough to make haste slowly, and also a victim to Wandering Millie, who can wreck a strong man's career and reduce a lesser mind to the point of near destruction.

This vast flat interior of the island continent was like a fly-paper, and Upfield just another fly ensnared. Here inside the coastal mountains, the coastal forests and the ever-growing farm-belts, dwells the Spirit that the aborigines have tried to describe and have named with many names. This Spirit dwells beneath the earth, on the earth, and above it. Always it has drawn Man to its net so that down all the ages the aborigines inhabiting the country were nomadic, restless, ever aware of the controlling Spirit.

The great white men came, and couldn't understand why the aborigines, living by water where there is plenty of wild life to keep them fat and contented, should abruptly leave Arcadia and travel into the gibber desert and across the burning sands, to return emaciated, reduced in number, without having achieved anything to be understood by the stranger.

You ask a man where he is going, and he names a town or a station hundreds of miles away, giving as a reason for the journey the certainty of employment. The reason is evasive. He wants employment, there is employment waiting within fifty miles. He wants a change of people with whom to work, there is the change within a few miles. Actually he is journeying to the distant place because he is influenced by the power which drives the aborigine from abundance to hardship in the desert.

A man will enter this land, take a look at it, and rush back to the city. Another will come, work a while to amass a wages cheque, promise his fellows he will return from the pleasures of spending and the bright lights, but never come back. Yet another, having knocked up a wages cheque earned over a full year and more, leaves for a city holiday. If he goes broke in the city he will tramp all the way back to the 'real Australia', Sometimes he may run away from the city and bring back most of his cheque.

Thus some men will see the interior and run from it, others will see and be captured by it and be happy to remain captive. The Spirit will fashion its captives to its own mould, the mould of space, mirages, flying sand-grains and silence alternating with the sighing of the wind. The white captive is re-shaped in the mould which created the black captive, and he holds in the depth of his eyes that which no stranger can decipher.

In all human history no people are closer to the Christian ideals than the Australian aborigine, and next to him is the white man who is captured by the aborigines' Spirit of the inland. Give an aborigine a pair of trousers, and another is wearing them the next day. Give him a hunk of meat, and he shares it all round. The white man is hungry, hand him a meal. He needs a coat, give him your spare one, and if you haven't a spare one, give him the one you do have. Christlike! It is insurance against your own time of need. And what is the edict 'Love your neighbour', if it isn't a form of insurance? A greater coverage, anyway, than an armaments race.

2

The bushman has a tremendous advantage over the city worker, living and working under conditions where he cannot spend; when going for a city holiday he can enjoy one gloriously uninhibited fling for a fortnight or three weeks. The city worker is broke to the wide the day before every pay-day. The bushman can live through an entire year without ever seeing a coin or a note, and without wanting to.

Some go no further than the nearest bush pub. They start off being Mister Smith; they end by being a body on the woodheap, which is an eye-sore to the cook and is kicked out by the rouseabout.

Upfield had to learn the hard way, for this way had become his early in life.

Possessed of a cheque, he went to market with a character called Sloper at a wayside hotel on the Darling. Sloper began on whisky; Upfield began on beer and graduated to whisky. At first Upfield was violently ill each morning, but great performances are invariably the result of practice. It began with:

"Good-day, Fred. Pleased to see you. Put 'em up!"

"Glad to see you too, Sloper. And you. What'll you have?"

"The same, Fred. Whisky for me," replied Sloper, producing his cheque. "Here, take charge of this and say when it's cut out. Well, good health. How's the missus?"

"Fine, Sloper. She thrives on a beltin' every mornin'. All right, I'll warn you when the tide's nearly out. Yours too, Arthur! Righto!"

It was on. Every morning at six when Fred opened the bar he found the drunks standing outside the door, eyes like fish, moronic faces craving the hair of the dog. When the travellers called, it was:

"Come and have a drink! The pub's on us."

Millionaires! Australia belonged to them! The pub was their own. They were the hosts, gracious and generous. All for twenty days. The long-pent dreams of good living, endless days of thirst quenched only by milkless tea, long weeks and months on monotonous rations, were banished for three weeks at the cost of two station cheques totalling almost a hundred pounds when a pound was a golden nugget.

"Well, boys," remarked the publican one morning, "the money's cut out. You had a good time, you shouted for all and sundry. I'm shouting a drink for the track. Here's some tucker for the road, and a half-bottle to carry you through."

It was March, and hot. The wrecks staggered up the river, humping their swags beneath a glaring sky they dared not notice, mouths slack, eyes semi-blind, the strength of dying whisky still in their legs, the next bend and water eight or nine miles on. The kookaburras mocked. The cockatoos jeered. For an hour neither spoke, when:

"What about a drink?"

A drink! They stopped and stared each at the other, swaying inward and almost cracking their heads, each seeking agreement to drink from that half-bottle.

"Open her up."

Cork in the bottle. To hell with the cork! The blunt side of a knife-blade spun off the bottle-top. Lips bleeding from the broken glass. Ah...the rush upward from the deepest depth, vigour coursing through the body. The empty tossed away without regret. Then all of three hours later the big trees marking the river appeared beyond the box trees on the endless grey fiats.

"Hug your chains, lad!" whispered Sloper. "Hug your chains! Kiss your chains, lad!" Silence, then: "Hug and kiss your chains, lad. They'll hurt less if you hug 'em and kiss 'em."

The blanket roll on the back, a ton weight. The sky above, another irksome weight, and the very innards of a man parched and shrivelled to a gibber. The voice of one crying in the wilderness: 'Hug 'em and kiss 'em!' The voice a croak like that of a scissored bullfrog.

The bank at the sharp bend was fully a hundred feet of perpendicular cliff, and so the wayfarers left the road and followed the river to where its banks were normal. But the recent rise had passed, and for the last twelve feet down to the water the steeply sloping banks were like grease, the colour of graphite.

"Hug 'em," Sloper managed to say, and proceeded along the bank until he found what he needed, a gum that had fallen to the river and down the trunk of which it was possible to reach the water. "You can get down by that trunk," he gasped.

"No fear, not me," replied Upfield—or thought he did.

"Ruddy Pommy! Strike me dead! Why did I take up with you? Gimme the billy."

Sloper was decidedly game, or desperate. With the billy dangling from his mouth, he proceeded to crawl on hands and knees down the inclined trunk of the great tree. Where the water had covered the trunk, the sun by now had dried it and made it firm. Slowly, now and then halting as though to banish dizziness, Sloper at last neared the water, and was within an ace of losing balance. Eventually he crawled the last couple of feet and managed to dip the utensil and fill it.

The return was less arduous. They made a fire and set the billy against the flames, and, long before the water boiled, Upfield stood by with a handful of tea ready to toss into it. Sloper sat on the ground, his face buried in his crossed arms, and now and then his entire body heaved with dry retching. When the tea was made, they sipped the scalding liquid which at first failed to burn through the coating of dust and saliva. The tea made them sick, but when some of it did sink to the bottom, both benefited from the rebirth of dead whisky, and they felt a little better.

Sloper lay on his back, his eyes closed, and Upfield did the best he could with a cigarette. Then he saw emerging from the inside of Sloper's shirt the green-brown head of a snake. The apparition froze him to stillness. The reptile finally left Sloper's shirt, when Sloper saw it, and cried mournfully:

"Hug your chains, lad. Hug 'em and kiss 'em."

Sitting up, he groped in a pocket for his pipe. He saw the snake and didn't believe it. Upfield saw the snake wriggle away from the fire, and he didn't believe it. Both watched the three-foot whip snake until it disappeared behind a bush, and still neither believed. They slept, and the sun was setting when they awoke, and then they noted the trail of the snake from the proximity of the fire to the bush. On leaving camp, they looked once again at the trail of the snake, and both refused to believe that too.

Drunks and babies are said to be immune from danger. Sloper when at the bottom of the log refused to believe in the snake, had waved it away as though it had no substance, and under his shirt was safety to the snake.

3

Eighteen months after Upfield landed in Australia, the interior had completely claimed him. No longer was he the smartly-dressed youth whose clothes and speech at once stamped him with the impress of his social status in the Old Country. His face and arms were varnished by the wind and the sun. His clothes were of dungaree or drill. His boots were elastic-sided and meant for horse-riding. His hips could accept the hardness of ground, and, awake or asleep, his lungs throve on air both dry and pure. His body was thus built to perfection of physical fitness.

A job boundary-riding was a short rest before again moving on with the load on the pedal-less bike. Work on a fence was terminated by the desire to see what lay beyond a low range of hills. Employment with an axe, cutting scrub for sheep in a dry period, ended with the partnership of one Irish Tim, who told glowing stories of fortunes made at White Cliffs.

So to White Cliffs, then thriving on opal. There were a dozen pubs, half a dozen opal buyers and two policemen; and a few stores where equipment could be purchased, and several Chinese from whom equipment could be hired by the week for a few shillings. It was a free country. You could dig where you liked, provided the shaft you intended to put down did not endanger another. Opal lies in pockets. You dig a hole and go down and down until you are tired, and then begin sinking another hole.

For a reason which, doubtless, biographers have recorded,

Queen Victoria abruptly banished opals from her ken, and the natural follow- on was that the opal fell into disfavour all over Europe and most of America. However, the harem ladies and the dancing girls of Asia were not so foolish, and at this time Australian opal found a ready market among people who appreciate mystic colourful gems.

Irish Tim and his partner found an old and disused hut within a mile of the township and decided to camp there. The waterman brought out the hired equipment, comprising windlass and rope and bucket and picks and shovels, and supplied a tank which he filled with water at sixpence a gallon. In the vicinity were many abandoned shafts of various depths, and the nearest neighbours were a thousand yards away. Abandoned shafts mean nothing to the opal gouger, as the stuff does not lie in seams like gold, nor in the rough sands of a dry creek, like tin. Irish Tim had been on this field several times, swearing that once he had found a pocket which netted him three hundred pounds, and at another period a pocket which sold to the buyer for eighty pounds. He stalked the country about the old hut, displaying acumen he didn't possess, and finally these two proceeded to sink a shaft and set up their windlass.

The days passed, and every Monday morning the Chinaman called for his rent, and the water-man came and sympathised over the absence of luck. The shaft sank deeper, one man picking and shovelling the mulloch into the bucket, and the other winding it to the surface.

Father Ryan came out and was welcomed by Upfield, who had heard about him and his geological knowledge. Irish Tim happened to be below, and, distracted by the coming of the jovial priest, Upfield inadvertently kicked a small lump of rubble to fall on Tim's head.

The language from the bowels of the earth was that spoken by One Spur Dick to his bullocks. Father Ryan beamed. He stooped forward over the shaft.

"That'll be enough out of you, Irish," he shouted. "That little lot will cost you half a crown at threepence a bad word."

"Be cripes! That you, Father, up there and all?" yelled Irish.

"Wait around. I'm coming up."

He was brought up by the windlass, to find Father Ryan making an entry in a small book.

"Half a crown, like I said," the priest remarked, stowing book and pencil in a pocket of his very old coat. "Any showing?"

"Naw, Father. Will you take a look-see? The lamp's down on the floor."

Now Father Ryan was locally famous, at least, as a geologist, and had been the cause of many discoveries of opal pockets off a shaft which would have been abandoned as barren. He descended by the bucket to the floor, where he slung the lamp by a string from his neck, and proceeded to examine the walls, tapping now and then with his hammer. Slowly thereafter he was drawn up, scrutinising the walls as he came, until finally he clambered out to say he had seen no promising evidence.

Irish Tim swore, and was fined an additional one and threepence.

"I shall see you in town," declared the priest, "and then you will settle."

Everyone did, too. In the pubs he would collect his money. Instead of a few shillings, he would often receive a sovereign. And with the money from swear-words he nursed back to sanity those wrecked by a bout of drinking, would buy them new boots and what clothes they required, and speed them on the track of another job far from White Cliffs and its temptations.

When the shaft sunk by Irish Tim and Upfield was down about twenty-odd feet, they were taking lunch in the shadow cast by the old hut and watching the approach of two men laden with pickaxe and shovel. Both men wore city clothes, and, what was worse, cloth caps, which blatantly betrayed the new chum. One asked with a Devonshire accent where they could dig, and Irish Tim airily suggested they might start a shaft where countless feet coming and departing from the hut had hardened the ground to cement.

The newcomers removed their coats, rolled their shirt-sleeves, spat on their hands and fell to with the implements. One picked a square, and the other shovelled away the loosened earth, and it was obvious that both were experienced miners. The fellow with the pick then proceeded to loosen the next layer of surface, and he was half-way over the square when his pick crashed through glass.

Irish Tim shouted and ran forward to stop the pick descending again in the same place. He assisted the newcomers to take out a pocket of opal worth twenty-six pounds an ounce, and for which a buyer paid five hundred and seventeen pounds.

The Devonshire men had arrived in Adelaide by the old *Orsova*, had come direct to White Cliffs. They returned to Adelaide, caught the *Orsova* on her homeward voyage, and knew nothing of Upfield and Irish Tim, who tramped north to Milparinka looking for work, and not particularly anxious to find it.

4

At this time in Australia proper there were three great slave masters: Red Gold, John Barleycorn, and Wandering Millie, and if one of these inserts the hooks deeply, there can be little hope for the victim. Of the three masters, the gold fever is the most powerful, trapping its victims with the promise of wealth by the discovery of other metals and gems as well as gold. Men will forsake John Barleycorn for Red Gold and men will forsake Red Gold for Wandering Millie, whose promises cannot be worded in any language. Her siren voice is heard only by the inner ear, the very soul of a man, forever calling to him from without the world encompassed by his vision.

Wandering Millie dug her hooks into young Upfield, thereby saving him from falling victim to Red Gold and John Barleycorn. There is little doubt that those aunts with their reading and their stories, those warships back from strange lands, and the tales of adventure provided by the Northcliffe press combined to groom Upfield for slavery to Wandering Millie.

He pushed his bike to Winton, Central Queensland, via Thargominda, and pushed it down again to Bourke, via Charleville, stopping now and then for short periods to eat at a table in the men's quarters of a station. He travelled thus for hundreds of miles, and thought he was seeing Australia, when he was seeing but a hundredth part of it, yet a thousand times more than is seen by the average city dweller.

A rolling stone gathers no moss. A turning wheel gathers no rust. Moss and rust amount to the same thing: a clogging agent.

He pushed the bike across to Hergott Springs, re-named Marree, and with a mate followed the overland telegraph line right up to Daly Waters, which isn't such a heck of a way from Darwin. There was then no highway, water obtainable only at the telegraph stations, and the aborigines still suspicious. Birtles had done this trip per bike, so Upfield was no trail blazer.

At Daly Waters, Upfield decided he was tired and hired himself to a droving outfit taking cattle across to Longreach, and he wished he hadn't, because he wasn't a good rider and stampeding cattle always made him nervous. Keeping ahead of a stampede in scrub country when the night is black is no pleasure to an imaginative man, no matter how good the horse under him.

Silent Eddie, the boss of the outfit, was tall, rangy, raw. Mounted, he looked like Don Quixote, for he appeared to prefer a small horse from which his feet dangled within inches of the ground. The large felt hat, deliberately holed to admit air to the shock of amber hair, the dungaree coat, the gabardine trousers and the elastic sides on the feet revealed a man for ever tilting at mental windmills, beside which problems connected with cattle-droving were of small moment. Nothing, even the stampede which occasioned a delay of a week, upset him. When Upfield shot off his horse as the animal abruptly slewed to avoid a rabbit burrow, and the others roared laughing; when two of his men deserted at a wayside pub and eventually caught up ten days later, sorry and near the d.t. stage; when storms accompanied by vivid lightning drenched everyone, and dust-storms obliterated everything within ten yards of a man's nose, he neither smiled nor scowled, commiserated or upbraided.

But always he was where most needed, and always a second or two at the right place before he was needed. Once a scrub bull came tearing towards the mob. Humped, thoughts of Paradise or something occupying him, Silent Eddie seemed unaware of the bull until it was within fifty feet of him and intent on goring his horse. With his right hand he plucked the rifle from the saddle scabbard, with one hand he pointed the weapon and fired it. The bull went down, somersaulted, lay properly dead. Back into the scabbard went the rifle, by the same hand. The horse didn't change its gait; the rider returned to his visions.

The Black Bastard was Silent Eddie's most important aide, for he was the scout, riding miles ahead and reporting after sundown the condition of the ground feed and the quality and quantity of waters. He had also to give notice of the cattle passing through pastoral properties, and carry through a dozen other such chores on behalf of the general who was moving an army of beasts across hundreds of miles. A half-caste, he was an expert cattleman at the age of ten.

When a hundred miles from Longreach, the Black Bastard reported that a station manager refused to permit the cattle to cross his area, on the plea that ground feed was scarce, and that three thousand additional cattle would make it still more scarce.

The market was right, and the owners had arranged with the railway department to have trucks at Longreach on a certain date, and already Silent Eddie had worked out in his mind the daily stages to deliver his cattle on time at the railyards. The refusal of the station manager to permit passage through his area meant a deviation of more than a hundred miles, many days' delay, and additional rail truck charges.

Silent Eddie lifted a lip to reveal yellow teeth, gave fresh orders to the Black Bastard, and went on with his dreaming. The cattle continued forward, opened out wide, feeding as they walked.

In mid-afternoon a few days later, the Black Bastard again reported. The cattle were in sight of the boundary fence of the station blocked to them, and on the far side of the fence a couple of dozen station men waited in command of the manager and his overseers. All were armed with empty tins and sticks with which to beat them. Guns also were in evidence. Clearly that boundary fence was to be defended.

Silent Eddie signalled to the men on the wings, and the herd was bunched and at the same time speeded forward. The peace of the afternoon was broken by the reports of stock-whips, and by this time Upfield could manage to crack his whip without hitting his horse or wrapping it round his own neck.

The manœuvre excited the herd. The bellowing drowned the whip reports, but soon the bellowing was submerged by the incessant clatter of beaten tins and the firing of shot-guns into the air. The pandemonium thus created baulked the cattle within yards of the fence, a six-wire cattle fence. Despite the efforts of the drovers they turned back, and a stampede was averted only by great effort and the herd brought to a stop about four hundred yards off the disputed barrier.

"Wheel 'em," commanded Silent Eddie. "Round the clock."

Yelling maniacs urged the twenty-eight hundred beasts into a turning wheel, compact like a circular dance-floor. The red dust rose like a gigantic willy-willy sober for once. Slowly the turning wheel of living bone and flesh approached the fence, the din made by the men on the far side vying with the uproar of frightened beasts.

Silent Eddie was everywhere. Even the cook, who drove four mules in a buckboard, was now astride one of his animals and joined in the fray. Thus was fashioned a force as irresistible as a landslide, in fact more so, because it had a cutting edge and was powered by the herd instinct, than which nothing in life is more terrible when agitated.

Once the wheel revolved it was comparatively easy to maintain the movement, and the steadily rising column of red dust based on a sea of horns, advanced against a barrier of less efficiency than strands of cotton braced to match-sticks. The fence went down, flattened under the hooves. The defenders were pushed away, scattered. The wheel went on revolving with slow and grinding impetus deep into the territory of the enemy, where it was gradually broken up, and the cook raced back to his heavy buckboard and drove smartly across the boundary before he could be stopped.

There was only one fight. A station man attempted to argue with a drover. The combat began on horseback and ended on the ground. The other drovers cheered while pushing the cattle into open order and onward to Longreach. The station manager shouted and threatened as he rode beside Silent Eddie, who rode without expression, without interest.

Doubtless there was a law-suit, but the cattle arrived at Longreach on the due date.

5

Droving sheep is less exciting than playing draughts, and yet demands experience and understanding of the animal's psychology. One lacking these attributes is apt to be trying, and such was Mr. Elkins, a small settler who lived in Cunnamulla and employed Upfield and another to mind his sheep.

The drought was on, and Elkins decided to send his flock by train to agistment nearer the border. He was a fussy man who believed he knew all, and who could never trust anyone. He arrived at his station, which was hardly larger than a farm, and fussed when the sheep were mustered, and was still fussing when they were started for the railway.

The mob consisted of four thousand head, and the travelling time to the railway about five days. Swags and tucker for the men were carried by two pack-horses, quiet mokes who walked with the sheep.

Elkins appointed himself to the left wing, placing Upfield to the centre, and an aborigine named Titanic to the right wing. Provided the drovers work as a team, the job is easy, slow and conducive to meditation. If the sheep tend to move out on a wing, the man there merely sends a dog forward to correct them, but Elkins was too prone to work his dogs and his voice, with the result that the flock was repeatedly thrust over to Titanic, who, of necessity, had to overwork his old and mangy dogs to correct the general drift.

Eventually Titanic lost his temper and began to swear. At first Elkins declined to notice the bad language. He was a Justice of the Peace who sat regularly on the bench in Cunnamulla, and also a regular church- goer. Following a fine performance by Titanic, he upbraided him, and for a little while the aborigine bottled his ire.

But what to do when the fault is persistent? Titanic called his employer a fool, a stubborn new chum, etcetera, with garnishing, and in rage Elkins told him, across yards and yards of animated wool, what he would do when he was on the bench and Titanic in the dock.

Titanic was deflated for a couple of hours, then he stood in his stirrups and waved his hands high above his head, saying nothing, but grimacing. This performance was repeated until the exasperated Elkins demanded at the top of his voice to know what the antics meant. Said Titanic, the allegedly bucolic savage:

"That's deaf and dumb for 'Up you!'"

6

When Wandering Millie thought she had her hooks deeply into Upfield, she decided to test for proof.

With another man, Upfield was engaged as a boundary rider on a northern station. They lived in a small hut beside a well, and each had two paddocks to ride every week, each paddock something like forty miles around the fences. Not that their work was merely to ride the boundary of 'fields' comprising 65,000 acres. The enclosed sheep were the responsibility.

Upfield's companion had travelled widely and was most enthusiastic about Northern Queensland. He talked of the money to be earned on the cane-fields, and the jobs to be obtained in the islands as a native overseer, and creating another mirage beyond the mirage.

Upfield set off for the cane-fields, taking train at Bourke for Sydney. The train left at eight in the morning and by midnight had arrived at Mount Victoria in the Blue Mountains. Here there was a stop for refreshment, and by now the train journey was a bore. Upfield asked the barman could he recommend an hotel for the night, and the barman said he was the licensee of the hotel across the way, and would happily put him up.

The next day was filled with mist and drizzle, but the scents wafted by the soft damp wind lured Upfield to stay on, for these were the scents of almost forgotten green pastures after the long period of the semi-arid interior. The following day was just as bad and, for something to do, Upfield walked up the main street and became interested in an open-fronted shop where an auction was in progress.

The auctioneer, the play-bills, the enlarged plans, the bidders, all failed to hold his interest. Outside was the mist and the drizzle so like the Devon moors; the softness and the scents of Hampshire in the month of May. The auctioneer was selling a corner block of land, and assuring the bidders that from this block one could see fifty miles over the surrounding mountains, and no one could build to foreshorten this panorama. So Upfield paid eighty pounds for the block, and then after arriving in Sydney realised he was short of money, having sufficient only to get him up to Brisbane.

How silly can a young man be! Stranded in a city. At the mercy of strangers all intent on their own way of life. Pawning a camera and a good overcoat for the wherewithal, he took a job, in desperation, with a vine-grower. Work, when outback had been comparative relaxation! Confined to a few acres after the freedom of unlimited square miles, Upfield passionately determined to save quickly for travelling expenses back to Eldorado.

Wine on the property, excellent port for a shilling, and good champagne for eighteenpence the bottle, the lights of Brisbane less than twenty miles away. Every Saturday night he went to the city, to remove the taste of grapes with the taste of hops, to visit one of the new cinemas, and from there to travel back to the job on the Drunks' Train at eleven-thirty. The Drunks' Train had windows fitted with iron bars in place of glass so easily broken. On Sunday mornings he was broke, nothing saved for the means of running back to the One Spur Dicks, the Titanics, and the Murrays.

Wandering Millie had lost her bet–or so it appeared.

On leaving the train, Upfield had to walk up a hill between houses in one of which a tortured soul was always screaming as he passed, whether from dementia or pain he never knew. Then the road sank to a shallow valley, now beyond the houses, to rise to a ridge and again to fall to the edge of a wide lagoon, where it turned sharply.

On moonlit nights this lagoon was a beautiful place, silvered and shadowed by the gums ringing it.

One Saturday night, shortly after leaving the train, and when opposite the house where the woman screamed, Upfield saw ahead a girl dressed in white. All Queensland girls wore white in summer, and this one walked the same road Upfield was following. As there were no houses beyond the girl, he guessed she was one of the boss's two daughters.

Now the boss was very wealthy, and anywhere in the world it is wise to marry the boss's daughter–if you are in the position of having to work for a boss. The night was soft and brilliantly illumined, and the figure in white passed from sight in the shadow cast by the roadside trees, then appeared clear and alluring in the moonlight.

Upfield hurried to catch up. The girl hurried that he might not. He called to her, offering escort. She took no notice, not even looking back. Upfield ran and she ran. When Upfield stopped she stopped, in black shadow.

'Hoity-toity,' thought Upfield. 'Too high in the social register to be escorted by a common working man. Blast her!' He continued, and the girl went on ahead. She passed over the second hill-top and she was down the far slope when Upfield saw her again. Thus they proceeded down the long incline to the turn at the lagoon, Upfield now drawing appreciably nearer. By now he was grim at a fancied slight.

At the bottom of the road, the girl went on, went on walking on the water over the lagoon. When Upfield reached the edge, she was half-way across. There she stopped, and he was perplexed. He rubbed his eyes-and she was no longer on the lagoon!

That port, and sherry, and muscat, and champagne! At a shilling and eightpence the bottle and millions of bottles down in the cellar two hundred feet long and as many wide! It was time something happened.

The next week, a minor event did occur. The auctioneer at Mount Victoria wrote offering on behalf of a client one hundred and fifty pounds for the block of land. How much sillier can a young man be! Upfield accepted the offer. Had he held the land for forty years, he could have sold for two thousand pounds.

The major event was the outbreak of war with the Kaiser's Germany.

Upfield joined the A.I.F. August 23rd, 1914, and became a soldier for five years. Wandering Millie wasn't beaten.

10. Upfield at his desk

11. The dray from the rear, where Upfield wrote *The Sands of Windee*

12. The Brooking Range, East Kimberleys: the background of *Cake in the Hat Box*

13. The Wolf Creek meteorite crater, described in *Cake in the Hat Box*

CHAPTER EIGHT

'WIRE FIVE QUID'

I

Although not a shot was lobbed and not a bomb dropped on Australia during the 1914-18 War, amazing changes took place inside the continent.

When Upfield returned to Australia proper, all Cobb & Co.'s coaches had disappeared from the mail routes; mail-cars were cutting time down to a quarter and less. The last of great bullock and camel- drawn wagons were lurching and swaying into the red dust of oblivion, and the Ford motor-trucks were moving a quarter of the loads in one- tenth of the time. The paddle-wheel steamers hauling their barges up and down the Darling were hurling their banshee wails in despairing defiance of the sentence of death pronounced by Mr. Ford. The Afghans, who with their long strings of pack-camels had served the far interior so well, were reading the writing in the dust and planning to return to their own country, comparative millionaires.

Upfield found Wilcannia, the once fair Queen City of the West, as though stricken by a plague. Half the pubs were closed. The sidewalks on Saturday nights were deserted, the hitching rails loaded with dust, the wharves beginning to rot. It was impossible to grasp the extent of the change, and impossible to determine the causes, until he talked with One Spur Dick.

Under the branches of a red-gum stood the house built by two sons. The sunlight was reflected in a blaze of silver from the walls and the roof composed of four-gallon petrol tins opened to sheets. Petrol tins! Petrol here!

A man sat on an ancient Windsor chair outside the door of the one- room hut measuring ten by twelve feet. His face was turned to the approaching visitor, and one gnarled hand was restraining a dog. His hair was almost white, and thirty years, not seven, had marked him since Upfield had last seen him.

The light was gone from his eyes. "Bet you don't know who I am," Upfield said when standing before One Spur Dick.

"You could lose. Gimme a chance," he countered, gently cuffing the dog to silence. "Say something."

"Young Tom told me where to find you. Grown up well, hasn't he? Told me, too, how you and he built this hut, as your eyes were failing. Said you wouldn't live in Wilcannia even though half the houses are vacant."

"Live in a ruddy town! Not me. I can sit here and listen to the birds. I can take me fish-line and make eighteen steps to reach the river bank. I can walk another way, making fourteen steps, to reach the axe and me wood-heap, and I can cut wood with me eyes shut. Say some more. Where you been? Long time since I seen you, anyway."

"Went up to Queensland before the war. Gallipoli, France and the rest. Only just got back," Upfield said. "Was married. It was a failure. Headed for the Back country."

"Yair. Could of told you you would, young feller. I know you now.

Arthur Upfield."

Upfield gripped the outflung hand of a ghost. For a space nothing was said, although a million thoughts cried for expression. He sat with the prematurely old man, and the dog accepted him as a friend. Then he remarked on the construction of the hut, its situation, the short distance from the town, and again silence fell about them, until One Spur said:

"Would you stay a bit and read us a book?"

"Why not?"

"No one ain't read a book since you was me offsider. Tom comes out now and then to tell me about the races, but he won't read no books. Up-river a bit two old blokes live together and comes along to gas sometimes, but they don't read—not them books you usta read at the camp-fires. Remember them camps, Arthur?"

Remember them! All through the years of exile Upfield had remembered those camps, the long mule team and the great wagon, the camp-fires and the warmth, and the face of a kindly human being.

Coach driver Fred Essen had gone into retirement at Broken Hill. Dave Steele had been killed in Palestine. Tim Redmond had come into property in Ireland. Murray was in Adelaide in the real estate business. Overseer Galloway had a selection over Ivanhoe way, doing well, too. Momba!

"That bloody Kidman got hold of Momba," snarled One Spur Dick. "Made another forchune, too. Bought it when there was no wire, no iron coming into the country. He had the fences tore up and sold the wire out of 'em, and all the netting off the vermin fences, and all the iron from the sheds and huts. And when he'd sold the lot he had the land, a million acres, for nothing. He's going to own all Australia before he's done, mark my words.

"The coaches! All motee-cars now, and trucks. Young Tom's savin' to buy a motee-car. Remember how he usta be flash riding horses? Flash spurs what tinkled when he sneezed? Tight trousers kept up with a red or blue thing? And a extra brim hat? No horse any good if it didn't rear and buck every ten minutes. Well, now he wants a motee- car. Horses no good to Tom exceptin' they're racing with a jockey up. Motee-cars! A motee-car killed old Bill Wilshire."

"When?" pressed Upfield.

"Three year back. Came in for a spell. Stopped at Ma Goonery's till he spent his cheque. Bullocks and wagon away out on the Common. Bill sets off for camp late one night. Half-way, he decided to have a sleep. So he sleeps. Everyone got a right to sleep when they wants and where they wants. He flopped down and slept on the track, and a cove came along in a motee-car without his lamps lit, and didn't see Bill. He heard Bill yell out when the front wheels went over him, but he couldn't pull up in time to stop the rear wheels going over him. I got no time for them motee-cars."

One Spur Dick wore old clothes, but he was tidier than when he drove mules. He made tea and offered his guest bread and jam, and afterwards Upfield walked back to the Wilcannia Hotel, and again made the trip loaded with a suitcase, meat and bread and half a dozen books he had borrowed where he might.

Wars may change the way of a nation, oil seeping from the earth may wipe out the horse and replace him with iron junk, but nothing will change individuals like One Spur Dick. His hut was tightly built. It had a fireplace and chimney opposite the door, a bunk along one side and the table and cases for seats against the other. But he wasn't truly at home until he had had hessian tacked to the inside walls as the interior of most other huts on the stations were lined. Even so, that was not entirely satisfying because, in every outback hut lined with hessian, the hessian was masked by Bulletin cartoons and drawings pasted to it. So it had to be with this hut, and for some time Upfield again admired the drawings of C. H. Percival, whom he had met in the A.I.F., as well as the art of the great Norman Lindsay.

"You still lookin' at me pictures?" asked One Spur. "I like that one best of old Billy Hughes standing on a chair and poundin' the table at the other coves what's at the Peace Meeting. About the last picture I ever seen before me eyes went wonky on me.

"D'you recollect So-and-so? Remember Brutus, that leader I had? And the sheep you couldn't kill? Then I took it on, and give it up 'cos it looked at me and wanted a damper crust?"

So it went on, and every blessed minute One Spur Dick dropped a month of ageing time, and in the end produced his great whip and they went outside, and he called once more to his team and smacked the whip like a gun and swore with verve Time couldn't depress. And then, laughing like a couple of idiots, they went in to dine off grilled chops and baker's bread, and more bread with jam and butter, as it was winter.

Upfield stayed with One Spur Dick for eleven days and read for hours every night. Of the books he had borrowed he was never to forget Louis Stone's *Betty Wayside*, a novel of insight and feeling than which nothing better has since been done. At the end, One Spur Dick said:

"I like that one, and I'll keep it in mind. What about the one with no covers?"

"It's gone three o'clock," Upfield said, his voice cracked. The tips of the fingers which had done a real man's share to fashion a nation felt for the hands of the alarm clock from the face of which the glass had been removed, and the ex-mule-driver exclaimed: "Why so it is, young feller. Better pack up. Day'll break soon."

2

Upfield sold the suitcase, a watch and a good pair of shoes to One Spur Dick's son Tom, and bought a second-hand bike, a blanket and a calico sheet, a billy-can and a fry-pan, and One Spur Dick sat outside his door and listened to the departing footsteps. When Upfield came again to Wilcannia, young Tom told him how his father had died, sitting outside the door of that little tin hut.

Upfield pushed the bike up-river, camping at sundown just where sunset found him, pausing often to gaze at the lazy river, or to watch an ant fight, or merely to sit on a log and stare into the vista of red-gums and grey box.

At the age of twenty-eight he was pilotless, rudderless, mere flotsam. A born idealist, he was bereft of ideals. A creator of illusions, he was now without the illusions which had carried him into youth and onward into early manhood. But one thing remained-the driving urge to see what waited beyond the next bend.

He met coaches, but they were motor mail-cars. He met stockmen, and they were riding motor-bikes. He met with teamsters steering motor-trucks. He hated them all because they now inhabited a world so different from the world where lived the One Spur Dicks, where the townships were not greatly removed from those described by Zane Grey and Clarence Mulford. Time was needed and miles to cover before understanding that this world of inland Australia hadn't changed, and yet a little more time and a few more miles to tramp over before realising that this inland hadn't changed since the last Ice Age, and wouldn't ever change until the next.

On Upfield's coming to understand this unchanging, eternal thing which he could not tell of but felt, could not determine but had to admit was here, his first reactions on returning from the war gave way to gladness that he had returned. Returned to what?

He had left home in England in 1910. He had spent three years in the interior of Australia, a year in Queensland, then two years of active service before returning on leave to his home in England. A total of only six years' absence from the place where he was born, nurtured and brought to the verge of manhood. Going home on leave was good. The parents were a little older, the large house was silent and empty, the business limited, through lack of assistants. Everything was the same, and yet nothing was. There was nothing there to equal the power of the Demon, the Spirit, whatever it might be, that ruled over the interior of Australia and himself.

That home-coming, warm and crowded with affection, was as nothing compared to this coming back to the bushland where all the birds, all the rabbits, all the ants, even the willy-willies and the thunder- clouds had been waiting patiently just for his return.

Perhaps Upfield was controlled by that same irresistible

prodding by Wandering Millie which sent Drake across the seas of the world, and Cook and Dampier and others, but they were loyal to the land which gave them life, and he had turned his back on his homeland to embrace this other world of sand and mirages, of dusty depressions and darkly glooming mulga forests.

Perhaps there was no such being as Wandering Millie, and Upfield was destined to be a wanderer simply because he lacked strength of purpose to make anything of his life. Perhaps he was doomed to push a bike from sandhill to sandhill and from creek to creek, until he grew old and sat outside the door of a tin hut and peacefully passed into the Beyond.

He might have been, were it not for Mary.

3

It was mid-February and very hot, and the moon was sailing the sky o'nights, and Upfield preferred to push his bike in lunar glow rather than when the shade temperature was something like 115 degrees, and the sun's heat up to a probable 300, anyway hot enough to fire an exposed match in a climate minus humidity.

The track wound over silvered glades and under sleeping trees where the shadows were black. No leaf stirred unless a foraging ant ran upon it. Sometimes a butcher-bird pretended it was day and began to warble a lilting song, this tempting a magpie to compete. Sometimes an owl or a night hawk was curious about the traveller.

The stars said it was two o'clock, Upfield being a pupil of teachers who don't need a watch, when he came to a side track where three great gums pointed a triangle. Here he made a fire and boiled water for tea, and then squatted over the embers to eat dinner of cold fish. He was then twelve miles from the last homestead, and about eleven off the next one. The side track surely would conduct him to a homestead in a bend.

A shearing shed, or any shed, is preferable in summer to sleeping on the open ground, because of the ants, and when Upfield heard a rooster far down the side track he decided to take it and find a shed where he could sleep in peace. An hour later he saw ahead the shining roofs of a homestead, proving to be that of a small selection rather than a large holding.

The first sign of dawn darted into the sky as he unrolled his swag on the floor of an open shed, and prepared to sleep by simply removing his boots. Hours after dawning, a man said:

"Good-day-eel Travelling?"

He was slight, bow-legged, grey-haired. The grey eyes were puckered as they regarded the 'tramp'.

"Thought you wouldn't mind," Upfield said. "Ants are bad this weather."

"They are so. Where you making for?"

"Up-river a bit. Nowhere particularly."

"Ah, well, you can sleep again or come in for breakfast. It'll be on in five minutes. Wash-house at the end of the house."

Thus the meeting with Mary's husband, Angus. Mary was taller than Angus, her face was rugged, and her complexion pale. Her hair was greying, and her eyes were large and brown. She served grilled chops and toasted baker's bread, jam and cream and coffee, and Upfield ate with them, fully appreciating the snow-white table-cloth, sitting on a real chair, eating from china instead of tin, and drinking from a china cup instead of a tin pannikin.

They discussed the heat, and agreed that Wragge was a good long- range weather prophet. They evinced no curiosity about the stranger's origin, didn't ask him how he liked Australia. In fact Angus asked only one question:

"Would you take a job with me for a few weeks?"

It could have been the table-cloth, or the china, or the well-cooked food, which created sudden aversion to endless tracks and abruptly dulled the siren call of that which promised beyond the next bend. It could have been the fleeting expression in Mary's eyes as they waited for his answer. Upfield was glad to stay a while and work.

"I want some help making two four-thousand-gallon tanks, and the stands to set 'em on," Angus explained. "Eat with us, and there's a room off the store shed you can sleep in. Station hand's wages."

They hitched a couple of horses to a buckboard and drove twelve miles down-river to the nearest neighbour, from whom Angus borrowed the roller necessary to curve the iron sheets, and the following day began the work proper. Angus knew the tricks of this job, and Upfield hadn't forgotten what he had learned on Momba, where his first job had been offsider to a tank maker. They worked in the shadow of the river gums, and it seemed that Mary was always calling them to meals and morning and afternoon smoko tea. The kookaburra chortled lazily and the magpies warbled, and the cockatoos screeched, and even the shadows gossiped with the sunlight and whispered of the aborigines' Being-Who-Created-the-World in the long past Alchuringa Days.

Angus liked talking; Mary liked to be silent and observant. At table she appeared to take keen interest in what the men said, but after a day or two the stranger realised it was an attitude, and that she was thinking and dreaming.

Their only son had been killed on Gallipoli, and Mary stepped right out of her dream world to meet the hired hand on that strip of beach backed by the escarpments within the horns of a crescent. Thereafter, Upfield was invited to spend the evenings with them on the mosquito- netted verandah, and there in the cool and the peace of dusk this female psychologist probed with never a betrayal of her art.

When the second of the two tanks was built, she knew all about Arthur Upfield, which was infinitely more than he himself knew. There was one subject on which he never appeared to satisfy her–those three lengthy novels written in longhand on neatly margin-ruled foolscap.

"You were how old when you wrote them?" she asked, not looking up from her sewing.

He told her, and attempted to brush aside the memory, but she wanted to know why he hadn't sent them to a publisher, and why had he written them. He was embarrassed when trying to explain why.

Mary never rode a subject to exhaustion. On balance the scales were loaded in favour of her husband, who had travelled the outback tracks in his youth much as Upfield had done before the war, and who reminisced from the depths of a canvas chair. Angus had once worked on Momba. He had never met One Spur Dick, but knew of him; he had known Manager Murray. It was when Upfield was talking about the reading sessions that Mary took hold once more and wanted to know the titles of the books. As the evenings passed, her interest in Upfield's background became more centred on books. Ultimately, she was constantly bringing him back to books, but this he didn't realise at the time.

The tanks were made and finally hauled to the tall stands, and connected to the river pump operated by the oil engine. Angus had other work he wanted done before the lamb-marking, but they knew by the signs that the hired hand wouldn't stay on, knew it when they saw him oiling his bike, when they saw him gazing away to low sand dunes beyond a flat. The weeks tallied five when Upfield again pushed a bike towards the mirages created by the March sun.

4

He left the river and took the track out through Dunlop to the Paroo, and on to Wanaaring. Milparinka, like Wanaaring, like Wilcannia, like all the other far-back towns, was but a shadow of its former entity. The pubs sold liquor, but only the remnants of a past generation still spent wages cheques and left broke and hugging and kissing their chains. A blight was falling upon the land and, later on, Kidman, when he bought station to add to station, was blamed for it, when he was merely far-sighted enough to profit by the blight caused by the coming of the petrol-driven vehicle.

Momba provided an excellent example of the change which took place during and immediately following War One. When Upfield travelled to Momba per Parcels Post there were about sixty men employed at Momba, then, of course, merely one of fifty vast properties. Wool was about threepence a pound, and wages and upkeep and development costs were on a par. The war had drained the outback of manpower, for it was the manpower from the outback, trained by the ex-non-commissioned officers from the British Army, which gave the A.I.F. its renown.

So the Kidmans stepped in and discarded wool in favour of beef, cattle requiring no great labour staffs to handle and relatively few men to drive the stores and fats to the railheads. Where once upon a time Momba employed sixty men on wool Momba on cattle needed but a dozen. As though to hasten the process of denudation of population, added to the distance-devouring motor-vehicle, was the policy of the Labour Governments, who, because of hatred of capitalism, proceeded to take slices off the pastoral properties and on these slices settle a man with a wife and family.

Where Momba employed sixty men, all politically Labour, Momba now supported but half a dozen families, all of whom quickly became Conservative. As cattle can travel quicker and farther than sheep to and from water, the sinking of dams dwindled to a fraction, the demand for fencing-wire fell to a trickle, and the great development of the country west of the Darling abruptly ceased. And the demand for labour fell away almost to nothing.

The blight extended far into Queensland and away into South Australia. Sidney Kidman was but one of several men who became overlords of vast tracts of country and vast herds of cattle, and the quip which appeared in the *Bulletin*: "It is understood that the Japanese Government has approached Sir Sidney Kidman, asking what he would take for his half of Australia" wasn't as facetious as might appear.

There was a station called Earoo, and late one day Upfield arrived at its out-station, making camp in the wool-shed which hadn't housed wool for years. The place seemed to be deserted; it was, save for the cook-housekeeper and her daughter, as the manager and the hands were all absent mustering cattle.

The women were starved for human companionship, and the mother insisted that Upfield take dinner with them. There was tension between them, the mother evincing a forced gaiety and the daughter being moodily silent. She was about nineteen, pretty and plump, dark and emotional.

After dinner the mother prevailed on the guest to stay a while and talk on the verandah. The girl sat with them, but spoke seldom. Eventually, supper was suggested and the girl went off to prepare it, when the mother explained that her daughter had been captivated by an aborigine youth and was being restrained from making a fool of herself. The youth was then away with the stockmen, and it had been arranged with the manager that mother and daughter would leave for the city immediately the mustering was over.

"Once away from here she'll be cured," predicted the mother.

Upfield left about ten o'clock, and was asleep in the vacant woolshed when awakened by the mother, who came crying that her daughter had taken poison.

Together they raced to the house and into a room off the rear verandah. The girl lay on the bed, her lips parted to reveal clenched teeth, her breathing rasping, her body arched in a horrible contortion. The mother fell to her knees beside the bed wailing:

"What have you done, Sue? What have you taken?"

Upfield had had several dogs poisoned by baits dropped to kill wild dogs. One he had saved by a time-honoured method. There could be no doubt that the girl had taken strychnine. There was, also, no doubt that the mother had become useless through panic. He rushed to the kitchen for salt and water and a wooden spoon. Emptying the salt tin contents into a jug, he ran back to the bedroom, where he found the mother still imploring the girl to tell her what she had taken.

A doctor would know what to do in such an emergency, but the nearest doctor was at Wilcannia, one hundred and forty-two miles away. The woman being useless, Upfield slapped her face and shouted at her. The blow sent her back to the floor, and he could hear her moaning as he tried to prise open the daughter's clenched teeth with the spoon. Then the mother was standing beside him, sobbing.

"Hold that jug handy," he ordered, and she recovered sufficiently to obey.

The paroxysm was passing. The jaws were easing the pressure of the teeth. The eyes were beginning to flutter down from the roof of the sockets, and the rigidity of the body was lessening. The rasping breathing slowly changed to harsh panting. Then the body became limp and wet with perspiration, and the eyes stilled and were glazed with terror. Upfield lifted her and shouted at her to drink the heavily salted water. She moaned:

"Why did I do it? Why...why...why! It's coming...it's coming back."

She took a little of the saline before the next onslaught caught her, when Upfield laid her down and managed to insert the spoon between her teeth before they clamped. He had to hold the girl down until the climax came and the horror was repeated. After it passed, he managed to persuade her to drink a tumbler full of the saline, and this made her retch instantly but did not prevent the following paroxysm.

The mother couldn't stand it, and ran screaming from the room. Upfield was possessed by that same urge to run from horror begotten by helplessness to stop the Thing which controlled the agonised body, the room, the house, the world. He had heard that a dog is often helped by slitting its ears to bleed, and he ran for a butcher's knife and nicked the girl's arms. If only the victim lost consciousness!

The end came to give blessed relief, not only to the unfortunate girl. Somewhere in the house the mother continued to shriek as Upfield hunted for and found a bed from which he took the sheet. And when he left the dead girl, he felt like dashing his head against the wall to obliterate the memories.

The telephone at the main homestead was in a detached office. No one heard his ring. He slapped the mother till she shrieked from a different cause, and then persuaded her to tell him where the manager kept his grog. He made her drunk and himself too. Only doctors and policemen can stand up to that kind of thing.

5

Until much later, anyone could purchase poison at any store. Strychnine, phosphorus, cyanide, were often parcelled with the groceries. At every station homestead these poisons were kept in large quantities, to be employed in the everlasting battle with the rabbits, foxes and wild dogs. Murray, like many another manager, always took with him on his buckboard a bucket of meat baits poisoned with strychnine, now and then tossing one out as he drove about the run. He was accused of tossing out baits when on the way to and from Wilcannia, but this was put about by the town butchers, who, when Murray was known to be in town, would rush out and scatter baits to collect the town dogs that worried their sheep.

Rabbits! A stockman returning one evening to a homestead reported that he had seen a rabbit on a sandhill. The last rabbits had died in the drought four years previously. Six months after the stockman reported his rabbit there were colonies of them. They were cleaning out burrows that had been sanded over for years. They were breeding at the rate of five kittens every nine weeks, the female kittens beginning when they were about nine weeks old.

It isn't possible to describe adequately the phenomenal increase, for estimates of thousands, millions, trillions, do not convey the picture. The rolling country covered with waving spear and rye grasses almost overnight becomes pocked by areas of bare earth, and the areas grow to acres, even to square miles. Take a couple of dogs for a walk, and they will choke the burrows with rabbits, leaving the last with its rump sticking out of every entry. A man with well-trained sheep dogs can gather rabbits into a vast mass, or walk through them, when they will open out in front and close in behind.

At sundown after a hot day you can sit on the bank of a dam and watch the rabbits come to drink, and crowd each other to get at the water. They will be arriving and leaving all night through until sunrise.

When the grass has gone, they dig for the roots, climb leaning trees and sever the living twigs to eat the leaves. They eat the bark at ground level and thus kill the tree. The dogs will refuse to chase them, will starve almost to death before eating the flesh. A stockman leaving the door of his hut open will find on returning a dozen or two rabbits hunting for crumbs and even lying down with the cats. If he has hens, he must yard them, otherwise the rabbits will rob them of the wheat he tosses to them.

At night you can hear the grinding of a million jaws. The darkness seems to be alive, wriggling, squealing, the very earth itself no longer having solidity. As in the dawning when human families lived in isolation, when the young men were hunted away by the old and formed marauding bands whose main object was woman-thieving, so eventually with the rabbits in plague proportions. All the young bucks are hunted from the burrows by the old males, they become nomads, and ultimately in their numbers and strength they fight the family males and the does, and so begin the final extermination, aided by the end of the good season and the beginning of the bad. If the rabbit host doesn't migrate, which sometimes it does.

Upfield, temporarily a northern boundary rider, sat on a case outside a hut. He was washing clothes, it being Sunday. With him was a half- caste stockman. From the hut the track lay straight across a narrow ribbon of red clay and straight through the mulga forest beyond. They could see along that road for two miles, hot and dusty, the first two miles to the main homestead, thirty-odd miles away. The half-caste said:

"That's strange. I saw a rabbit."

"A rabbit!" exclaimed Upfield.

"Yes, I'm sure. It crossed the road just the other side of that dead needlewood."

"By George, you're right, there's another." Neither had seen a rabbit for many many months. A third rabbit crossed the road, then a fourth. The dogs raced away in excited uproar and gave chase to a rabbit that ventured to pass the hut. The washing was forgotten, and together they left the verandah as though seeking further proof to nail an illusion.

For four days, and presumably during the four nights, rabbits continuously crossed the road from the south side, never in the opposite direction. They passed from south to north either side of the hut, and as far along that road as the men could see. When out riding their paddocks, they found that the width of the migration was something like a mile, that the rodents were not packed into mass formation, and that their progress was not intermittently halted to feed. They were not bothering to eat when making from one point to another.

"No does," remarked the half-caste, called Tracker Leon. "All bucks. The survivors. Tell me, if you can, why the rabbits in western New South Wales invariably migrate to the north, why east of the Darling they migrate south to the Murray River, and why over in South Australia they always come from the great lakes to the north-east?"

Tracker Leon spoke like that, carefully, almost pedantically. Upfield accepted his questions as implied statements of fact, and never in the subsequent years did he encounter hostile argument, although many book-raised naturalists, who never dared the discomforts of the inland summer, expressed doubt that these migrations ever happen.

It is a pity that the moving camera-men are not more venturesome than the naturalists.

In 1927, Upfield was patrolling a section of the dog-proof fence marking the boundary between South Australia and New South Wales. There were a few rabbits then on either side of the fence. One morning there were many more on the South Australian side, and the next day there were rabbits impossible to estimate, running the South Australian side of the netting, trying to chew the wire, seeking temporarily the shade cast by dead buckbush. When the sun had done its work there was a swathe of carcasses eleven miles long, eighteen inches to two feet deep against the wire, and some ten feet wide. It was no illusion to a man who had to rake away the carcasses and burn them, so that the wind-driven sand would not pile up against the barrier.

While the rabbits are plentiful, the fox and the eagle are the pastoralist's best friends, for both subsist on Brer Rabbit. It is when the rabbit has been temporarily wiped out by drought and disease that the eagles and the crows attack lambs; for which they cannot be upbraided as they have to eat something. It is in times of drought that the crow, the pastoralist's greatest friend, will become his worst enemy.

Crows will attack weakened sheep, plucking out their eyes for a beginning. The eagles work more often than not in pairs, one knocking a heavy lamb off its feet, the other swooping to knock it down again as it struggles up, and so on until the animal is utterly exhausted. And what an eagle can do with its iron talons and beak is something. Foxes will attack a grown sheep even in broad day; but prefer to mark a starved sheep or weak lamb and wait for darkness. It so happens that after a bad summer, when the ewes drop twins, they will abandon one that the other may have sufficient milk to survive. Thus bands of deserted lambs will be found cowering in tree shade and bleating pathetically at the approach of a man who is unable to help them. When night falls, the foxes gather to run among them and slash with their fangs.

Perhaps the rabbit is the very greatest pal of the pastoralist. Not that the sheep man would ever admit it, not even when the land is empty of rabbits and he visits the troughs at a well at night, carrying a lamp, and finds himself ringed about with thousands of red lights-the red eyes of foxes.

Brer Rabbit has survived all the assaults on him. The sun has slain him in countless billions. Poison by the ton has terminated his life. Man has erected thousands of miles of netted fences to confine him, and has exterminated him in comparatively small areas. Now myxomatosis is employed–an agency more cruel than strychnine, and less effective, because Brer Rabbit is building resistance to it.

6

Upfield worked with Tracker Leon for five months, and five months living in a hut to which rations are delivered once a month by a youth driving a ton truck and wearing a cloth cap back to front will achieve either intense hatred or great regard. This partnership was ended only by Wandering Millie.

He was a strange man, this Tracker Leon. About thirty, he was under medium height for a white man, tough of body and lean.

The colour of his skin was brown, and his eyes were of that penetrating blue associated with the seafarer. On chest and back he bore cicatrices of the fully initiated, and this was unusual, as those of mixed blood are rarely so favoured by the aborigines.

Tracker Leon was ever conservative in his opinions, eager to impart what knowledge he had in store, pedantic in speech, always calm. Upfield was quick to take offence, slow to forgive, alternately humble and arrogant. Tracker Leon often countered with a proverb, always with an understanding smile, and, after the first two weeks, gained Upfield's respect, and soon afterwards Upfield acknowledged himself to be in the condition of One Spur Dick, relatively to this half-caste.

He was of North Queensland origin, having been found with his dead mother in the shade of a sandalwood tree. It was assumed that the mother had been killed by her relatives for breaking the law, and how the babe escaped the avengers could not be guessed.

The child was taken to a near-by mission, and the matron adopted him for her own. At the Mission School he showed such promise as to be sent to High School. For several years he had been attached to the Queensland Police Department as one of its most reliable and gifted trackers, because he added to his natural abilities as a tracker the honours of white education.

Following the sojourn as a northern boundary rider with Tracker Leon, Upfield drifted south to Broken Hill, decided to take a trip to Adelaide, passed on to Melbourne, and went completely broke. The greatest catastrophe to happen to a bushman is to go broke in a city. Try it, and learn how cold the people are, how indifferent.

Realising when staying at Menzies Hotel that after paying his he'd have about fourpence, and shuddering away from previous experience of humping a suitcase back to home and friends, he wired to a pal on a station for a fiver, which amount would just meet the fares.

The next morning he received a telegram saying: "Wiring ten pounds". Collecting the ten pounds, he bought rail accommodation to Mildura and booked his seat on the motor mail-car to Menindee. On returning from the station he was given another telegram, this also reading: "Wiring ten pounds".

It must indeed be a duplicate, but a visit to the post office proved otherwise. Twenty pounds! Good for another day at Menzies, where the second waiter and the chef proved good companions. The train left Spencer Street at seven something, and Upfield was tempted, was actually reaching the climax with Satan, when the third telegram arrived, worded precisely the same.

The third ten pounds was loaded against Satan. Thirty pounds was a dead horse too heavy to work off when station wages were two pounds and fourteen shillings a week, plus keep, and Upfield caught the train and then spent most of the night moaning at being such a fool as to leave the flesh-pots. The story at the other end went like this.

At morning smoko, the blacksmith told the men that Arthur was broke in Melbourne and had wired for five pounds. Having decided that five pounds was ridiculous to send to anyone in Upfield's situation, he had made it ten, telephoning to the storekeeper at Menindee to wire the cash.

They considered the matter and the Boss Stockman then asked: "What's ten quid to a man stayin' at Menzies? Wouldn't pay for his breakfast. I'll fix it."

From the office he telephoned the storekeeper and had the second ten pounds wired. The morning passed and the men were called to lunch. After lunch the Chinese gardener approached the blacksmith, saying:

"You teleglath this ten pound, eh? Twenty pounds no damn good Arthur in Melbun."

7

To press on without a predetermined destination is merely lust, and when the September sun promised faithfully a hot summer to follow, Upfield pushed his loaded machine deep into South Australia. The track took him through vast areas of desert flowers, for the winter rains had come at the right periods. It crossed low ridges blazing with diamonds-specks of mica-and masses of white quartz chips, sufficient to cover all the graves in the world. Eventually the track rose to the lip of a great basin, and here he paused to gaze downward at a gigantic gold nugget.

The track led down to the floor of the basin, when the nugget of gold looked immense–a hill four hundred feet high and completely covered with wild buttercups. Now he could see a small stone house and, about a quarter-mile from the house, a windmill about which rose dust.

The track skirted a fence, which he followed to the gate, and he was closing the gate when dogs barked from the house verandah. Dogs bark menacingly, joyfully, or expectantly. The barking was that of sick dogs. They came to meet him–two kelpies and a fox-terrier. Their tails drooped and their legs dragged. They lurched as they walked, and when they met the stranger they lifted their lips, whined softly, and stared with bloodshot eyes at the nearly empty water-bag hung from the handle-bars.

At one end of the verandah stood, low to ground, a large rain-water tank, and one of the kelpies made for it and there looked back at the stranger. Under the tap they had scooped a large hole, and beside the hole was an upturned wash-basin.

Leaning his machine against a verandah post, Upfield knocked at the only door, waited a moment, although realising that no one was there, before turning the tap of the water tank and being mobbed by the frantic dogs. Allowing the water to fill the hole, he sat on a corner of the wood staging and rolled a cigarette. The dogs lapped and nuzzled at the water, vomited water and returned to it, and the suspicion grew that tragedy extended beyond these famished animals

Again Upfield knocked at the door. He found it unbolted and opened it, and the smell which met his nose confirmed the suspicion. Within was a dead man, the owner of the dogs. There was a room beyond the first, and on the bunk in the far room was the body.

Outside again, with the door shut, Upfield felt better.

There was no wire indicating telephonic communication with the outside world, and the incident was easily explained. The man living here had felt ill, had gone to his bed and died. The unfortunate dogs had…But why hadn't they gone to the mill to drink at the trough there? The three dogs followed him to the house corner when he could see the distant mill amid the rising dust. The mill was shut off. The black dots of crows edged the square reservoir tank and were settled on a dun-coloured mound, and other things moved in the dust the wind was carrying low to ground. Drawing near, the extent of the tragedy became clear.

The sheep had come in to drink at the trough. The water in the reservoir tank had been exhausted. The sheep had crowded into the empty trough line. The first had been trampled to death, and others had been trampled above them, until some three hundred animals lay dead in the mound. The crows and the eagles had attacked the dead, and tufts of wool lay scattered about. The din made by the birds was increased by the baa-ing of sheep and he turned to see a flock consisting of some four thousand hoggets. Although they had three months' growth of new wool, their drawn flanks bespoke the lack of water.

On his releasing the control bar setting the mill to work the well pump, the sheep ran forward to surround the mound of dead animals, the tank and himself. There was frantic urgency in their baa-ing. The water spurted from the pipe into the reservoir tank. On the outskirts of the flock appeared in the dust some two dozen horses.

Through the dust pall the rays of the westering sun painted the horrific scene with the colour of blood. On the other side, the golden buttercups glowed.

Upfield faced a problem. It would take several hours to drag the dead sheep from the trough, and immediately he removed the last carcass jamming the ball-valve and so released water from the tank into the trough-line, those four thousand sheep and the horses would rush and trample to death those first reaching it. One person could not clear the trough and lead the sheep to the water, and the dogs were quite unfit to work.

Problems multiplied. From this point he was unaware of the direction and distance of the homestead. He cursed the squatter for being penny wise and pound foolish, for had he gone to the expense of erecting a telephone wire, the man in charge, when desperately ill, might have obtained help for himself as well as the stock. Upfield prospected about the house, and found three tracks going from it, any two of which would terminate at a lonely well and mill. Under a bough roof shelter he found an old truck, several poison-carts and horse harness, and several forty-gallon petrol drums, only one of which contained petrol. The truck had been employed on all three tracks, so its distinctive marks gave no assistance.

Not over-familiar with trucks, it took Upfield an hour to get this one moving, and by now the sun was setting, and the horses came charging from the well to circle the house and smell the water left by the dogs at the tank. He thought of giving them water in the wash-basin, but they were so maddened that to attempt it was to be knocked down.

A Mr. Murray or a Tracker Leon might easily have solved these problems, the most difficult of which was to identify the track leading to the homestead. Again he examined each in turn, following it for some distance, and eventually decided that one had been used more than the others and doubtless was the oldest—the first track made from the homestead to here.

Upfield tested the truck's lights, and found the battery quite flat, the engine being run on a magneto. So that was that, as only an albino or a cat could see an unknown track in the dark.

That night he camped by the truck parked some distance from the house, and during the night he heard the horses fighting at the rain tank, and all night through heard the continuous uproar of the sheep at the distant mill. At sunset the wind had dropped, the mill had stopped pumping, and but an inch or two of water would have been raised to the reservoir tank.

When day dawned he took the dogs to the mill and managed to put the kelpies to work keeping the sheep back, and the little fox-terrier to do his damnedest to shoo away the horses, while he dragged out dead sheep to free the ball-valve. Fortunately, with the rise of the sun, the wind came to work the mill, and as it conveyed water to the big tank, so did Upfield slave to drag heavy dead animal after animal clear of the trough, watched from a distance by the sheep guarded by the kelpies, and by two of the horses being yapped at by the terrier, the others seemingly determined to kick the water out of the house tank.

Four hours of this exhausting labour resulted in sufficient of the trough being cleared, and about a foot of water run into it. Then, of course not before, there appeared a fiend on a motor-bike who came to a skidding halt and calmly asked:

"What's burning, Dig?"

Upfield's choice of track was good enough, and the homestead was eleven miles along it. In less than an hour there were half a dozen men on the job, including the boss and a cook. Again, when the sun went down, a policeman arrived, and, the boss acting as Justice of the Peace and a Coroner, the dead man was buried. It was known that his heart had been erratic, and all the circumstances indicated he had died in his sleep.

As well there, of course, as in a palace.

CHAPTER NINE

THE AMATEUR BULL-FIGHTER

I

Late spring one year, Upfield found himself again at Milparinka and decided to prospect out to Yandama, a property of three thousand square miles, and famous for its horses. Yandama occupies the far north-west tip of New South Wales, and is reached by crossing high plains and stony flats, then abruptly dropping down to the sandhill country, where the homestead lies athwart a small creek.

The Yandama Creek meanders westward from the homestead, crosses into South Australia and enters a depression joining Lake Callabonna with Lake Frome. North-west of the homestead is Sturt's old camp, named Fort Grey, and a mile or so beyond this you can brew tea in New South Wales, toss the leaves into Queensland and water South Australia, for here the boundaries of the three States meet, here at this angle meet three great dog- and rabbit-proof State fences.

Upfield accompanied the camel-rider patrolling the northern section of the South Australian border fence, and saluted the three States in the time-honoured manner. One of the gates on this section barred a track leading to the homestead of Tilcha Station in South Australia; the track did not pass beyond the homestead, for beyond Tilcha live only the buckbush and the flies. To this homestead was yet to come a woman who wrote a fine book entitled *No Roads Go By*.

Subsequently, Upfield took over a section of the fence west of the Quinambie homestead, the section being twenty-two miles long, and pack-camels used for transportation. The fence is dog-proof, being six feet high of wire netting topped with barbed wire, and it runs due north and south, this particular section an endless switchback over gigantic sand ranges.

These sand ranges run east-west for miles, and from the eastern highlands to the shores of Lake Frome, like the waves of a petrified ocean, waves of red sand forty and fifty feet high above the troughs of narrow, hard flats.

With two camels to carry his equipment, Upfield discovered that his section of twenty-two miles was twenty miles too long. Across flat and over sandhill, the fence had to be not less than six feet high, the minimum height to stop dingoes; and the eternal battle was to prevent the fence being engulfed by sand.

The quiet and crisp winter days and cold nights of inland Australia present a markedly different country from that ruled by the summer sun. In summer this world comes alive and what is termed the Dead Heart fights and bashes men and animals, and brings flies, snakes, iguanas and perentis, stomach and eye troubles, and the conviction of lunacy for being there.

Yet Upfield gained much from it.

Come November, the flies are such that the white tarpaulin over the pack-load is made black, and the only relief in this cattle country is to keep one's face in the hot air rising from a fire, and there eat your salt beef and bone-dry soda bread. Cooking is done and dinner eaten after dark.

But you are not alone in this misery; your two camels are equally victims to the pest, and they will often demand the application of kerosene mixed with fat to their eyes, and frequently they will thrust their heads either side of your own, to gain a share of the hot air rising from a fire. So you take two bites of a hunk of bread and give a bite to each of your comrades. And, as Upfield did, you come to understand that these animals do think, and do reason, that they have appetites, and do feel pain, such as that caused by rheumatism and strained tendons and the like.

These two camels, for instance. One was an old gentleman bullock, and the other was an elderly lady-like cow. They were individuals, each a personality, and the idea becomes a conviction that man, as an individual, is the beast, not the animal he controls and looks upon as fodder for his own voracious vanity.

As Upfield and his camels patrolled twenty-two miles of this State border fence, being but one of a number of men who had patrolled it since its erection, he was seeing yet another of the thousand facets of this limitless land, and was still enthralled, still intensely absorbed by it. The buckbush was born in the heat of early summer, appearing on the sandhills and the slopes like green dots on red velvet. It had to be hoed up along both sides of the netting, so that the coming wind-storms which energised the sand would not pile it against obstruction at the wire, but blow it through the mesh. It grows swiftly to round balls of living filigree, providing excellent feed for stock until, when twice the size of a football, it dies and becomes useless straw.

The wind will snap the ball from the parent stem, drive it over the ground, and send it hurdling over low obstructions. The west wind is the worst enemy of this vermin fence. Before its hot breath, the buckbush comes charging from the reddish murk to dash against the wire, and gradually the 'slain' will provide a rising step, so that eventually the buckbush charges over the six-foot-high wire barrier into New South Wales. The entire surface of this chaotic world will continue to move eastward during the hours of wind, and when the wind has finished its sport the wire fence has become a straw rampart bedded in sand.

At the beginning of a wind-storm the fence may be the regulation height at the apex of a sand-wave. The patrol man may find, the next time he comes, that the fence has been reduced in height to a foot, instead of the original six. This means he has to fell trees for posts, lash the new posts to the posts of the old, run wire from post to post and stretch new netting over the new section. A day's work, perhaps two days. Then, when he is at an extremity of his section, another storm will rage, and again, coming to the new section, he may well find that the crown of the hill has been blown away, and he will have to dismantle his recent work, and perhaps the fence under it, for here the barrier had been built fence upon fence, three, four, even five times.

It might be thought that working under these conditions would send a man crazy, that only a complete moron could possibly continue, despite the good money paid by the controlling State Department. Upfield was happy enough to stay seven months.

There was the battle between two eagles and a handsome pure-bred dingo. The dog had been caught on the centre of a flat by the two birds. He had been sitting, tongue lolling, watching the eagles, when one of these great birds came down at him and knocked him over with a wing pinion, lurched, and continued its flight on and up. Immediately, the other repeated this manœuvre. So it went on, and the wretched dog was given no chance to run for cover. The power of the birds, their grace and timing were superb. The dog, instead of lying prone, continued to fight and be knocked down, courage never failing, even to the end when it lay prostrate and feebly snapping at the elusive wings.

Finally the dog gave up and the eagles landed within a few feet of it. They there remained, motionless, waiting for the animal to die, as though knowing that the sun, allied with exhaustion, would deal the death blow.

One day Upfield met King George and the perenti almost at the same moment. The perenti is one degree advanced from iguana to alligator, and, although very rare, is occasionally found in the great Lake Frome- Callabonna Basin. Upfield watched this perenti from behind a buckbush on the summit of a sand-wave. It was about six feet long, smooth-skinned like the iguana, and possessing a head and jaws having distinct resemblance to the saurian.

Behind Upfield, lower down the sand bank, were his camels, and movement by them caused him to look back and down, to see a white-haired aborigine astride an ancient horse. That he was King George was proved by the information painted on a sheet of tin swung from his neck to rest on his chest. In reply to Upfield's signals, he dismounted and clambered upward to join him.

"Big feller perenti, eh!" he whispered. "You shoot him, eh? No good you miss him, no good you wound him. You wound him, he find out and come here. By cri, him bite like hell."

"Bet you I stop him," boasted Upfield, but King George objected, explaining that only half a mile along the flat some of his people were camped and saying, if Upfield would watch the perenti, he would call his young men to deal with it.

On Upfield's agreeing, he retreated, mounted his horse and almost succeeded in persuading it to trot. The reptile went to sleep anyway, it closed its snake-like eyes and rested its head on the ground.

Twenty minutes later King George returned, accompanied by several young bucks, lubras and children. The bucks crept up the sand-wave to join the white man, then retreated down to the flat and went into a huddle, because these people cannot do anything without a ceremony of some kind.

They produced two waddies, reminding Upfield of the Irish shillelagh, and, with motion only, the chief ordered the women, the children and uninitiated youths to sit with their backs to the few bucks, who then squatted and proceeded to 'sing' power and accuracy into their waddies. Afterwards they ran away along the flat and King George joined Upfield, saying:

"You wait. You gibbit bacco, eh?"

Down on that wide flat lay the perenti. About him was scattered tussock grass which would not give cover to a chicken. The reptile continued to sleep, or pretended to. Minutes slid out of New South Wales into South Australia. The scene remained the same until Upfield saw a fire-blackened log over beyond the perenti, and another fifty yards behind it. He could not recall seeing those logs previously, and was astonished when one moved and proved to be a naked aborigine.

How they reached those positions baffled him, for he had been steadily watching the perenti, and the area about it.

Suddenly there were two of them. Only when they moved were they human beings; they appeared able to change shape from a man to a log, and back again to a man when they moved forward.

Now and then the perenti would open an eye, but there must have been blind spots, and those aborigines knew just where to conceal themselves in those blind spots. Sometimes the perenti would raise its head, not unlike a dog sniffing suspiciously at the air wafted to his snout. And with what seemed to be short and jerky jumps, the two logs gradually closed upon it.

One of the stalkers was within a few yards of the perenti and was in the act of rising to move forward, when the reptile raised itself on stiffened four legs, and, like the iguana, began to swell its neck in fearsome menace. The stalker froze to immobility the instant the perenti rose, and he held that position for minutes with not the faintest movement; half crouched, one foot off the ground, one hand supporting himself, the other gripping the waddy.

Presently the neck swelling subsided and the stiffness went from the legs of the perenti, whereupon the second stalker moved forward, the first remaining completely still. On the second stalker again becoming a log, he coughed. The sound caused the perenti to flash to his direction, and the first stalker then leapt to his feet and charged over the remaining four or five yards. The watchers could see the wide jaws, the flattened snout, the whirling tail. The waddies rose and fell. The victory was won. Men and women and children yelled and screamed and rushed madly down to the flat to congratulate the victors.

2

Whilst awaiting the opportunity to visit Lake Frome, one of the worst storms for years provided Upfield with a memorable experience. Westward of that great sand waste extending beyond the northern tip of the Flinders Range and north-westward past Lake Eyre, and on across the Simpson Desert, a north wind was born, to grow lustily and run south to dance with a west wind, whirling and throbbing in the ecstasy of union. They kicked up the sand, gathered the buckbush, smashed the straw balls to tiny fractions, and soon countless tons of sand and debris were lifted thousands of feet into the sky to become a cloud having a flat golden summit and a body of jet-black chaos.

It was the grandfather of all willy-willies, those tall and drunken spiralling columns which march across hot Australia.

This particular black storm moved to the south-east, to Upfield, who was working on his fence, to stockmen in their camps and to the blacks who were doing merely 'what they oughta'. The day was very hot and strangely still, and Upfield, as usual, had worked from four in the morning, when day dawned, until eight, then again from five in the afternoon until dusk fell at seven.

There was no warning, no weather portent. Even the birds and the camels, quite often reliable alarms, were tricked. As day departed the full moon rose into the bottle-green sky and appeared to stare with cold disapproval at the sun's aftermath of blood staining the western limits.

Blessed relief from the flies, no larger than house flies, which will not enter a house or hut. Upfield cooked a meal, and afterwards baked the daily loaf and boiled the usual portion of salted beef. About the fire was the camp equipment, the tent not rigged, the stretcher set up under the open sky. Close by, the lazy clanging of the camel bells told that they were lying down contentedly chewing cud.

About nine that night Upfield lay on his stretcher, wearing only pyjama trousers, and not bothering to cover himself even with the luxury sheet of unbleached calico. The moon gained height to pour its radiance upon him, but he slept on.

When the sun had gone down, the frenzied dance of the north and the west winds ended abruptly, from sheer exhaustion, leaving in the upper air those uncountable tons of sand. The echo of the dancing winds propelled the sand-mass towards New South Wales and the sleeping Upfield.

He was awakened by the unfamiliar noise, a low throbbing, as though the alleged Dead Heart of Australia was actually beating deep in his own consciousness. He sat up. The camels were still, their bells silent. Then he saw them on the flat, standing motionless, both looking to the west as though they knew from which direction the throbbing was coming.

Upfield looked that way. Beyond the fence was a sand dune that wasn't there the previous day. Even as he watched it the sand dune became higher, and lengthened towards the north and the south, seeming to advance as a titanic black wave. The moon, not then at the zenith, failed to penetrate the surface, but did reveal the speed of this oncoming monster.

As it approached, so did it grow in height, and soon the black face presented to the moon changed to dull red, and even the red dunes are not red in the moonlight.

It was the camels who energised Upfield. Had they bolted he would have bolted too, not even bothering to slip on his boots. They swung their rumps to the sand-mass and went down to their knees and settled their long necks and heads on the ground. There was, of course, no escape. Within minutes the advancing sand dune was towering high above animals and man, a mighty spectacle which even Jules Verne and H. G. Wells could not have imagined.

The face of the mass was palpitating, vast areas being gently sucked inwards, and corresponding areas gently puffed outwards. The declivities were jet black, the protuberances livid crimson.

From deep inside the horror originated the pulsating beat which seemed to be born in the depth of the mind.

Upfield had snatched up the tent and spread it over the stretcher. He was without hope of living under this avalanche of sand, and the flimsy protection of the tent was the result of frantically clutching at a straw. When he slid in under the stretcher he tried in vain to wait calmly for the end, not only of himself and the camels but of the world, for what could possibly survive this advancing mountain of sand?

There was a crack in the tent wall, and without thinking, Upfield maintained it to permit air to the last possible moment. The camels didn't move. He waited for the hurricane motivating the sand-mass, and it didn't come. The moon shone as brightly and as calmly, and apart from the beating of the monstrous heart the night was entirely devoid of sound. One moment the world was a bright fairyland, the next it vanished in complete night. It was as swift as switching off the light in a curtained room.

The absence of the expected wind and the expected grinding of millions of tons of rolling sand made the ensuing silence even more terrifying. The throbbing ceased, and against the straining drums of Upfield's ears there came far-away elfin singing, like the bursting bubbles of sea foam to be heard beneath the whispering wind.

It occurred to Upfield that he was still breathing; he panted and proved it. He listened, hearing only that unearthly and yet beautiful chanting. Inertia followed tension, and this phase passed, to be replaced by keen curiosity to know what was going on outside.

He possessed no means of measuring time, and refrained from guessing how long he had lain under the stretcher before the light began slowly to return. He ventured to widen the crack, and there entered a cool draught of air to chill his sweat-drenched body, and what he could see of the world was unrelated to the normal. He crawled out.

The tent over the stretcher bore inches of sand and the world was dim in a murk of dull brown, rapidly thinning. He looked for the camels, and two humps of sand cast shadows and revealed their position.

He found them still resting their heads on the ground, but instead of heads were humps of sand, and instead of necks were wide ridges of sand, and instead of humped bodies were small mountains of sand. Thinking both had been asphyxiated he nudged a head mound with his foot, and the mound lifted and the head came up and was shaken, and the calm black eyes regarded Upfield serenely. On their clambering to their feet, masses of fine dust fell from them.

All that remained of the sand cloud was a dark mist withdrawing to the east, and the dawn came to reveal the aftermath. As though the grains of sand falling from the sky when the wind was slain from under them were flakes of red snow, so every object was piled with them. The branches of trees, the small shrubs, dead wood, the camp equipment, even the wires of the fence were loaded with sand. When Upfield tossed a stick against the fence it rained sand. He tossed another into the branches of a tree, and the entire tree was masked by falling sand.

The windless sand-storm exhausted itself a few miles east of the fence. Temporarily, it wiped out all the tracks to the bores and to Lake Elder.

3

Every fourth day Upfield watered his camels at the bore nearest the point he happened to be. There were three, two of them in South Australia. All were artesian, all brought water under pressure to pour strongly from an angled pipe, flow for a mile or more to form a lake, and finally disappear into the sand.

At the bore head the water is hot and too loaded with alkalis to drink, therefore it is necessary to fill water-drums far along the channel or at the small natural lake, where much of it has been separated to form a white substance at the edge. Even then the water is unsuitable for tea, and only passable for coffee.

One of the South Australian bores was a hundred per cent up on the finest washing machine ever invented. All Upfield had to do was to hang a garment on the point of a stick and hold it in the gush of water for five seconds, wring it and wave it in the sunlight, where it would dry within a minute. Six such washes, and the garment would fall to. pieces. A billy-can stained dark brown by brewing tea or coffee would, when so treated, become silver bright in half a minute. Even at the extremity of the surface flow the water was still loaded, so it can be imagined what seven months of living on this water will do to a man's interior.

It has been stressed in this chronicle that Upfield was being constantly urged to seek what lay ahead. It was now proved that animals sometimes suffer from the same irresistible urge.

Late one day Upfield had come to a bad break in the fence and next morning he worked on the repairs. When done, the noon heat dictated rest in the shade of several matured mulga trees. So the camping equipment wasn't packed, and the camels were lying down in distant shade, when a bull topped the nearest sand dune. He came over it, hugging the fence, came on steadily with tail swishing like that of an irate cat. On seeing the camp he launched himself down the slope.

The French have a polite word to describe this bull's condition, and it was then greatly in vogue in the current romantic literature on the French Foreign Legion–*cafard*. The Anglo-Saxon, who must find humour even in a funeral, invented the word 'wonky'.

This bull was decidedly 'wonky'. It could be surmised that he had been hunted from the herd by the younger bulls, and thereby severed from that which plays so important a part in the life of cattle, as well as human beings–the herd instinct.

Having been cast out by the herd, which might then be twenty miles away, as the country had received no rain for a year and therefore there were no pools of water, this specimen had marched up and down the fence until he was decidedly wonky, although still agile, speedy and cunning.

He was down off that sand dune and charging across the flat before Upfield realised it was his turn to be a perenti, and he had but ten seconds' grace to scramble up a tree, and ten seconds were far short of the period needed to cross twelve yards to the riding saddle where the .44 Winchester was slung.

It is certain sure that an Australian bull gone wonky would not play the game with a Spanish matador, for it has no time for rules. This one, on arrival in a small dust-storm, tested the tree with his head, then tested it by leaning against it, knowing that when fifteen hundred pounds of meat and bone is leaned against a tree, the tree may stagger and fall. He had done it often merely to show off before the cows.

Fortunately for Upfield, this particular tree withstood the assault, and so the wonky bull almost calmly trampled flat the stretcher, horned the bedding, then smashed the tucker-box and flattened the billy-cans. The camp-fire was now a mound of red coals, and instead of charging this as your Spanish bull would have done, he looked at it, pawed the ground, snorted hard enough to blow the embers apart, and went off to rub a tick in his hide against another tree.

Excepting that his horns were short and neatly pointed, there was little of the Shorthorn about him. His mother must have said 'yes' to a buffalo, for all over him was the buffalo's mean look, its latent power, the buffalo's dirty cunning.

An Australian mulga tree is the last place on earth, excepting the middle of a wait-a-bit bush, for a man to take his ease, the mulga being too spiny, too hard, and too close-branched.

The bull dozed, and Upfield moved down the tree, purposing to steal quietly to the riding saddle and the rifle. The bull rested with his nose to the ground, his eyes closed, and Upfield was about to leave the tree when the bull was up and charging. Knowing that Upfield intended to escape again, he halted on straightened legs, snorted, and went back to his shade. All this was repeated twice again in the following hour.

The bull's playmate must have been a tom cat, for that was how he played with the mouse in the tree; and he was so wonky that he had forgotten how thirsty he was. He intended to play that game of his until the treed man fell.

Eventually the bull changed the plan. He lurched to his feet and again tried to push down the tree. Then he examined the two five-gallon water-drums. He kicked both and sniffed, and prodded them with his horns. He upturned the straw-stuffed pack saddle, and trampled across the riding saddle as though he knew all about the rifle and was determined to smash it.

By this time Upfield's situation was desperate. He cursed the bull, but believes no sound issued from his gummed throat. He cursed himself for being on a job like this, where there is so much poison laid for dingoes that to have a dog isn't possible. The bull again laid himself down and pretended to sleep.

Some time later, the camels agreed to feed and their bells clattered abruptly and loudly. The noise startled the bull, who flashed to his feet and stood staring in the direction from which it came, from beyond a low sand ridge. He snorted and strode to the ridge.

By now Upfield was learning to exercise what brain he had. Instead of climbing down the tree, he fell from it when the bull's rump was towards him, and he was hidden by the trunk when the animal flashed a look. Seeing no movement, it went on to prospect the bells, and as Upfield had seen the blacks stalk the perenti, so now did he stalk his own rifle, freezing to a stump every time the bull turned.

Under the dominance of a craving for water, Upfield was

beyond fear, and possessed by hatred. He reached the rifle at the moment the bull topped the low ridge. On seeing the camels the bull bellowed, swung about and came charging, as the camels held no interest for him. For the man to run meant being caught. Pumping a cartridge into the breech, he fired at the great head.

The bull bucked, roared, missed his stride or crossed his feet, and fell. Then he was up again, standing quite still, save for the wicked eyes searching for the man taking cover behind the iron riding saddle that wouldn't give cover to a rabbit. From a moving picture, it became a still. The bull was looking at the tree where Upfield had perched, and Upfield had yet to pump out the used cartridge and pump in another, and this cannot be done without movement.

It is all very easy for big game hunters on safari in Africa, but Upfield was only a common working man in Australia. The big game hunter wouldn't have missed with his first shot. Upfield didn't miss, either, but his first try wasn't good enough to stop this bull. This bull stood, waiting for movement to betray his victim, and he appeared unconcerned by the blood dripping down a flank. The job was to pump another cartridge into the breech and fire before the bull could cross nine yards of country, but the vital achievement was to plant a bullet in his brain, there being no possibility of a third try. Upfield watched the flaring red nostrils trying to smell him. He watched the vicious red-flamed eyes searching for him, and he was stiff with horror, and tortured unbearably by the flies crawling into his eyes and his ears.

And the flies were doing just that to the bull. He blinked his eyes, shook his head, rubbed his eye against a foreleg and became really angry. He snorted and again shook his head and bellowed, and during that bellow Upfield pumped the magazine lever. Thereafter the show ended. The bull dropped with a bullet in his brain, and Upfield staggered to the water-drums.

Anticlimax came when, having gathered his camels, Upfield walked the twelve miles to the station homestead for new equipment, and the manager expected him to pay for the bull! But then the manager had been too long away from the bright lights and was wonky, too.

4

During his last month patrolling the S. A. border fence, Upfield was presented with an opportunity to visit Lake Frome. He travelled with two dog trappers who owned a Ford truck, and, having arrived at Lake Frome, he sat on a tall sand dune for half a day, looking at it.

He saw a bare expanse of grey mud stretched taut to the far distant mirage 'water', and knew that the mud continued beyond the mirage to the west shore some forty miles away. The bare red dunes ran away to the north and down to the south to form the horns of a gigantic crescent also disappearing into the mirage. The mirage played fantastic tricks, supporting the rugged summits of the Flinders Range, making of them celestial islands, cutting into the shore dunes and raising ridges to sky-towering cliffs having glass faces. The wind brought across the mud to the seated Upfield breaths of fire, and tipped the sand ridges with feathers of red smoke.

The sun had crisped the surface of the mud to the formation of fallen leaves, and, beneath, it was glutinous for several inches down the hardening bottom. Here and there were what appeared to be cattle pads, but these paths had been made by the wild dogs said to be the sole inhabitants of 'islands' in the mud.

Such was Lake Frome as seen by Upfield–a desolate waste of mud baking in high temperatures and surrounded by red sand tossed into cones and ridges, funnelled and gullied, and in constant movement. A feeling of numbness in the left foot warned Upfield that the absence of green vegetables from his diet was at long last having effect, and when he dimpled the flesh and the cavity took minutes to fill up, he knew what he faced if he ignored the warning.

So down to Broken Hill for the cure which is so pleasant to take. Plenty of beer, meals of pickled onions and of sliced potatoes, pickled overnight in vinegar. No tea or coffee.

By this time the smelters had been transferred from Broken Hill to Port Pirie, and the 'Hill' had become the most healthy city in Australia. Its people have always been entirely free of snobbery. The incidence of crime is exceptionally low, and drunkenness is rare, because everyone is well seasoned to beer. A wonderful spa for a cure.

5

Old Havelock Ellis had much to say about sex, and a great deal of what he recorded is true.

Throughout this period of wandering from job to job, Upfield was troubled less by sex than by other demands, and following a full week on the 'cure', and the condition of his foot being good, he went exploring the 'Hill' in the cool of the early night.

Argent Street provided the bright lights proving that it isn't well for a man to live too much alone for too long. The people one met on Argent Street were always cheerful and passionately in love with life. The men were well dressed in white shirts and trousers, and the women were enjoying that ugliest of fashion termed the H line, and cloche hats which emphasised their formlessness.

Crystal Street is the antithesis of Argent Street, being a quiet thoroughfare bordered by small houses having reserved and respectablefronts. Here resided the ladies of easy virtue. The police knew all about them, never interfered unless one kicked over the traces, or permitted a rowdy party, and because of this, and for no other reason, Broken Hill is the safest place on earth for the wives and daughters of its citizens.

It was a quiet night between pay-days at the mines when Upfield strolled down Crystal Street, without knowing of its fame. The houses are set a little back from the footpaths, and most have small gardens and shrubs behind a picket fence. From the darker shadow cast by a flowering tree a woman said:

"Won't you come inside for a little while?"

Upfield halted and lit a cigarette, the flare of the match revealing a woman in her late twenties, buxom and wearing a light dressing gown. The woman spoke again:

"It's very quiet tonight. Won't cost you much."

"I'd like to stay an hour. How much would that be?"

"A pound suit you?"

"Yes."

The woman opened the gate and he followed her into the lighted passage, where she indicated a bedroom and then closed the front door. He sat on the bed and when she came into the room he asked for a cup of tea. Surprised, she nodded and departed, and within a few minutes returned with a tray bearing cups and saucers and a plate of biscuits. The tray she placed on the bed and then sat on the far side of it.

She was younger than the match flare had indicated, and less buxom. Her features were regular, and her complexion had nothing to it of depravity. The bed, the furnishings, her gown, all bespoke prosperity. There was a painting on the wall, and photographs in expensive frames on the dressing-table. A pound note Upfield folded and slipped under his hostess's saucer. There was no pouncing on the money; merely a cool nod of acceptance.

After ten minutes of somewhat stilted question and answer. The conversation became easy. The woman liked the horses and music. Upfield preferred books and the boxing at the Trade's Hall Stadium. He confessed that he was English, and spoke of his travels and general doings. They smoked many cigarettes, and the hour flew and another began to pass, when the woman said:

"You're a funny man. Aren't you going to have me?"

Upfield slipped the second pound note under the saucer. "Some time, perhaps. I came in only to talk. Haven't really talked to a woman for almost a year. After living on salted beef and damper bread and black tea for seven months, talking is all I'm fit for. You being bored?"

"Of course not. But talking's costing you a lot of money."

"Worth it, but you mightn't believe it. Are you going to the races tomorrow?"

"N-no."

"Would you go with me?"

"Why not? I'd like to."

So Upfield took her to the races, where they bet in five bobs, and on returning to the city they dined at a restaurant, then went to the cinema. And after the show he escorted her to her home in Crystal Street, and she invited him for supper, and no charge for the time. What he paid was little for the feminine society which no man can do without.

When he became normally human, he was broke.

CHAPTER TEN

HEN-HOUSE BREW

I

In the spring of 1924 Arthur Upfield came again to the small station property off the Darling River, to be warmly welcomed by Angus and his wife Mary. Always lean, he was now verging on gauntness, and his face and arms were as dark as the skin of many half-castes. His hazel eyes were partially hidden by the leathery puckered skin about them, and there was in him a tenseness not there at his first visit.

That evening Angus asked him whither he was bound, and he said he thought of running down to Melbourne for a spell. As formerly, Angus was interested in Upfield's wanderings, and his way of gaining the picture of a township was to establish how many pubs were still open for business, then compare the figure with the number open in his time. He would shake his head sadly because of the steady depletion of population due to so many causes, chiefly the new motor transport. A little abruptly, Upfield asked for a job.

"Times are tough," Angus said.

"No rain this past winter, and feed's so scarce I have to ration cake to the sheep. You know what a drain that is on the old bank account."

"I can guess," Upfield agreed, adding: "I don't want wages. I have money. I don't really want to trip down to Melbourne. I just want to..."

He drifted into introspection, and gently Mary asked: "What is it you really want?"

He seemed not to realise precisely what he wanted, but because they were silent and waiting he was compelled to bring to the surface that which had been stirring for some time. His hand indicated the soft light and shadow of this quiet and peaceful world; he pointed to the verandah roof; nodded towards the sitting-room.

"All this," he replied. "I didn't know it until this minute. I'd like to stay a while. You see, I haven't slept inside a house, or even a hut, for a long time. Haven't been inside a pub or stayed at a town overnight. You understand how the open sky gets at a man, too much of it, as though he's a rabbit caught far away from the burrow.

"I've come too close to a kind of precipice and something is warning me about it. I know what I should do, all right. Go down to the city and have a good old bender, but the city hasn't any appeal any longer. That's wrong, too. Let me stay a few days. I'll earn my keep doing something or other. It's the sky I want to get away from. I want to sit at a table with a white cloth, and talk and listen."

They regarded each other, Angus and Mary. Mary nodded and Angus said:

"Stay as long as you like, Artie. You can sleep in the spare room.

And between sheets. We know how it is."

2

Angus had had several tons of sheep cake trucked to him to eke out the natural feed, and every morning at eleven he and Upfield loaded a ration of cake on to the utility and drove to the back paddocks. The earth should have been covered with new grasses and herbage, but the river flats were barren and only beyond the sand dune, four miles from the river, was there still a little rubbish , for the sheep.

Sometimes the sheep were waiting for the truck, and with

much uproar would surround it and follow it, to pick up the broken cake tossed out by one man while the other drove about the paddock. When the sheep were not present to greet the truck, all that Angus had to do was to sound the hooter, and they would come charging over a dune or across a fiat.

Other than cake-feeding those four thousand sheep and maintaining the water supply at a well, there was very little to do. Upfield chopped wood for Mary's stove. He trolled for fish on the river, or took Angus's double-barrelled gun to wing a duck or two. He pottered about the little homestead, finding jobs to occupy him, and at night he lounged on the verandah and talked, and was watched by Mary without being aware of it.

There is more than a mile between squatting on the heels to eat a meal beside a fire–to keep warm in winter, or with head thrust into the hot air in summer to defeat the flies–and sitting on a chair at a white- covered table and eating a tastefully prepared meal. The distance is as great between rolling in a dusty blanket on a claypan and slipping in between sheets on a soft mattress. And even a greater distance lies between talking to a camel and talking with an intelligent woman about books, or with an intelligent man about raising oneself in this tough old world.

It was what Upfield needed–to cross those distances from the one extreme to the other, and Mary knew it when she saw him absently fingering the pattern of the table-cloth, or easing himself into a chair as though nervous of it. She was like the grandmother and the aunts who were convinced that grown men are children, and more often than not proved it. She proceeded to unearth his background from where she had been obliged to leave it at his first visit.

Women! A man hasn't a chance.

Mary tended a tiny garden. She placed flowers on the bedside table in Upfield's room. Where she obtained the new slippers, he was never to know. The little comforts gradually inserted into his life after so long an absence all amounted to the opening skirmishes in a battle timed and planned. Her hair was white and bountiful. Her face was lined. Her hands were large and work-spoiled. Her eyes were gentle and understanding. Another grandmother! Another aunt! She waited for the signs of restlessness in him–the next onset of the same walkabout fever to which the aborigines are constant victims.

"D'you ever think of taking up your writing again?" she asked.

"Writing!" he echoed. "Why, I wouldn't make enough at writing in a
year to buy a tin of jam."

"How do you know that, if you don't try? Now don't put me off, please. I'm serious, and I'm going to talk and you are going to listen, because you've done the talking and I've done the listening. How old are you?"

"About thirty."

"About! Don't you know?"

"Not to the year. I had my birth certificate when I left home, but I don't know what happened to it. As for writing–what chance would I have? It couldn't be done when boundary riding, or opal gouging, or droving. Besides, I'd have to anchor somewhere, and I don't intend to anchor to anything. Not now, after years of getting around."

Thus the skirmish. Then the battle, a week later.

"Did you speak the truth when you said you wrote three long novels before you left home?" Mary asked.

"Yes. Why?"

"Did you have two articles published by the London *Daily Mail*, and two short stories in the *Novel Magazine*?"

"Yes, Now, would you like me to tell you a story?"

Mary wasn't in the mood to be side-tracked by flippancy.

"Why don't you write about your experiences here in Australia?" she suggested. "You said the other evening you couldn't bear to think of settling down and writing. I read a book once about a man who wrote and wrote until he made his writing pay, and eventually he was able to travel about the world and he still went on writing because he was inwardly driven to it.

"Don't speak. Listen. None of us have talents one week and none the next. It is sinful to toss back to the Eternal the talents He has given. Try to understand that life is so very short, and roaming here and there, year after year, is just plain silly. And think of the hopes your father and mother had of you. You told us you never miss writing to them once a week. The next time you write, ask them to tell you candidly if they are or are not disappointed in you. And then sit on a sandhill and look at yourself in the mirror of a mirage. Good-night! It was nice of you to hear me out."

3

The rain came in the middle of the night, without warning until the first heavy drops pinged on the corrugated iron roof. The sound, the small but magical sound, woke everyone more swiftly than a ton of dynamite exploded at the back door could have done. The pinging became a roar, and Mary and Angus and Upfield stood on the verandah and watched the darting streaks of water falling through the blaze of the pressure lamp. The needy earth released its long withheld scents into the atmosphere, and Angus produced a bottle of whisky he had had planted for twenty years.

Two days later the slopes of the sand dunes were stained light green. On the fifth day the grass and young buckbush were high enough for sheep to nibble. It rained again within a fortnight, and at the end of a month the aridity and the deadness were but memories banished from a re-created Eden.

Hundreds of miles to the north storms dropped inches of water over central and southern Queensland, and Upfield watched a river running up-hill. Once again a northern boundary rider, he lived in a tent protected from the wind by a brushwood fence and set up beside the Paroo.

This river hadn't run for many years. Its course is marked by mile- wide flat clay-channels connecting a chain of shallow depressions, and unless you know north from south, it is difficult to determine the natural flow of water.

Every other day, Upfield rode across a mile-wide channel to inspect a well and windmill, where two thousand sheep came to water. The flat floor of the channel was cracked, the cracks were feet deep and the general pattern hexagonal. The clay half an inch below the surface was hard enough to defy the point of a crow-bar.

Returning to camp one afternoon, the horse became nervous immediately on stepping on to the channel, and the dog as anxious as the horse to get back to camp, halted and cocked his head, then sniffed into a crack. A rabbit, or perhaps an iguana? The day was hot and Upfield, too, was impatient to reach camp, but such was the persistent behaviour of horse and dog that he dismounted. The wind was strong, and wind in the ears will defeat sound, so that it was not until he stooped to peer into a crack that he heard the noise of water, at first refusing to believe it. There was water running happily many feet below.

That evening he sat on a box near the fireplace from which he could see the channel, and there was no difference in the view which had been static for several years. It was, of course, before radio came into general use, and the camp was not in telephone contact with the homestead some eighteen miles away. The sun went down and the stars came out–to quote a famous line–and the wind died down, too. Like an invisible army, strange sounds advanced from the channel.

One sound was not unlike sand being sparsely dropped on to stiff paper; this sound persisted without interruption. Under or behind it was the sound of something slithering across a waxed floor. Now and then a rabbit squealed, not from pain, but sudden fright. Later the dog became vociferous and charged a monarch iguana that entered the firelight and took possession of the tent.

As it is unwise to wrestle with an iguana when excited by a dog (for the reptile might mistake a man for a tree and take firm grip of his hair) Upfield had to shoot this one, and an hour later shot a carpet snake which also took refuge in his tent. All the inhabitants of the channel were migrating, and he wished they could have done so in daylight.

The next morning the channel was the same. On his going down to it and stepping a hundred yards from the bank, the water could be seen in the cracks, about a foot down, and on his stamping on a hexagonal mass of cement-hard clay, a tremor indicated a softening base.

Back on the low bank again, Upfield gazed northward, from where the river flow must come, because all the maps proved that the water came from the north to empty into the Darling River. On seeing the water glinting in the sunlight far to the south, Upfield squared himself with the shadows.

Too long alone! Was living alone with a horse and a dog now having the usual effect? Next day, if not before, he would be setting double knives and forks on the sheet used for a table, or placing the wash-basin upside-down on his head in lieu of a hat.

There followed proof that the river was running, for the water was approaching from the south. No! the north. No! the south. There are two fears deep in the mind of a man situated as Upfield–fear of becoming hopelessly lost, and fear of becoming 'wonky'. Rather it is fear of the fears, for if either becomes the master the end is sure.

The water came on, slowly. Then opposite the camp a pool appeared, a pool of gold gradually changing to silver and extending. Other pools appeared, and presently the main flow found them, and the flow began to pass the camp, flowing to the north...or was it to the south? Later still, the water was passing up the Paroo River as far as the eye could follow the broad channel. On it floated herbal rubbish, and small tree boughs used by snakes and lizards as rafts.

Upfield no longer doubted that he was wonky, and that the river was flowing up-hill. This it continued to do for about two hours, when the flow stopped for an hour, and then proceeded in reverse to follow natural laws. The water in the channel deepened to about three feet, and all the depressions were being changed to sparkling lakes.

The explanation, of course, was simple. The water first ran on the real floor of the channel through the myriad cracks in the upper clay. Down-river was a bar of rock or of sand which had dammed the water, making it rise from the cracks, finally causing it to flow backward until it topped the bar.

It is to be regretted that Henry Lawson had a chip on his shoulder when he carried his swag into this country, for he has described it so well in verse. Free of that chip, he would have felt its slumbering majesty and its hidden powers, which tend so strongly to humble a man and eliminate inferiority complexes.

Additionally it is unfortunate that he lived in the latter part of an era when class hatred was so strong, when dislike of the competing immigrant often verged on hatred, and when even dislike of men born in another State amounted to absurdity. Lawson was good; he might have been magnificent.

Upfield met with this hatred in the old-timers who clung to the sheep stations where they were employed. It was something he could not accept, for he did not believe that all men better off than himself were enemies.

When Upfield came to Australia the pastoral workers were being organised into the Australian Workers' Union. He could find no objection to joining this Union, for the rations, known as 'keep', plus the wage, amounted to only a fraction of the wages paid to the pampered city workers. In those days, the farther from a city the lower the wage, when it ought to have been the other way about, to compensate for greater hardship. The men producing the wealth on which the city dwellers were battening ought to have been paid the highest wages and amenities.

There was the bunch at Yiparoo homestead. They had been without potatoes for some three months, and the next supply rested on the arrival of the mule wagon from Broken Hill. There was still a supply of sweet potatoes. A couple of the men persistently moaned about lack of potatoes, and were supported by several others. All were elderly men who had been employed for years at Yiparoo.

Young, lacking experience, fed up with the moaning, Upfield suggested striking for the blasted potatoes, and immediately he was elected spokesman. As is customary, the following morning at seven, the men gathered outside the manager's office to await the orders for the day. The manager appeared, and Upfield stepped forward saying that there would be no work done until the promised potatoes arrived. Just like that! As though the damned spuds could be brought over hundreds of miles of virgin bush on a magic carpet.

The manager flushed red, eyed the malcontents, ignored their spokesman. To one he said:

"Fred! Are you going to strike?"

"Well, er, Mister Blank, you see, we gotta have pertaters, ain't we?" replied Fred.

"We are getting them, as promised. What are you going to do? Work and wait, or strike and go for your cheque?"

"Well, er, Mister Blank, we don't wanta be hard on you, but them spuds was promised months back and…"

"You put a horse into the dray and go out to Needlewood Yards with Harry. What about you, Harry?"

And so they went back to work, one by one, leaving the spokesman to stand alone.

To Upfield, Mr. Blank said:

"As man to man, you're a ruddy fool. You leave strikes to the Union, who has all the proper weapons. You fellers aren't alone in wanting real spuds to eat. There's me and the book-keeper and the overseer and the rest all hungry for a potato, and now I'll report this threatened strike to the owners and hurry up the supply. You go along to the office for your pay cheque, and when you have it, come to me, and I'll give you another job, having done my duty."

Upfield collected his cheque and did not ask for another job. His faith in the Australian working man in the aggregate was for ever shattered, and thenceforward he became an individualist.

4

The rains came, the rivers flowed, the herbage bloomed, the sheep multiplied. Following War One, the price of wool and meat rose, but the number of men employed on the runs was never to reach the height ruling before the war.

Upfield waylaid the manager of a property consisting of eight hundred thousand acres, and sheep flocks totalling sixty thousand head, and the manager asked if he could cook.

Although the country was prosperous, there were more men than jobs at this particular time, and Upfield had found that a cook could always find work when a stockman wasn't wanted. He had too, at odd moments, recalled what Mary had said about taking up writing, and had discovered still within him the urge to write. He was aware that sustained writing wasn't possible for the casual worker on sheep and cattle runs, who had to live with others as closely as the sailor with his shipmates, and that station cooks, because of the hours they worked, were provided with a room to themselves.

It would almost appear that Angus and Mary were constantly crouching over a small aboriginal fire and pointing a pen at Arthur Upfield, instead of a bone, and when the manager of Albermarle offered him a temporary cook's job he was on the verge of refusing, because he lacked confidence that he could quickly become proficient in baking yeast bread, a cook having also to be a baker.

However, Mr. James L. Hole of Albermarle wanted a man to take over the men's kitchen, and said he would arrange for the cook at the big house, colloquially named 'Government House', to do the extra bread-making *pro tem*. Thus Upfield found himself cooking for a dozen to twenty men, and the occupier of a room off the kitchen.

These were days when rations were more plentiful and varied than when he entered Australia. He could roast and boil meats, cook fish from the river, manufacture a passable curry and cook vegetables, but he was unlucky with pastry and cakes, and had to start at scratch with bread-making. Fortunately for his victims, the cook at Government House possessed a copy of the *Workers' Cookery Book*, the most helpful book on the subject ever published, because commended ingredients were measured by the handful and by the pint pannikin and no scales were necessary.

When the permanent (more or less) men's cook returned from his annual binge, the manager wanted Upfield to cook for the Mustering Camp, which moved from one part of the run to another where yards had been built. Following this, the ultimate of the 'pen pointing' by Mary and Angus was achieved when Mr. Hole said:

"How would you like the idea of cooking at Wheeler's Well?"

Knowing this Wheeler's Well, and what would be required of him, Upfield gladly accepted.

"All right, you can go out tomorrow," Mr. Hole decided. "There's no one there at the moment, but I'll be sending a couple of stockmen out to you in a day or so."

The overseer conveyed Upfield and a heavy supply of rations on a utility truck to Wheeler's Well, situated between the main homestead and the out-station, and twenty-five miles either way. There was a telephone, and every evening, at the same time, the manager rang to say he would be sending the men the following day. But this and that upset his plans, and for five weeks Upfield merely had to cook for himself.

The well was named after the contractor who sank it, and the site was chosen by a water diviner who knew his job or proved to be lucky, because the water was pure and plentiful. Over the well bestrode the windmill, raising the water to a square-shaped reservoir tank from which a ball-valve serviced a long line of drinking troughs for sheep and other animals. Near-by stood two huts, each built of pine logs and roofed with corrugated iron. There were shutters for windows, and a solitary ancient pepper tree gave adequate shade to stockmen's dogs, and shelter to half a dozen hens which no one owned. One hut was occupied by the men, when any were there, and the other was used as kitchen, dining-room, with the cook's bunk in a corner or on the verandah.

Twenty-five miles either way to a homestead! All about, as though situated in the centre of a basin, Wheeler's Well was surrounded by low sand dunes, beautifully fashioned by the wind, gloriously tinted by the setting sun, and furies of dust smoke when the gales raged. Once a week, Upfield watched the track crossing the little plain to where it topped the sand dunes, watching for the manager's car or the overseer's utility to appear, welcoming both with genuine warmth, for they brought the mail and papers and any rations ordered.

He asked for, and was supplied with, wire and netting, and he built a fence about the reservoir tank and grew a garden. With the assistance of a stockman he cut and collected cane-grass, and with it built a connecting wall and a cane-grass roof giving cool and complete shade between the huts.

That 'pointing pen' kept him there for nearly three years, with occasional short breaks in Broken Hill.

Mr. Hole one day was taking Dalgety's Broken Hill manager to the out-station, and as the car topped the dunes he said: "The feller here is writing a novel, I'm told."

The other man gasped, for the day was extremely hot and

dusty: "Writing a novel! My God! Here!"

5

At Wheeler's Well, Upfield found and accepted responsibilities. There was Paddy, the pet sheep, who would follow a man all day if given a pinch of tobacco now and then, and who was used to lead a flock across a narrow bridge when the river flats were flooded. Paddy was twice the size of an ordinary wether, and ten times more cunning. Then there were two galahs, each with a wing slightly clipped to prevent flying, and a yellow cat about to give birth. What with the senative inhabitants, a couple of dogs and the hens, Upfield's life was crowded solitude.

The cat liked Upfield's bed, and obviously determined to produce her litter on it. So he made a nice soft bed in a case and put the case in a dark corner. Constantly he watched that cat, removing her from his bed to the box a dozen times and more, but she beat him and proudly showed him her five black and white handsome offspring.

He put the cat and kittens in the box, turned his back and the mother carried them up to his bed. He removed them, and again the mother returned the family to the bed. In the end she won, and every night the mother and five kittens claimed the place where he would have liked to put his feet. As they grew older and became heavier, he was compelled to sleep with his feet dangling from the edge of the bunk.

After five weeks of cooking for himself and seeing that the sheep did not lack water, the manager sent a party of stockmen to muster several near-by flocks, and after they had gone Upfield had the place to himself for many weeks.

The summer was hot and the wind-storms were few, and when the sun was going down and people in the cities were making ready to go to the theatres or to the beaches Upfield poured water over himself, dressed in clean pyjama trousers and cotton vest, put on canvas shoes and took his companions for a walk.

By this time, wherever he went, Paddy the pet sheep followed. As did the two galahs and the six cats. The birds, unable to fly, fell over their own feet, became angry at being left behind, and screeched protest, their rose-coloured combs raised. So they were lifted on a finger and rode on the sheep's back. A couple of hundred yards, and the cats protested, and one by one they were added to Paddy's load. Thus would the party arrive at and mount the summit of one of the encircling dunes.

There Upfield sat to watch the sun go down, himself withdrawn. Paddy nibbled at odds and ends of herbage, the dogs lay about with tongues lolling, and the cats pretended to be stalking something other than the two galah cockatoos. When darkness began to shadow the flat between the dunes and the distant huts, Paddy lay down and chewed cud, the cats came close and formed a mound of fur, and the birds climbed Upfield's arms and sleepily prepared to roost on his shoulders.

And as they had arrived, so they returned to the huts, where the dogs were fed and chained to their shelters, the birds lifted to their perches, and the cats also fed and given powdered milk. The hens were independent of man.

When seated on the sand dune made vividly red by the afterglow, Upfield, for the first time in years, felt no compulsion to see what lay beyond the range of dunes. It was as though Wandering Millie had tired of him and had taken on another victim.

As though seated beside him, he heard Mary urging him to make something of life, to employ the talents given him, and slowly that impulsion of so long ago returned, propelling him back to the huts, followed by Paddy carrying the cats and with the sleepy birds perched precariously on his shoulders.

Seated at the kitchen table, without any sign of mental effort, he worked out the plots and the characters of six short stories. He sent an order to Norman Brothers, Melbourne, for reams of foolscap and a fountain-pen and wrote the six stories, watching with indescribable satisfaction the filled sheets grow to a thick wad. Back over the years, fifteen of them, and back across the world to become again the boy who wrote novels-never-to-be-published.

He was satisfied to look at that amount of work, to re-read the stories now and then, to savour his reaction to them. Some he re-wrote, others he re-wrote in part. And then, with the mail brought to him one day was a complete issue of *The Times*, containing the *Literary Supplement*. He sent a cable to his mother asking her to post out every week *The Times Literary Supplement*.

After those lonely weeks at Wheeler's Well, life became normal. Two stockmen were stationed there, both men being middle-aged, both avid readers of anything, from the sporting pages of the newspapers to paper-backs and expensive autobiographies, for your real dyed-in-the- wool bushman is more widely read and more intelligent than the above- average city worker, whose leisure is captured so much by other interests.

It being hot these summer months, the riders set out at about six in the morning, and returned shortly after noon. The first part of every day was, therefore, Upfield's. At night the men read or played cards in their hut across the way, leaving Upfield to his eternal scribbling. If the cook preferred to waste his time that way, it was his affair, especially as the cooking continued to be as good as they would enjoy at one of the homesteads.

Upfield continued to take the menagerie for a walk at sundown, and those golden minutes atop a dune did much to bring him to see himself as Angus and Mary had seen him.

He lacked ambition, had no plan, no purpose. This he had glimpsed when he turned to novel-writing in boyhood, and he might have established his writing career much earlier had he then been impressed by the necessity of equipping himself to write, instead of merely finding pleasure in telling a story, like one who finds pleasure in playing the piano by ear and is unable to read music.

When writing those short stories he had recaptured the almost forgotten joy of creating characters in action and moving to a climax, and now found himself as the man who contemplates a journey and is well aware of the hazards.

How many young men and women, per million, have the urge to write? The answer might be astonishing. How many per hundred of those who attempt it, persevere? Very few. How many of the few go on and on, and ultimately produce a work to be reviewed in *The Times Literary Supplement*? And how many of that elite advance to fame and fortune? Upfield, when at Wheeler's Well, had the advantage of knowing all the answers to these questions, or believed he had. At that time such questions were relatively unimportant compared with the growing hunger within him—a hunger which those short stories failed to satisfy.

The ants had excavated a nest in his garden, and seemed to be doing little else than running up to the circular mound about the entrance to the underground, then running down again. So what?— to be vulgar. The rabbits in a particular district always migrate to a particular point. Why? Superficially, silly questions. But not to Upfield.

He discovered for himself what probably a hundred scientists had already discovered: that the ants were bringing up tiny pebbles to heat in the sun, and taking down sun-heated stones to maintain warmth for their eggs. Among the tiny stones was a fragment of glass, and he watched an ant take this up and carry it below, and waited thirty-two minutes for an ant to bring it up again for re-heating.

Glass! It might well have been a ruby or a sapphire from a girl's ring, proving that a girl wearing a ring had stood close by at some time or other. See the ring, minus the gem, on the finger of a girl, and there was proof that she was the girl who had stood or passed by the nest. Did a boomerang in flight contact a tree trunk, and did the weapon have a number of indentations on the sharp edge, denoting the tribe of the thrower, then the mark or scar on the trunk would reveal the weapon that had caused it, and also reveal the tribe of the man who had thrown it.

Such clues, and there were hundreds of them waiting to be employed, would be a refreshing variant of the bloody knife, the distorted bullet, the finger-prints, with which most mystery novels were loaded. Then, in his mail, and to be found all over inland Australia, was the *Wide World Magazine*. Question! Why do people read the *Wide World Magazine*? Who are they, and how many? They are to be found in all walks of life, readers who desire to learn about far countries, the customs of the people, all presented in the form of adventure, romance, mystery. They would accept a clue provided by the ants, and be blasé towards the clue of the bullet.

Upfield proceeded further. Supposing he were to write a mystery novel, would it not be foolish to compete with Edgar Wallace and S. S. Van Dine? He could have little hope of success there. But not one of the world-famous writers of detective novels could compete with him against this background of Australia, could use so intelligently the extraordinary clues, atmosphere, motives and what not. Here was a mine of pure gold waiting for someone to open it up. Any competent novelist could stay a week or two at an Australian homestead, preferably in the winter when the climate is comfortable, and turn out a novel of the people at the homestead and a stockman or two to emphasise the social standing of the owner and his friends. Shove in a few gum trees, add some aborigines for comic relief–and behold the Great Australian Novel!

Thus developed the flame of ambition firing the urge to tell a story. He began his first mystery novel early in March, and drove onward until the musterers were quartered on him during the shearing in July, and by that time he had covered ten sheets of foolscap, with an average of three hundred and fifty words every day. Having completed the work, he left it for a month, revised and began its second writing when he found that the mental rest from it enabled him to see many errors of construction.

This first mystery centred on the fact that some half-caste children are born white and begin to change colour only after they reach the age of ten. A full-blooded aborigine was found dead near a Darling River homestead. He had been hit with a weapon having a sharp edge, and as all local aborigines were away on walkabout, it was suspected that one of the station men had committed the crime. A white detective having a fine reputation as a bushman was sent to investigate; and at the end of the first writing Upfield thought he had done a reasonably good job.

He was half-way through the second writing when one afternoon the dogs barked at the coming of none other than Tracker Leon, with whom he had worked and with whom he had watched the rabbit migration crossing the track. There were no stockmen quartered on him at the time, and the welcome to Tracker Leon was naturally warm. He was invited to stay the day and, having watered his horse and freed it, he was conducted to the kitchen for afternoon tea, and couldn't fail to see the work on which his host had been engaged.

Far into the night they talked of old days, of places and men and events, and there was still much to be said when, before sunrise next morning, Tracker Leon mounted and continued his journey to Ivanhoe. He had been, as formerly, reticent about himself, even for a half-caste, but the subjects he had discussed ranged from weather prediction to the political turmoil in Germany, where a new personality was beginning to stand clear.

Tracker Leon had suggested an exchange of books, and he left two books with Upfield and departed with several issues of the *Wide World Magazine* and *The Times Literary Supplement*.

From the back of the huts Upfield watched the man and horse dwindle until they topped the distant sand dunes and vanished, and in that moment came the impulse to change his white detective to a half-caste. The advantages were instantly apparent. No white man could track like an aborigine or as expertly as a half-caste, and no white man in all the world could read the Book of the Bush as knowledgeably as Tracker Leon.

Upfield fingered the two-hundred-odd pages of the second writing of his fourth novel, and decided to scrap it and introduce a half-caste investigator, Tracker Leon, who possessed the acume of the aborigine plus the reasoning ability of the educated white.

No matter what his attainments, the aspiring novelist faces many stiff hurdles, and when Upfield changed his white detective for an Australian half-caste, he himself built a hurdle higher than all those confronting him. Days later, he glanced at the books left by Tracker Leon. One was *The Last Days of Pompeii*, and the other was Abbot's *Life of Napoleon Bonaparte*. Napoleon Bonaparte! Why not! Aborigines were known as Pontius Pilate, Little Willie, Sir Galahad. Why not Napoleon Bonaparte? So for the third time Upfield began what was ultimately to be published under the title *The Barrakee Mystery*.

6

On his way from the homestead to the out-station Mr. J. L. Hole brought to Wheeler's Well about twenty pounds of the famed River grapes, and, in error, the overseer who came the following day left a similar quantity.

What to do with all this fruit! And only one stockman with Upfield!

Upfield possessed a handy little book entitled *A Thousand and One Recipes*, telling how to make anything from cement to pills having household names, and from it he found the answer to this grape problem—grape wine.

The grapes were pounded with a bottle and the juice placed in a large dish. For three days the scum had to be removed from the liquid, and then a little bread yeast was added to start fermentation. After a further period, when according to the book the stuff was ripe, the liquid was bottled and stored in a cool place for ten days.

The ceremony at the end of ten days was impressive in its simplicity. The stockman and the cook stood one of the twenty odd bottles on the kitchen bench, where Upfield cut the string tying down the cork, and solemnly worked it free. There was no fizz, no cascade. The liquid was flat and unpalatable. One sadly disappointed man regarded another equally sad.

A post-mortem was held. The directions from the book were checked and found correct, but there was slight doubt that the condition of the bread yeast had been as good as it ought to have been.

"I think," Upfield said, "we'll empty the bottles back into the basin and give the brew another shot of yeast. Come to think of it, the stuff wasn't too active when we bottled it, and I happen to have a fresh supply that's working well."

"My old man uster make a fine dope outer spuds," remarked the stockman. "What about adding a slice or two to each bottle?"

"It's a potato yeast, Ted. We could add six or seven raisins to the bottle. Anyway, we'll see what she's like in the morning."

The stockman wouldn't leave for work next day until he had seen the brew in the basin, and he had no doubt that the liquid was active. They decided to defer bottling until that evening, when once again the light scum was removed, and the tasters dipped their spoons.

"Seems better," said the stockman.

"But not much," objected the cook.

"A drop of pain-killer might give her a kick," suggested the stockman, and the cook agreed.

So a full bottle of pain-killer was stirred into the mixture, and as now the concoction was experimental, they added a bottle of chlorodyne for luck. Then into each bottle were dropped six or seven raisins and a dessert-spoon of brown sugar, and the re-bottled brew was returned to the cool place under the cook's bunk.

A fortnight passed when a gang of musterers was quartered temporarily at Wheeler's Well, and after they had departed the brew was forgotten, until one night the boss telephoned to say that he was sending Fred to check the well pump.

Fred was a valuable man on any station, but he had one incurable failing. Even to smell liquor meant demanding his cheque and clearing down to Menindee for a prolonged bender. If this happened, Mr. Hole would smell more than liquor, and it was decided by the distillers to plant the stock under the perch in the hen-house. And there it remained for several weeks, until the bullocky and his offsider arrived.

The bullocky was an outstanding character. In the long ago he had participated in a pub brawl and on recovering was unable to speak, but could make himself understood by what amounted to grunts and high-pitched yells. This unfortunate disability did not detract from his bullock-driving, because he was a master with the whip, and he was also employed about the station on odd jobs. His offsider was a youth who was not mentally one hundred per cent, but the two got along very well, and the offsider, through long association, was able to interpret the grunts and yells.

After dinner on the day of their arrival, Sam the Bullocky produced a full bottle of Scotch, enabling hosts and guests to pass a pleasant evening. The following day the bullock men went out to gather a load of firewood, and again after dinner a full bottle of Scotch was produced. After dinner on the third day there was no whisky, and the matter worried the stockman, in that the guests had provided the drinks and the hosts could offer no adequate return, until he remembered the brew buried under the hen perch, and suggested trying it out. The two visitors being 'safe' men, Upfield agreed, and several bottles of alleged champagne were brought in from the cellar.

Sam the Bullocky was most interested. He was tall and like wire, and his blue eyes blazed with anticipation. Upfield warned him that the brew would probably be a failure, and having removed the string he levered up the cork, which flew to the kitchen roof, to be followed by the entire contents of the bottle. Everyone present beamed.

By arranging two buckets, the next bottle was saved, and to its contents were added the contents of several others. Now solemnly pint pannikins were filled and judgment awaited.

The distillers were instantly congratulated. Sam the Bullocky grunted genuine appreciation, emptied his pannikin and grunted for a refill. His offsider was right behind him, and the stockman declined to be left out. As a party, it swung into instant success.

The stuff had a remarkable lift. It tasted like a mixture of Chablis and new bread, and the bouquet included just the right whiff of a hospital operating-theatre. It both pleased and tickled the palate, and merely to sip it like wine would be to offer insult. Sam grunted and yelled, and Upfield, turning to the offsider to interpret for him, found the young fellow staring into his pannikin and unable to direct his gaze from it. Sam slapped the fellow between the shoulders to draw his attention, and the offsider fell forward over the table like a robot knocked off its feet. The stockman sat down and began to recite 'Clancy of the Over- flow', and Upfield tried to hush Sam because he wanted to recall every detail of the picture of Fred Essen singing it atop his coach.

The stockman proceeded as far as the third verse, when his voice faltered into a giggle and he tried to rise to fill his pannikin once more, and provided irrefutable truth of the proverb about the pitcher.

Upfield saw Sam's eyes change from washy blue to brilliant black, and instead of a few dark stumps, his gums were lined with brilliantly polished teeth. His mouth was opening, opening wide to emit words.

"Coo! You're drunk, pal. Haw, haw! Your own brew 'as got you under. Now me..." He began to sing 'The Face on the Barroom Floor', then his legs folded and he hit the deck. Upfield swayed over him, collapsed and crawled round to stare into his changing face and say:

"D'you know you're talking? Good English, too."

Sam blinked and the wonder of it momentarily sobered both. "Thought I was dreaming," he said. "Cripes, so I can. Let's have one on me."

Upfield does remember his last effort to arouse Sam to talk once more, but there was not sufficient of the potion left to prove the miracle, and Sam never talked again.

7

The shearers were coming, and soon the stockmen would be quartered at Wheeler's Well, and forwarding to the shearing shed at the main homestead flock after flock comprising thousands of sheep. From the back fences of the run to the shearing shed the distance was eighty miles, and Mr. Hole must place his riders and the cooks in strategic positions to move this four-legged army of sixty thousand sheep.

The boss telephoned Upfield that he was sending a man to cut fence posts and stack cooking wood for the truck to collect later, and next day there came one known as the Storm Bird. He was tall, lank, and the worse for wear.

The Storm Bird sat on the form at the kitchen table and with calloused hands pressed to his head tried to control its shaking, and as though he did not exist the driver who had brought him out calmly remarked:

"Been on the booze properly. Broke to the wide and won't be fit to cut his throat with an axe, let alone cut fence posts. Wants nursing for a day or two."

One of the pet galahs clawed its way up Upfield's trousers, up his shirt, to perch on a shoulder. It rubbed its beak against an ear-lobe, and when Upfield gently puffed air into its impish eye, it raised its comb and shrieked. Whereupon the Storm Bird leaped to his feet, glared wildly about, tore at his sparse hair, and again slumped to the form, muttering.

"That's 'im," observed the driver. "He'll be having the dingbats in no time. Best thing is to wooden him with a shovel. Well, I'd better be getting back. Got any mail to go in?"

At seven o'clock that night the manager rang as usual and this time asked after the Storm Bird.

"He's parading around the huts at the moment," replied Upfield, and, extending the chances of the Storm Bird's earning a few pounds: "Probably come good by morning."

Mr. Hole advised where among the surrounding dunes were the best trees for posts, and rang off. Upfield went out to persuade his 'guest' to come in for dinner, his heart filled with sympathy, having himself been in a similar condition.

"Dinner!" moaned the Storm Bird.

"Try some soup I made."

"Lemme alone. I gotta walk, keep ahead of 'em. You ain't gotta bottle be any chance?"

"Holbrook's Sauce, plenty. Lace the soup with it, settles the stomach."

"Yair. Help, perhaps."

The Storm Bird sat at table, his head continuously shaking, the wide mouth slack, and pale blue eyes washed out like rags. Upfield gave him soup in a pint pannikin and passed the sauce. The guest knocked the soup over the table and, seizing the bottle, drank the entire contents without evincing the slightest discomfort. In fact, it appeared to steady him.

"What did you booze on?" Upfield asked.

"Whisky."

"Only whisky?"

"Yair, I stuck to it–three weeks and a bit. Then the bastard publican said I'd cut out me cheque and chucked me out with a half-bottle to face the track with."

"Seen them yet?"

"No, but they're around. I kep' me half-bottle for last night at the homestead. Seen the boss for a job this morning. Now I'm stuck here, and there ain't a dose in sight. Sure you ain't gotta a bottle?" His breath caught, then he screamed. "Look out! Look...look!"

Leaping to his feet, he brushed things off his hands, his arms, from his neck and face. In the lamplight his face glistened with sweat.

Snatching up the empty sauce bottle, he swiped hard at something perched on the sugar bowl. When the enemy withdrew, he sat with every muscle taut, his eyes constantly alerted for the next visitation. Upfield mopped up the mess, cleared the table, and ate his dinner at the cooking bench.

Shortly after nine o'clock, the Storm Bird was fighting fit. He gave his forehead a terrific wallop, danced back from something on the floor which the blow appeared to have dislodged, and implored Upfield to stamp on it. Upfield obliged, but apparently missed, because it proceeded to stalk the Storm Bird around the table. It is impossible to convince a man in this state that what he sees isn't real, and it becomes tiring for the co-operator in mass extermination of imaginary monsters. Abruptly, the Storm Bird leapt to the table, reached for the cross-beam and swung himself up to lie along it, to glare downward and indicate the position of monster reinforcements to be stamped out.

As from midnight, Upfield lost interest in the study of delirium tremens, for the exhibit refused to come down from his beam and retire to the men's hut across the way. As did most bushmen, he had several bottles of chlorodyne, and a stiffener of chlorodyne is often helpful in such a case, although he had never tried it on himself.

A further two hours were spent persuading the Storm Bird to descend from his perch to partake of the cure, and by now Upfield was worn out, desperate and angry. He assisted the object to the men's hut, induced him to lie on one of the bunks, and gave him a goodly dose of chlorodyne in a little water. The instructions on the bottle said from ten to twenty drops. Upfield added two full teaspoons for luck.

Ten minutes later the Storm Bird was asleep. Back in his own bunk, Upfield began to worry instead of sleeping the sleep of the innocent, and he carried the lamp to see how the patient was faring.

The Storm Bird wasn't faring at all. His blotchy-red face was now a uniform blue. His mouth was open, his breathing not discernible. Despite effort, he could not be wakened. Upfield hauled him up, wrapped a long arm about his own neck, and walked him outside.

When day broke, he was still walking the Storm Bird to and fro along a hundred-feet beat, and the corpse was showing signs of returning life, imploring in mumbled tones to be left alone. He was dropped, and Upfield departed for the kitchen, where he brewed tea, his legs and arms trembling with fatigue.

On taking a pannikin of tea out to the Storm Bird he found Paddy, the pet sheep, steadily rolling the body over and over with his head, in an effort to get at the plug of tobacco in a trousers pocket, and examination revealed that the Storm Bird was sleeping normally.

Paddy was given the tobacco, and after lunch that day the Storm Bird went out to cut his fence posts.

8

At the end of Upfield's first year at Wheeler's Well, a three-inch-thick wad of foolscap represented his first mystery novel. The year was 1926, the publishing trade was booming outside Australia, which was importing tons of cheap reprints, and as Paddy had rolled the Storm Bird over and over, so the world was now being rolled over by Edgar Wallace.

From *The Times Literary Supplement* Upfield learned much of the industry of literature and nothing of the people revolving about it like dust motes about a lamp. *The Times Literary Supplement* gave the major portion of its space to what may be termed serious literature, plus a few novels, and towards the end of the journal a long list of short reviews of general fiction. Among these reviews appeared the work of Edgar Wallace, as well as books by authors even more widely known.

Someone sent Upfield a book by Australian Roy Bridges, which he greatly admired for its historical background of Tasmania, as well as for Bridges' style, and he was set back a little when subsequently he read a *Times Literary Supplement* review of it in those columns he called the 'Also Rans'. The reviewer was complimentary, and the publishers were advertising the fourth and fifth impressions. Unaware that the birth, life and death of a book isn't wholly dependent on the valuation of an editor or a critic, and finding Bridges' book among the Also Rans, he compared it with the writing on that block of foolscap, did nothing with the MS and proceeded to the writing of the next novel, merely because creation of it gave him pleasure.

That he was creating characters and situations, whereas the works of the historian and biographer given full space in *The Times Literary Supplement* were merely first-class reporting, did nothing to foster the slow growth of confidence.

Months afterwards he read a small advertisement in *The Times*, inserted by one George Frankland, who offered to advise on, criticise and offer MSS to publishers, and because the tone was so different from the advertisements of the large outcrop of literary agencies, Upfield wrote to Frankland at his Buckinghamshire home.

It proved to be the most fortunate move he ever made, and at the right time. George Frankland dealt at length with *The Barrakee Mystery*, tearing it to shreds and applauding some of the pieces; he complained of repetition, praised the general construction and expressed enthusiasm at the choice of a boomerang as a blunt weapon. And sent it back.

Upfield checked the story with Frankland's report and found the criticism one hundred per cent just. Those blows between the eyes cost Upfield three guineas, but they established a friendship which continued until Frankland's death fourteen years later.

Stowing *The Barrakee Mystery* in his case, he began *The House of Cain*. Life at Wheeler's Well went on, and the Australian world of mirage and space continued to reveal more and more of itself. In England, Frankland thought there was yet another budding author who could not take criticism.

There was no mystery in *The House of Cain*, and no orthodox detection, it being what is termed a 'straight' thriller. Like the straight novel, it possessed none of the intricacies of plot and development so essential to the build-up of a mystery. Someone said that writing a straight novel is as easy as writing letters. Upfield found a degree of truth in that.

And so summer passed, and autumn showed how fiercely hot the sun can be. The dogs and Paddy clung to the pepper tree shade, and the cats were appreciative of cold water being poured on their tummies. The galahs had deserted, their clipped wings having been permitted to grow.

One was most proficient in Australian language. Having been compelled for two years to hop about the ground, when its wings became normal it made no attempt to fly, and had to be taught by being tossed into the air. One evening during these flying lessons, a number of his fellows came to the trough to drink, and when they rose, the tame galah flew proudly to join them. Away they went, about a hundred of them, flying about the mill and the huts, some chuckling softly, others raucously screaming. Then from among them one said:

"Hell with you! Hell with you!"

The flock converged, and from it spun one to come swooping down and land with scrabbling feet on the iron roof. It stood there, cocked its head and yelled:

"Hell with you! Hell with you!"

The next day he rejoined his cousins. This time they accepted him, and it can be surmised that eventually he was weaned from the influence of the depraved companions of his youth.

De Rougemont, or someone, claimed that he was conveyed by a willy-willy for a considerable distance and set down uninjured. Artists have portrayed cats, dogs, sheep, farmers and their wives being carried to high heaven by a willy-willy. But when a dog at Wheeler's Well chased a rabbit clean through a powerful willy-willy, it led Upfield to experiment.

One of medium velocity came over the sand dune and across the flat, and Upfield went to meet it. He was accompanied by a dog. The willy-willy moved along a course with but slight variation, and at a speed enabling Upfield to walk with it. About its foot the sand and rubbish were caught and drawn to the revolving column; above its foot the air was wildly drawn as though to a magnet.

Remembering the incident of the rabbit and the dog on impulse Upfield stepped into the column, intending to pass through it. He found the interior void of sand, and almost without agitation. He discovered that it was possible to maintain himself within the cylinder, walking with it, the circular wall revolving so fast that he could only faintly see the dog without.

Whistling made the dog frantic, but the animal made no attempt to join him. He walked inside the willy-willy for perhaps a full minute before it gained speed and left him behind.

Some of these giants move with the speed of express trains, and create as much noise, and seldom do they travel at man's walking pace. So yet another little oddity for the mystery story that must be different. Instead of the great detective trailing the master criminal along a rain-swept city street, this new investigator could trail the suspect by walking in the interior of a willy-willy. The odds are a million to one in favour of the aborigines having done it, for to them there is nothing novel or new in this ancient Australia.

Perhaps for their magic men the following incident, which was to be as a curtain-raiser to a drama in which Upfield played a part, would hold no mystery.

It has been mentioned that during the hot weather Upfield slept on a stretcher bed on the verandah of the kitchen, a verandah wide enough to take the bed set against the kitchen wall. At the foot of the bed stood the washstand he had made, and on the wall above it hung a mirror about one foot square.

Life was normal, and although Upfield had been alone for something over a week, there had been the daily contact with the homestead per telephone, the garden to tend, the pets to companion, and his writing to do. This night he wrote until about eleven, as usual, made himself yet another cup of tea, and took it to the case beside the bed, on which he sat to smoke the last cigarette.

There was nothing abnormal about the silence and the beauty of the moonlit night. The small birds inhabiting the pepper tree were asleep, the rooster in the yard was too old to be wakeful, and the dogs were at peace with their stick-fast fleas.

Seated on the side of the bed, Upfield sipped tea and pondered on a development of his story. The cup emptied, the cigarette consumed, he kicked off his slippers and was about to swing his legs to the bed when he saw, with excusable astonishment, a man standing before the washstand and adjusting his tie with the aid of the wall mirror.

The moonlight which reached to the centre of the bed also reached to the man's waist. It revealed his body, the shape of his head and his face in profile. He was tall, well-proportioned and good-looking, though his chin slightly receded. He wore fawn gabardine trousers, a silk shirt, and the tie he was adjusting was in good shape.

He was a stranger to Upfield, who could see him as clearly as though by day, and Upfield said:

"Good-night!" a question in the greeting.

Then the fellow wasn't there. So convinced was Upfield that the figure was real, he believed the man had merely side-stepped and entered the kitchen. He took the lamp to the kitchen, which was vacant. He carried the lamp to the men's quarters, and they were empty. When again between the two huts, he recalled that the dogs hadn't barked.

Puzzled but not uneasy, he slept until morning. Still puzzled, he spent half an hour examining tracks outside and all about the mill, and found no strange tracks indicating that a man had come and had left.

A moon trick? No. An illusion created by a tired mind? Perhaps. Anyway, the illusion was perfect, the picture accurate in every detail.

Three days later came temptation to desert Wheeler's Well and his writing for a few months. A man arrived in an old truck; he was going out to the back of the run where the rabbits were thick at the dams and about the lake now filled with water. He wanted a mate, and Mr. Hole agreed that Upfield could do with a change.

Those two netted the dams and caught two thousand rabbits every night in the netted cages, for the rabbits had to drink or perish of the heat the following day, and the erected wire netting formed runs leading to the cages. Upfield bought a utility, traps and equipment and began the winter trapping rabbits about the lake. He employed sixty traps, and should the night's take be less than sixty, it was poor judgment. The skins in March were worth two pounds a hundred. In May and June they were up to four pounds a hundred. When, the following year in mid-summer, the lake dried up, there were millions of rabbits killed by the sun within a few hours. They all died in one gigantic heap over the last drop of water.

Again at Wheeler's Well, Upfield completed his fifth novel, sending it to Frankland for criticism together with a series of articles on offer to the *Wide World Magazine*.

The rains failed. The grass and herbage was blown away by the wind and carried off by the willy-willies. The rabbits vanished, and the foxes were a menace to the new lambs.

In April, Upfield went after the foxes, and in nine weeks trapped eight hundred and thirty-three. The skins averaged ten shillings, and he was paid station wages and rations for trapping them.

It was like digging for opal, chasing after gold. It became a fever to beat records. Eight hundred odd pelts all pegged the same way to dry board-hard. The beauty of fur is like the wonder of opal. Upfield hated to bale his skins to be sent down to Sydney.

The overseer called one day with the mail, and among the letters and papers was the cheque for the pelts and a cable from George Frankland, reading:

"Hutchinson accepts novel. *World* takes articles."

CHAPTER ELEVEN

IT IN SATIN PANTS

I

The week passed, and Upfield duly applied himself to the third writing of *The Barrakee Mystery*, in which, without leave, he introduced Napoleon Bonaparte. Eventually he posted the thick wad of MS to England, and then one afternoon two rabbit trappers called at Wheeler's Well, ate a light meal, left the mail and departed for the out-station. Among the mail was his first publisher's contract.

All that late afternoon and far into the night, Upfield did nothing but sit at the kitchen table and stare at that contract. The dogs and Paddy and the cats sulked because he had forgotten them; the walk to the sand dunes had become habit for them, a never wearying adventure. The cable hadn't lied, the impossible was reality. Here in this iron hut beside the mill and well, surrounded by red dunes, in the interior of Australia, and twenty-five miles from the nearest house, a man having no literary background, no literary associates, had written a novel to be published in far-off London.

He had to read the contract again the next morning before he kindled the fire to boil water for breakfast tea, and still it was unreal, something not to be accepted, something to be fought to avoid dreaded disillusionment. Only when he wrote about it to his mother, and also to Mary the pen-pointer, did his mind return to normal, brought to this state by the task of setting out truth in bald statement.

Then he was attacked by restlessness which could not be appeased, the drive to move on springing from a source other than the urge to roam. He arranged for two weeks' leave of absence, and drove in his utility to talk with Angus and Mary, without realising that what he hungered for was to share this stupendous thing, that he might be fully convinced by those who had pleaded that the talents given him by the Eternal be not flung back in His face.

"It's the most wonderful thing that ever happened to us," they told him, and it was not until he was about to leave them four days later that he recalled this statement and sought enlightenment. Mary said to Angus:

"You tell him."

"There's nothing much to tell," Angus began. "Some of it we think you'll understand from what you told us about your early life. Ever since you were here last, both of us, sitting of an evening on the verandah, have thought about the same thing: for you to take on the writing so you'd stop your gallivantin' about and get some place. Every night we both prayed about it, about you writing a book." They regarded Upfield with eyes strangely bright, and Mary said:

"That's the wonderful thing that happened to us. It's even more wonderful than it is for you. Think about it sometimes. It will carry you on. And do remember to read John 14, v. 14."

Still unenlightened, Upfield left for Broken Hill and took train to Adelaide, where he visited the bookshops, admiring the book jackets and finding pleasure in handling new books and smelling their bookish odour. At one shop he was asked if he needed assistance in choosing a book, and so met Jeremy Long, which shall be the name.

Long guessed, and it wasn't a notable effort, that the customer was from the inland, and customers from the inland invariably had money to spend. He had watched Upfield browsing and had noticed his absorption in jackets. First he learned that Upfield was mainly interested in books issued by Hutchinson, London, and then he learned with some degree of astonishment that

Hutchinson was to publish a book by this fellow. Scenting a story, he invited Upfield to lunch, and there followed invitations to dinner at his own home for several consecutive evenings. And it was then that Upfield became aware that many dream of writing a novel and never do.

It was the era of enormous sales, and fortunes to be won for writers themselves and not for the taxation departments, and Long, who was practical in friendship, gave Upfield a collection of novels that were selling in their tens of thousands.

"Read them when you get back," he said. "Study them and locate the common denominator that takes them over the hundred thousand sales mark, when crime and mysteries rarely sell more than ten thousand. Edgar Wallace is about the only writer today making a fortune out of mystery thrillers.

"There's something else, too. The public these days shies away from Australian novels. Offer an Australian novel and the customer almost impolitely declines it. So put your scene and characters anywhere except in Australia. I'll tell you what I would do if I had the time to write a novel. Like to hear?"

Upfield said he would–this being the first of many occasions when he was advised what to write.

"All right," proceeded the confident Jeremy Long. "Now study the people on the street and you'll think that everyone is bent on earning money or spending it. Study the audiences at the picture shows. The same people, but after something different. Yet all of them all the time are motivated by the same thing–Sex.

"The people we see on the streets, in trams and taxis, in the theatres and the hotels, aren't merely human beings. The plain girl, the old maid, the beautiful woman, the pretty chit and the married woman–the major portion of their thinking is of Man. The successful executive and his junior clerk, the foreman and his slaves, think chiefly of Woman. Sex is the force which spins the world, is the spur to human effort, is the universal key subject. There's more hard cash in Sex than in any commodity.

"Now, your best-selling novelists," Long continued earnestly, "are expert psychologists. They know that the vast majority of human beings are law-abiding, decent, intelligent, also that in every one of 'em there is the sneaking dream of mating with beauty loaded with dynamite. Your best-sellers know that Sex in the raw is universally disapproved of. And they know that the only successful way to sell sex is to clothe it in satin pants. Now and then the pants must have tiny rents in them, but never must the pants be removed. Those novels I've given you are all world bestsellers, for in them Sex is presented in a glamour garment of gossamer silk which just barely frustrates the eye.

"That's my advice to you, Upfield. People don't want to read about Australia. Remember what Nellie Melba said–'Give 'em muck.' Well, you give 'em muck dressed up in satin pants, and the money will roll into your bank account so fast the tellers won't have time to count it."

Returning to Wheeler's Well, Upfield read the best-sellers, and agreed with Jeremy Long's common denominator. By no means a prude, he was startled by the rents in the pants, for it must be emphasised that this was 1926, not 1956. What attracted his attention was the statement opposite the title page of each novel, giving the number of impressions, and in some cases the bald statement of total sales.

Foolishly he attempted to produce a novel of It in satin pants. His failure was due to many reasons, for his mental gifts, his early training and subsequent life in Australia were against such writing. It was a case of the cobbler not sticking to his last. The result was that he involved himself in such a spiritual and physical upheaval, under circumstances so clearly known to Havelock Ellis, that he rushed again to Adelaide for a purpose far different from that which had previously enabled him to meet Jeremy Long.

2

When the six presentation copies of his first novel, *The House of Cain*, reached Upfield, the reaction was less powerful than that produced by the contract. He was now familiar with the 'idea' of having written a story good enough to be published. That, eventually, it received only one review in Australia was balanced by what *The Times Literary Supplement* said of it, even though the review appeared in the section Upfield called the 'Also Rans'. And when he found that the proceeds from this book did not entirely cover Frankland's fee and commission, plus the typing expenses, he was undaunted. Ultimately, he received the presentation copies of his second novel, *The Barrakee Mystery*, in which his friend Tracker Leon appeared for the first time as Napoleon Bonaparte.

London wasn't fired, and Australia remained coldly indifferent.

Wandering Millie returned to attack him, and he packed his gear on the utility and went rabbit-trapping. The season changed and he hunted kangaroos, and when the kangaroos migrated or died of disease, he set off with a mate for Western Australia, taking the little known track across the continent via Eucla, from which the telegraph staff, a bare three months previously, had been withdrawn to the railway at Cook.

It was the beginning of summer and the season was spent scrub-clearing down the south-west tip of the State, and he made two trips to the lonely Leeuwin Lighthouse, was almost drowned and almost caught by a bush fire. At the beginning of winter he moved to the eastern wheat belts beyond Merredin, and then west again to the coast about Dongerra, just south of Geraldton, and it was at Dongerra that he found material for his third novel.

The inspector in charge of the southern section of the number ; one vermin fence offered him a job patrolling one hundred and seventy miles of it, and it might have been that the inspector was influenced by Fate to call Upfield to play a part in an impending drama.

It is said that this fence is the longest in the world, being eleven hundred and thirty miles, and bisecting the State of Western Australia from the Eighty Mile Beach, south of Broome, to the South Coast. Its erection was quite a job. It is also said that the first man to gain a contract to build portion of it had brought a load of live rabbits across from the East, rabbits being regarded as the poor man's food. By the time the fence was completed it became less a problem of keeping the rabbits back from the State's agricultural areas than coping with the problem of rabbit migration.

The inspector's house and headquarters were situated at Burracoppin on the railway to Kalgoorlie, and Upfield's section began at the railway line, extended northward for 170 miles and terminated at the Government camel-breeding station called Dromedary. Here young camels were trained to draw heavy hooded drays for the patrol man. Here was a stone homestead of three rooms, a well, and mill and yards. And here was a man employed by the Rabbit Department, who was also destined for a dramatic role.

Upfield found the country and the transport vastly different from what he had met hitherto on State fences. This fence was easier to maintain. On his section there were no high and moving sand-waves, and beside the fence, all the way, was a fairly good track. The public was liable to prosecution for using this track, for the simple reason that no driver of a motor vehicle seemed able to avoid being mesmerised by the fence and driving into it.

Equidistant apart were five rain-sheds–iron roofs to catch rainwater to conduct into reservoir tanks. There were rock holes off the fence containing fresh water and protected from animals and birds by wire netting. The country varied. From the railway northward, the fence crossed arid land broken by outcrops of rock, then it passed over a wheat belt, and from this entered a beautiful salmon gum forest, which changed abruptly to low desert scrub for almost a hundred miles before changing again to the saltbush and mulga of the pastoral lands of the great Murchison District.

Transportation was by dray drawn by two camels in tandem, the hooded dray serving the patrolman as a travelling house. Into the shafts was harnessed one camel wearing blinkers like a horse, and ahead of him was the leader. Prop-sticks under the shafts and at the rear of the dray maintained its level when the camels were freed, and it had front and rear canvas drop sheets and an iron roof.

All the way the scrub came to within a few yards of the fence on one side, and to the edge of the track bordering the fence on the other. North of the wheat belt there were no farms and no stations and not a house until the camel station homestead–140 miles. As travellers seldom risked prosecution by using the track, Upfield rarely encountered anyone from Burracoppin to the Government station during the fortnight he was scheduled to make the journey.

For one man with camels harnessed to a dray, the job was not without risks. Injury from a camel or from a dray, snake bite or incapacitating illness, might easily prove fatal, because of isolation from help and no means of contact with any base.

Although the dray was large and heavy, and its iron tyres were six inches wide, the roadway was so good that one camel could have drawn it, but camels, being much more sensible than men, will not travel alone. Heavy brake blocks were fitted to clamp against the tyres by turning an iron handle at the rear of the vehicle, but when aroused it mattered nothing to the camels if the wheels were locked.

Like all camels, these two were distinct characters. Curley, the shaft camel, was young, dark, handsome, wilful and boisterous. Millie wasn't much older. She possessed feminine cunning, and feminine contempt for a man. She had a brain and used it, and she spent most of the time as lead camel plotting to outwit the man. She resented having to leave all her friends at the camel station, and she evolved plan after plan to return to them. This was clearly evident when she conversed with Curley, her eyes coaxing him to support her plots.

They would swing placidly along, the dray rumbling easily over the hard ground, the man walking to the rear and within jumping distance of the brake. Then Millie would signal, and in perfect unison, from a loping stride, both animals would leap into a top gallop. To walk behind the dray enabled the man to attend to small matters along the fence without constant stopping and climbing down from and back into the vehicle, and as the stages were never more than sixteen miles a day, Upfield invariably walked.

But if you follow a never-ending fence all day and every day, ultimately you meet the truth–that familiarity breeds contempt. Although Upfield watched the passing wire barrier, his mind was more occupied with novel-writing, and so sometimes his pace became faster than that of the camels, and instead of being just behind the dray, he would be walking alongside Curley. Then Millie would prove that she had a brain. She would lurch into her harness, Curley would heave into his, and Millie would deliberately try to jam the man between the dray wheel and the fence.

When handling these two, hobbling them, putting them to the dray or taking them from it, they were reasonably matey, but it was essential to watch Millie's plottery and ever be a jump ahead.

To permit them hobbled freedom at night was to walk ten miles next morning after them. They would certainly be found on the fence track, shuffling along, to the north towards the place where they had been bred–the Government camel station. Millie wouldn't even wait for Curley, who wanted to eat. It meant cutting scrub and piling it against a tree and neck-roping them to a tree apiece. And this in turn meant an early start in the morning.

Upfield completed his stages before noon, and spent the afternoon reading in the dray away from the ants, and in the shade provided by the roof. The evening was devoted to writing the new novel at a drop-flap table he fitted to the side of the dray. Sometimes a thunder-storm disturbed him. Sometimes a plague of moths or flying ants put out the hurricane lamp. And sometimes the silence distracted him. Windless days in this desert scrub, followed by windless nights, are something to experience. It is like looking at a painting of a wilderness, for nothing of the picture moves, and no sound comes from it. Often Upfield kicked the sleeping camels to their feet merely to make them clatter the bells suspended from their necks.

In early summer the emus came south, walking the fence along the track, seeking an entry to the forbidden land westward of it. There might be a hundred and more in one party, and the fence would lead them eventually to the wheat belt where desperate farmers tried to protect their crops. In winter it was not uncommon for a pack of dingoes to set up a howling like wolves. For the first time Upfield met with the banded ant-eater, a little furry fellow about the size of a cat, banded by white stripes and having a stiffened tail like that of an enraged cat. Here he found the caterpillar chains composed of twenty or so creatures closely following one behind the other. When he turned the leader round to catch up with the rear of the last one, they continued in a circle, until, compassionately, he broke it. The bell-birds were a delight. Perched on a branch near-by, one would imitate bullocks or camels being brought to camp, at first softly distant, and gradually becoming loud and still louder, until they entered the camp itself. The love-birds passed in clouds, whispering sweet nothings.

The cut line, in which were the fence and the track, was as straight as a rule for many miles, and the country was gently undulating, so that at two places, when Upfield camped on a low ridge, he could see where he would be camping the next night–all of fifteen miles.

Governed by these circumstances, he wrote his next novel in this camel dray. *The Beach of Atonement* was not a thriller nor a mystery. It could be termed a psychological novel, or a straight novel. Anyway, he found it infinitely easier to write than the complex mystery, and this could be why straight novelists only pretend superiority over the Edgar Wallaces and the S. S. Van Dines.

3

There was, of course, always the unexpected. More often than not, Upfield would complete a round trip and see no one between the extremities of his section. On sighting far along the track a black dot, it meant watching it before he could decide if the mirage was teasing or if it were really a car coming. If a car, he would pull his team off the track and wait, note-book in evidence. The meeting followed along the now familiar lines:

Upfield: "You must know by the notice on every gate that this is a Government-controlled road, that you are liable to a fine up to £100. Your name, please."

Driver: "Jack Brown."

Upfield, noting registration number and make of vehicle: "That's official. To hell with it. I fine you twenty minutes of time to boil the billy."

So the travellers piled out, and Upfield brewed tea and enjoyed a gossip, and often the travellers left a paper or two, and sometimes a book. They were warned not to do it again, and thus a good time was had by all.

When Upfield had been patrolling this fence for a year, with, of course, breaks at Burracoppin and down to Perth, the curtain was lifted on the prologue of a drama having all the elements of a Greek tragedy.

One quiet and peaceful day when he and his team were

travelling southward and were walking upward to the summit of a long land swell, there reached him the report of a rifle and, a moment later, the hum of a bullet passing over him. The emus were travelling the fence, and it was obvious that on the far side of the land rise some lunatic was firing a .303 rifle at emus coming towards Upfield. When several more bullets passed low to the roof of his dray, he drove the team off the track and into the scrub.

More shooting was heard, more bullets sang along the track. Then a couple of emus raced past Upfield and his camels to be followed by several more. Still other birds flashed by. Then rose the swelling hum of a car, and repeated rifle reports suggested an advancing army.

With a roar the car approached. It appeared in the short view of the track and fence, seen from the protection of the scrub. There was no windscreen. One young fellow was driving, and another crouched forward over the bonnet firing a .303 at the emus. For the next two days Upfield constantly came across dead and dying emus, having to drag the dead off into the scrub and despatch the living before he could induce the camels to pass. When, three weeks later, Upfield again reached the camel station, he mentioned the incident to George Ritchie, the man in charge, and Ritchie, knowing solitude as did Upfield, chuckled and said that apparently they were just a couple of irresponsibles and they had passed the homestead, but a hundred yards off the fence "going like hell and waving like ruddy lunatics"

About this time Upfield was receiving the notices on his *The Barrakee Mystery*, and these were more numerous and much more encouraging than the reviews of his first novel. *The Times Literary Supplement* still declined to front-page Upfield, but did warmly commend it, and as the straight novels being written by Australian metropolitan writers were also being included in the 'Also Rans' Upfield was not downcast.

He was, however, making a grave mistake by putting out a

variety of work. His first novel was a thriller, his second was a mystery, and his third, *The Beach of Atonement*, a psychological novel. When this appeared his English notices were even better, but in Australia it was ignored, save in Western Australia, while the novels of other Australian writers were receiving large space and much favour.

On coming again to the problem of the next book, he decided on another mystery featuring D. I. Napoleon Bonaparte. He hadn't used the clue of the ants who took down a piece of sun-heated glass to warm their eggs, so there was one contribution. And this next job had to be good, because the 'Also Ran' columns of *The Times Literary Supplement* clearly proved the tremendous competition by writers ranging from university professors to parsons, generals to sergeant-majors, diplomats to Civil Servants.

Detective fiction of the time had already dealt fully with the Locked Door mystery; in fact every writer of note had tried his hand at it. What had not been fully explored was the complete disposal of the victim's body, leaving no proof that the person had ever lived. To be sure, Dr. Crippen had tried in reality to dispose of the body of his wife, and others had tried and failed. Only in fiction with the aid of acid baths, or a plentiful supply of dynamite, had murder been adequately covered, for there Haigh and others who copied the fictioneers were yet to appear.

To strike an original note, Upfield required a method or process of body disposal, brilliant in sheer simplicity, with the aids easy to the hand of ordinary people, not scientifically trained, nor even members of the medical profession. It was a problem which nagged at this vermin fence rider.

A few weeks after the meeting with the sportsmen chasing emus, Upfield again arrived at the camel station, where he usually spent two days, in lieu of two Sundays when he travelled. George Ritchie, who sometimes saw no one, black or white, for a week and longer, was always happy to see Upfield's team halt at his house gate, for his only visitors were Upfield and the northern section rider, and a chance station hand from Narndee, a property partially surrounding the Government station.

On this occasion Ritchie had much to talk about.

The owner of Narndee Station had bought all the mules from the Government station, and his men had mustered the mules into the Government camel yards to be broken before being taken to Narndee. Several of the Narndee men were supposed to be good horsemen but the Government mules tried them out and the breaking did not proceed smoothly. Then arrived at the camel station a young man on a motor-bike, and naturally Ritchie invited him inside to eat and gossip. The stranger said he had come from Perth and was hunting a job, and Ritchie informed him that a job of breaking-in mules was waiting in the near-by yards.

"Anything of a horseman?" he asked.

"Oh yes. Done a spot of riding now and then. They having some trouble?"

Ritchie said it looked like it, and later they strolled over to the yards, where several men sat on the top rail gazing despondently at a mule which had a saddle under its belly. One of the men was sick, having been tossed, and the others were urging an aborigine rider to 'have a go'. The aborigine wasn't keen, and Ritchie's visitor offered to try out the mule if they got it into the crush, and the saddle on its back.

Now men in this country don't snigger at the stranger, being well-aware that there are two-legged dark horses as well as the four-legged variety often rung in at country race meetings. This stranger was fairly tall, splendidly proportioned, almost handsome in a blond way. His eyes were light-blue, his laugh came easily, and his legs and feet betrayed the power to wrap themselves about a horse's barrel.

So up into the saddle went the stranger to give a performance that raised enthusiastic cheers, and the result was that Mr. Bogle, the Narndee owner, offered the job of handling the lot to him, and on enquiry was told that his name was Rowles, usually called Snowy. When Upfield arrived, Snowy Rowles had broken all the mules and had taken them to Narndee, where he was now employed.

Another month passed before Upfield called at the camel station and heard more eulogies of Snowy Rowles, who was now working from a hut and well on Narndee just beyond the camel station boundary. There were Narndee bores to the north of the Government property, and to reach these Rowles had to pass by the camel station homestead, using his motor-bike. So that George Ritchie saw him at least once every week.

"Today's Wednesday, isn't it?" Ritchie asked, and Upfield said it could be, but he wasn't sure. Finally they agreed that it was Wednesday, and Ritchie explained that on Wednesdays Rowles always visited the outlying wells, and often brought fresh meat with him.

Fresh meat! The only fresh meat Upfield had seen was down at Burracoppin, and the only fresh meat Ritchie found was when his dogs caught a kangaroo. A month is a long time to live on tinned meat and fish, and when they saw Rowles coming they made a fire in the stove and scoured the fry-pan.

The house was built of stone and contained three rooms—kitchen, living-room and bedroom. Through the window in the kitchen wall could be seen the track to Namdee flowing down a slight incline to pass the yards, and thence over a plain in the middle of which sat Dromedary Hill. From the kitchen the men could see Rowles on his motor-bike approaching from a distance of almost two miles.

He arrived with a skittering roar, laughingly shouted good-day, and asked if there was any tea going. He was told the billy was on the stove, and where was the meat? He had forgotten the meat. Forgotten it! Didn't he know they were starving for fresh meat? What kind of a pal was he?

"If it's meat you want, I'll go back and get some," Rowles declared, and departed on a roaring machine sending upwards a cloud of red dust. He had to travel some twelve miles to his hut, and when Upfield looked beyond the window ten minutes after he had left, he was astonished to see Rowles coming around the foot of Dromedary Hill on the return journey.

Rowles was then off the track and racing over country pocked with rabbit burrows and humped by boulders often hidden by oldman saltbush. They could see the sunlight reflected by his machine. They watched the endless dust-cloud behind it, and both decided that Snowy Rowles had gone mad.

Minutes later they could see what he was at. He was riding down a kangaroo so that, no matter what evasive tactics the animal tried out, the man on the bike blocked it. Eventually Rowles mustered the kangaroo past the yards, past the house, and into the wire-netted fowl- run.

"That tea brewed yet?" he asked, laughing. "Your meat's in the chook house."

So here were three of the actors in the coming drama– Ritchie the manager of the camel station, Snowy Rowles the debonair stockman, and Arthur Upfield the fence rider and budding novelist. Away in New Zealand a young man was taking his wife-to-be to a jeweller for a wedding ring, and another young man in Adelaide decided to come over to Western Australia, where jobs appeared to be plentiful. Yet another man, an ex-seaman , who sank bores and erected fences, was becoming tired of his old car and thinking of buying a utility.

4

It must indeed be dull to know what you will be doing within the next hour, to look at an appointment pad and read that Mr. Blank will be calling, or that you have to be at the office of So-and-So Limited. Can you but snap your chains, life is no longer tedious.

When Upfield's team topped a rise he noted far down the land swell a mysterious object entangled with the fence. At first it looked like a huge dog standing on its hind legs and peering over the barrier, or an emu arguing with another on the best way of knocking down the fence. The last living things he had seen were when crossing the wheat belt: a farmer riding a stump-jump plough, a crow who had turned away instead of following him into the desert scrub—and that had been four days previously. So that this thing, obviously alive, was of special interest.

When it was clear that the object was a man, the normal question arose: what was he doing there? He leaned against the fence and seemed to be studiously admiring the scenery, which at this place was remarkable for its horizon-wide spinifex belt. He must have been deaf, or entirely captured by the scene, for he took no notice of the camels and the dray when the animals stopped of their own accord.

Upfield called:

"Good-day, there!"

The man, dressed in rags and without boots, slowly turned and said calmly:

"Day, mister."

He did not remove his hands from the top wire, and Upfield automatically looked for tracks, expecting to see the imprints of the naked feet on the track coming from the north, as this was the only road through this desert. Beside the road was a hessian sugar-bag. There was no evidence of any transport. Casually he asked:

"Travelling?"

"Yair." Blue eyes looked a trifle vacantly at him.

"Where have you come from?"

"Oh...a bit this side of Southern Cross."

"But you haven't come up the fence."

"No. Took a straight line."

A straight line from this point to Southern Cross was a couple of hundred miles of desert scrub, with water only in scattered rockholes. Upfield had to believe him because there was no evidence of the fellow's tracks along the road in either direction.

"You know," said the derelict, "the old blue will swallow the old brown one of these days."

"Likely enough," agreed Upfield, now seeing that the man's legs were weak and that he was actually clenching the wire to support himself. Emptying the sugar-bag, he found that the contents comprised a partially eaten iguana and a sauce bottle containing a little liquid. Nothing else. Upfield backtracked the man and saw the truth, for the fellow had come from the east direct to the fence to which he now clung.

Upfield put him into the dray and proceeded to the next timber belt, where camp was made. He suggested that the stranger might make a fire to boil the billy while he unharnessed the camels. He was removing Curley's blinkers when a roaring noise attracted his attention to the huge fire, which would require a fifty-foot pole under the handle of the billy to place it against the flames.

The traveller across uncharted regions wasn't famished. He sipped his tea, ate his damper bread and tinned beef as though he had but recently eaten. He was sure of the place from which he had come, and to which place he was going–another hundred miles westward before he came to open gold-bearing country, small towns and prospectors. The old blue and the old brown to which he made constant reference, were the sky and the earth. Had he been this way before? Oh yes! But to his annoyance he had 'hit' the fence about three miles south of the point aimed at when he left Southern Cross. How did he catch the iguana? Easy. Had seen it dive into a rabbit burrow and had dug for it with his hands. Where did he find the water in the bottle? It wasn't water. It was sap he'd got from a wait-a-bit bush by breaking a surface root and firing the entire bush by heaping dead rubbish about it.

He was harmless enough but gave Upfield many long and anxious moments when he handled Upfield's Winchester repeating rifle, and seemed disinclined to part with it. After that Upfield took the rifle to bed with him, as there was no secure place in which to hide the cartridges. He had this odd companion for eight nights, when they reached the camel station and Ritchie took him to Narndee, where he was collected by a policeman for proper care in a home. That he had crossed the trackless desert from Southern Cross was subsequently proved.

One night when Upfield and Ritchie were talking in the kitchen, the conversation turned to the subject of Upfield's next book, and he mentioned what he sought for his next mystery plot.

"I'd pay a pound for a simple and perfect method of wholly destroying a human body with aids to be found at any homestead."

Ritchie chuckled, saying:

"Easy. Give us your quid."

"You know I haven't the actual money, but it's yours, if you earn it."

"Earn it easy enough," asserted Ritchie. "Supposing I wanted to do you in. I'd kid you into the bush a bit and when you were nice and handy to plenty of dry wood, I'd shoot you dead and burn your body. When the ashes were cold I'd go through the lot with a sieve, getting out every burnt bone and all metal things like buttons and boot sprigs. The metal I'd put into a bottle of sulphuric acid, and at every homestead they keep sulphuric for tin-smithing, and your burnt bones I'd put through a prospector's dolly-pot, and toss out the dust for the wind to scatter. There'd be none of you left."

Sulphuric acid and a prospector's dolly-pot–a heavy iron object fashioned like a gun shell in which ore thought to contain gold is crushed to sand with the end of an iron bar. At every homestead, at many deserted camps, there would be a dolly-pot and sulphuric acid ranged beside the coffee canister. These items were, of course, at the camel station.

The perfect murder needed only time, say three days at longest.

The plan was perfect. There was no breaking it down. Upfield gladly paid the pound. He made only one test. Unburned animal bones would not grind to dust in the dolly-pot; they merely splintered and shredded. Burned bones became fine greyish dust that the lightest of winds easily wafted away. But one moment! Assuming that scientific examination of the ashes proved that flesh had been consumed, what then, Ritchie?

"Easy, Arthur me lad, easy. On the fire-site you burn a couple of kangaroo carcasses. We always burn carcasses about a camp or a homestead to keep the flies down. Burning a carcass would also shunt suspicion of why the fire was lit in the first place. Getting away with murder is as easy as falling off a log if only you use your brain. Try it some time and see."

5

Before the drop-table in the dray, with the soft flame of the hurricane lamp burning steadily in the motionless air, and all about him the silence which can become in the mind a material Being that watches and waits, Upfield plotted his next book and experienced that ecstasy known only to the imaginative writer. He created the major characters, listing their physical features, mental attributes and the rest, so that they became living beings, his companions for weeks into months. He chose the background, invented the motive for the crime, and outlined the history of the case to the point of the discovery that a man had vanished into thin air. He brought in Napoleon Bonaparte, and Napoleon Bonaparte, alias Tracker Leon, said in his soft voice:

"Very clever of George Ritchie to present through you the perfect murder. Your victim's body has been wholly destroyed, so there is no trace, no proof, that he ever lived, and not one pathologist in the world is able to gather together those specks of grey dust tossed from the dolly-pot. You wish me to investigate and prove–what?"

"Yes, I see, but you are infallible. What I have built and shall build, you can pull down. You must, Bony."

"You set out the perfect example of the irresistible projectile meeting the immovable object."

And that was all Upfield had achieved–thus far.

It became a problem question. If a man did such and such, where would he make a slip? He has to make a slip, just one. Yet the method of destruction must be carried through in its entirety.

Down in Burracoppin, Upfield had friends who were not bereft of intelligence, and friends in Perth who had passed through university. To them he posed the problem and they strove to find a solution.

There seemed none. Autumn came, and Upfield still was stumped. Winter came, when writing in the dray was prohibited even had he wanted to write, for the winter in Western Australia brings sparkling frost or wild and cold winds. Winter nights were endurable only when close to a roaring camp-fire, occupied with a book. And lurking in the shadows still was the tantalising problem of a mystery without a solution.

One morning Curley got out of bed on the wrong side and determinedly went on strike. As usual the camels had been freed to feed for an hour before work, and when Upfield approached them with the nose-lines, Curley refused to be led back to camp, even going down on his knees, shuffling forward and bellowing protest. He looked extremely silly. Millie stood by in an attitude of lofty disdain, but encouragement in her large black eyes.

Having almost to drag Curley back to camp, Upfield finally downed him to be harnessed, and in his present mood a rope about his neck had to be hitched to a tree to prevent his turning and biting as his blinkers were put on. When he felt the rope, he knew what was coming, and he bellowed and blew out his red throat bladder, danced about on his knees, and, as One Spur Dick would have said, really performed.

Being by this time not in an animal-loving mood, Upfield

slipped the blinkers over Curley's snout and managed to avoid the stream of cud. The bladder looked as though it might explode, but the blinkers went back into place and the throat strap was buckled. Upfield stood away and laughed with mocking triumph, and Curley opened his jaws still wider and gaped at him. And in that instant, even as he gazed into Curley's throat beyond the buck teeth, the solution of the perfect detection of the perfect murder flared into his mind.

He was so astonished that he reclined against Millie's hump and rolled a cigarette, and, despite frozen feet and hands, proceeded with the writing of *The Sands of Windee* and completed it before Christmas.

6

When George Ritchie said he had had enough of the camel station, the inspector put Upfield in charge.

Here were conditions remarkably similar to those ruling at Wheeler's Well, and, having sent *The Sands of Windee* off to his agent, Upfield began another thriller, not a mystery. He put ninety thousand words to paper in fourteen days and nights, and then, when he read through what he had written, found it mere rubbish and burned it. About once every week a car sped past as though the driver feared prosecution, and about once a fortnight a traveller would call, giving Upfield the pleasure of hearing a human voice. The only other visitors, and they were rare enough, were Snowy Rowles and Larry and Emily.

Two Murchison aborigines, Larry and Emily were young, good-looking, and in love. They were typical station workers, but like all their race could not stay put. They would arrive driving an ancient horse in a light dray piled high with dunnage, crowned with five or six hens. When put to ground, the hens remained, like black china birds, under the dray, and Emily would have with her a few kittens, and sometimes a baby kangaroo which she exhibited with shy giggles.

Still, they did have lovers' tiffs. On one occasion Emily showed a bad gash on a shoulder, and Upfield having applied iodine, which made her giggle, and adhesive tape over lint, which brought further giggles, she insisted that the 'doctor' receive a fee of a splendid foxskin. The next week they came again, this time for medical attention to Larry. He had been badly scalded at the back of his head and neck, and, when being treated, roared with laughter because Emily had got her own back by tossing boiling tea over him.

Heat seemed to agree with them. They liked curry much hotter than hot. When Larry was bitten on the big toe by a snake, he scarified the wound with a quartz flint and thrust the toe into the embers of the camp-fire. They were delighted when Upfield asked them to show him how to find the honey ants, those strange insects that are so crammed with honey by the workers that they become living food stores, their bodies so distended that the legs cannot be put to ground, and consequently are helpless prisoners deep in the caverns. They gave him letter-sticks and told him what the markings on them meant, and because they always had foxskins or scalps, and no traps or poison, Upfield prompted them to solve this mystery.

White men all over Australia worked early and late dragging a trail and laying poison baits for foxes, but the ignorant Australian 'savages' revealed more intelligence than the mighty white man. They walked casually about, and almost indifferently glanced at this rabbit burrow and that. Then Emily went forward to the burrow, and Larry made himself comfortable with a single-barrel shot-gun. Emily stooped and coughed loudly into a rabbit hole enlarged by a fox, and quietly withdrew. In a moment or two the fox thrust out his head to see what had made the strange noise, and Larry gathered another skin or scalp, for which the bonus was a pound. He bagged four foxes inside an hour and a half.

Once every month or six weeks the inspector appeared, driving a truck with a smart canvas hood, and bringing stores and the mail, and it would happen that a few days after he had gone south to Burracoppin the camels raced in to the troughs by the well, where several had fought and one lay injured.

Upfield found him the next morning, and he could not determine how badly injured he was. For three days he cut scrub and dragged it to the camel, a magnificent beast that Ritchie and he had broken in to buckboard work only a few months previously. It became a problem. To shoot him meant having to hitch camels to a rope to drag the carcass far away, and it would require a better man than Upfield to make camels undertake that job. Had it been a horse, yes, but not one of themselves. So, daily, for eight or nine days, Upfield fed and watered him, patted his head and talked, and the camel got to look for his coming.

One morning Snowy Rowles turned up in an old car and agreed that the injured camel wouldn't walk again. He suggested the obvious, and Upfield flatly said he couldn't shoot the beast. Rowles said he would do that, and did. After Upfield had cut off the brands for the Government records, Rowles found that his old car was incapable of dragging the carcass away from the trough to the distant scrub. Cheerfully he called for the axe, and with knife and axe divided the carcass and hauled each part away. To him nothing was any trouble.

He was on his way to Youanmi, a small township clinging to a once-important gold mine, for a few days' spell, and asked if he might shower and change, to which, of course, he was welcome.

"I'm thinking of slinging in the job and taking on the dog trapping an foxing," he said. "More money in trapping, and besides I want to be my own boss. What d'you reckon? Pink strychnine is easier to get, but some say it isn't as good as the white."

Upfield said that experience had taught him that pink

strychnine is less effective than white, because the substance used for the colouring arouses an animal's suspicion. He mentioned the easy method of fox-hunting adopted by Larry and Emily. To this Rowles laughingly said he couldn't persuade them to partner him, and that he had tried the coughing stunt and nary a fox would poke his head up.

"Might get the old grandfather to back me with a good utility," he said casually, and proceeded to strip on the earthen floor of the verandah. "Be seeing you."

Naked, he raced the quarter-mile to the well and reservoir tank, where he splashed about for half an hour before returning with the homestead dogs prancing around him. He dressed in clean underwear and put on a new pair of gabardine trousers. Upfield provided hot water and together they entered the bedroom, where, before the mirror on the wall, Rowles proceeded to shave.

Upfield sat on his bunk, and they gossiped until Rowles began to knot a tie under the soft shirt collar, when he exclaimed:

"Why, I've seen you before. Years ago."

"Not likely," argued Snowy, shooting a glance at Upfield, and then leaning closer to the mirror.

"It was over in New South Wales, at a place called Wheeler's Well."

"Couldn't have been. I've never been out of W.A."

Promising to be back in a few days, Snowy Rowles left a greatly perplexed Upfield, because he was quite sure that the man who just a few minutes before had shaved and adjusted his tie before the mirror was the very same he had seen doing this at Wheeler's Well, New South Wales, and something like two thousand miles to the east and several years in time. The stance of the figure, the face in profile, the shape of the head, and the manipulation of the tie was an exact repetition. A mystery without a solution. Or was it?

One morning there came to the Government camel station a man Upfield had not previously met, a well sinker and fence contractor named James Ryan. Ryan was one of the army of wanderers of which Upfield had been a member before the writing virus settled for ever in his blood. These casual workers appear, stay a while, move on.

Ryan was short, grizzled, leathery and tough. He had once been a sailor, had worked on various mines, and now was working on Narndee sinking a bore. He was on his way down to Burracoppin, and thence to Perth for a spell, and he told Upfield he intended selling his ancient car and buying a used utility, and that he would have to pick up a suitable mate if he could find one, as bore-sinking was too much for one man to handle.

On Snowy Rowles returning from Youanmi, Upfield naturally talked of Ryan, and Rowles expressed doubt that Ryan would buy a utility as he was a renowned 'booze artist' and wouldn't be likely to get beyond the pub at Burracoppin. He knew that Ryan wanted a mate, and he had himself thought of joining Ryan on the bore job. He had brought from Youanmi a leg of fresh pork and real potatoes and apples, and he stayed that night at the camel station.

Time passed, weeks of time. Ritchie came now and then, and one day Snowy called to announce that he had sold his car to Larry for so many pounds plus so many fox scalps.

"But Larry can't drive," objected Upfield. "Oh yes, he can," countered Rowles casually. "I gave him a lesson the other day."

Ritchie turned up in his truck, and shortly afterwards Larry and Emily appeared. They parked the light dray in the shed, freed the ancient horse to find company with the Government horses, and loaded their dunnage into Rowles's car.

It was amusing and yet strangely pathetic. Larry, dressed in nothing but a pair of trousers, climbed in behind the wheel. Beside him squatted the hens. On the rear seat was piled the dunnage, on which sat Emily. She was wearing her best clothes–a white cotton blouse, red poplin skirt, and red Court shoes. On top of her straight black hair was perched a small blue hat. Never was a girl more thrilled, and between giggles she behaved precisely as a white woman.

"Now you, Larry, you be careful. Don't you bump nothing."

"I'm gonna drive. You shut up."

"You can't drive."

"I can you. Shut up."

"Now, you all set?" enquired Snowy. "Right, I'll wind her up, and don't you do anything till I get out of the way."

Emily bounced on the load, forgetting English, and back-seat driving in the aboriginal tongue. The engine roared and Snowy leapt for the throttle on the steering-wheel.

"Work her up from normal," he said. "Don't forget you got to bring her back to idling when you want to stop, as well as tread on the brake. Know where the brake is? Yes, that's it. Now press on the other pedal and jerk in your stick. Like I told you."

Emily continued to bounce herself up and down and giggle and shriek. The men stood away, and Larry did things which tortured the insides of the car. Then he started with a jerk and Emily fell back on the load, her legs in the air until she righted herself. Fortunately the track was level and clearly followed. The several shallow water gutters across the track Larry took with a leap which would have wrecked a modern car, and after the first mile appeared to be driving a little less erratically. Rowles accompanied Ritchie in the truck to repair all the gates Larry was bound to drive through.

Larry and Emily had a wonderful time until the tyres blew out or were punctured and the naked wheel-rims could no longer stand up to the bashing. And then the curtain was raised on Act One.

14. Upfield at the time he met the original of 'Bony'

15. Upfield with Mr. James L. Hole in 1950

16. The rain-shed where Rowles and Ritchie found Ryan and Lloyd, the former on a continued 'bender'

17. John Thomas Smith, *alias* Snowy Rowles, with the utility to gain which he murdered Ryan and Lloyd

18. The residue of fires which consumed the body of Carron

CHAPTER TWELVE

THE DEBONAIR MURDERER

I

Ritchie, having worked so long for the Government and saved his wages, was a little capitalist who now enjoyed relaxation by driving around between Youanmi and Narndee, and he happened to be staying with Upfield when Snowy Rowles came asking after Ryan. Saying that he had heard Ryan had left Burracoppin, he decided to run down the fence and prospect for him, and he and Ritchie left together.

Ryan had bought his used utility, and he had found a mate in a young man named Lloyd who had come from Adelaide looking for work. Lloyd was the kind of mate a man like Ryan needed. Lloyd didn't drink and could look after Ryan, who did. Lloyd could play an accordion, and generous Ryan bought an accordion. Ryan liked to sing when drunk, and even when sober, and Lloyd proved to be a good accompanist. Lloyd wrote to his wife in Adelaide that he had found a job.

They left Burracoppin, Lloyd driving the utility, and on reaching the rain-shed and hut at the ninety-six mile, Ryan let himself go on the whisky. That was where and how Ritchie and Rowles discovered them, and, knowing that the inspector was due the next day, they persuaded Ryan to come on and planted all the bottles and other evidence of occupation.

By then it was clear that Snowy Rowles was most anxious to join Ryan. Having sold his unreliable old car to Larry for a few pounds, he told Upfield that he had written to his people to finance him in the purchase of a truck with which he would undertake dingo-trapping and fox-poisoning as a full-time occupation, and such was Rowles's address that his expectations in this direction appeared to be solidly based.

When Ryan left Narndee he had completed the bore-sinking, had been paid to date, and on his return would have only to equip the bore to complete his contract.

It was understood, and Upfield could never recall the source, that on completing the contract for Narndee, Ryan seriously thought of going farther north, where money was more plentiful, and of taking Rowles. Anyway, this 'idea' fitted with Rowles's annoyance on discovering that Ryan had already picked up a mate. They arrived at the camel station about four in the afternoon, Ryan in a happy mood, Ritchie likewise, Rowles seething, and Lloyd quiet, sober, and anxious because the days were fleeing and he wasn't yet earning money.

That evening they lounged on the verandah, Lloyd playing the accordion and Ryan singing his chanties, and the next morning they packed up to leave for the new bore. Ryan was still bemused, and no one asked him outright what were his future plans. Lloyd drove the heavy utility, which was in excellent condition. When they had gone, Ritchie drove off on business of his own, and returned just short of a week later with a story having the hallmark of authenticity.

Several miles up the fence, and beyond the extremity of the Government property, was one of Narndee's outlying wells, and at this time an old man, who was partially dumb, was stationed there to supervise stock watering. He told Ritchie that Ryan, Lloyd and Rowles had stopped at the far side of the vermin fence, and that Rowles had climbed the barrier, had walked to the well and told him they were all headed north. To have reached this point, they must have left the Narndee camel station track, to pass behind Dromedary Hill to reach the fence on the wrong side, and driven beside it to the next gate. Both Ritchie and Upfield were slightly hurt that they had not called to say good-bye.

It would seem that they travelled as far as Mount Magnet and that there Ryan began another bender. Snowy Rowles, who had a girl at Youanmi, borrowed the utility for a week-end to visit her, and after that no one took further interest in them, save to wish them good fortune wherever they might be.

The weeks ran into months, and as Inspector Coleman was unable to locate a man accustomed to camels, he placed a man at the Government station and returned Upfield to his section of the fence, where he heard only scraps of gossip about those in the vicinity of the camel station. And among these scraps of information was the item that Ryan had gone completely broke at Mount Magnet, had sold the utility to Snowy Rowles, and had drifted northward with Lloyd.

The Great Depression brought changes to the Rabbit Department no less severe than to other departments. All the men were put off save returned soldiers, and the resultant re-organisation reformed Upfield's section to one hundred miles north of Burracoppin and one hundred southward of the town, transport being by way of a draught horse and light dray, feed for the horse being dropped at points by the inspector's truck. This meant that Upfield did not travel nearer to the camel station than the ninety-six-mile rain-shed and hut.

The change suited Upfield. No longer had he to worry about losing camels. The dray was provided with a roof and drop-sides, and he quickly built himself a table. The contract for *The Sands of Windee* had been signed, and he was engaged on writing his next book when the inspector, then proceeding north, reported the astonishing story that Snowy Rowles was in serious trouble.

Rowles was just the type of devil-may-care fellow to land himself in trouble, but not to this degree.

"Seems that he was working with a man named Carron, and Carron has disappeared and they're looking for Snowy Rowles," said the inspector. "Last they know of Rowles is when he bought a case of beer at Paynes Find with his mate's cheque. Looks pretty bad."

"Must have been a booze party in the bush, and the mate was killed," surmised Upfield.

"Could be," agreed the inspector. "Anyway, I'll probably learn more on this trip."

He did. A week later, he said:

"The police are well on the job. Been all over the country. They found the remains of several big fires at the one-hundred-and-seventy- three-mile bore and hut. Going through the ashes when I stopped. Wouldn't talk–much. I got the feeling that Rowles put that book plot of yours into action."

"Then they will never prove anything," Upfield said with '. conviction. "If Rowles and his mate did have a drunks' fight and the mate was killed and Rowles destroyed the body as per Ritchie's formula, there will be nothing to prove."

"Ought to be interesting. You better tread lightly."

The inspector departed, promising to let Upfield have further news on arrival at Burracoppin, and leaving him with the horse and dray, and the fence, and the banded ant-eaters. 'What a fool,' ran Upfield's thoughts. Better for Snowy to face up to the brawl and its tragic result than to set off a police hunt.

Rowles certainly knew of the complete disposal of a body. He was there at the camel station homestead that evening when the wind howled and the fire leaped in the open hearth. Also present that night were Ritchie and the patrolman on the northward section, and his wife, who travelled with him. The problem had been put to the gathering: if a man did such and such, where would he make a slip? It was a good brain teaser on a cold and windy night.

The subject had died through lack of concentration and Ritchie invited Rowles to tell the company of an experience when employed by a buck-jumping show, and Rowles proved he could tell a story against himself. It appeared that Rowles and a companion were hired by the proprietor to start the show by riding their 'best' horses, and each to be deliberately thrown to encourage members of the audience to believe they could ride better.

"It was easy money," Rowles declared, "until one night my cobber got on first and he was a bit careless. He was thrown properly and badly hurt and then it came to my turn to mount the same horse, and I was so damn frightened that I couldn't fall off. So I was sacked."

Upfield remembered Snowy's smile. He could still hear Snowy's laughter as Larry drove off in the old car after only one lesson. He saw again the lunatic bike-rider mustering the kangaroo into the chook yard. And he remembered seeing Snowy Rowles on two occasions–at lonely Wheeler's Well, when adjusting a tie, and again in Western Australia doing the same thing. Only when drunk could such an admirable fellow have killed a man.

Thus Upfield, and many others, felt and thought similarly on hearing of police activities about the Govemment camel station.

Several weeks passed before Upfield again met the inspector on his trip south to the junction of the fence with the Southern Ocean.

"Looks even worse," said the inspector. "They're hunting for Ryan and Lloyd, and they've been out to the bore Ryan sank, and taken a look-see at the ashes of several big fires close about Ryan's old camp. Ritchie says Snowy left with Ryan and Lloyd after spending that night at the camel station. That's right, I suppose?"

"Yes." Upfield found it difficult to speak. The terrible inference about Ryan and Lloyd banished the smiling Snowy Rowles, and created a monster. His mind was divided. It refused to accept the monster and strove to recall the incidents and statements which, together, built up Rowles's assertion that he had come honestly by Ryan's utility.

"West Australia is a hell of a big place," he reminded the inspector. "Fellers come and leave, vanish for months, even years, and turn up again. This isn't a city. What of that lunatic I found clinging to the fence? If he had perished no one would have missed him. And, remember, Ryan was boozing at Mount Magnet when Snowy borrowed the ute for that trip to Youanmi."

"Could be. Let's hope so. Bogle tells a story. Bogle says that when he heard that Ryan was back at the bore, he went out there in his car, and found Snowy Rowles at the camp and several large fires burning close by. Snowy said Ryan and Lloyd were at the bore, and he was cleaning up the camp because they were all pulling out. The bore is half a mile through dense scrub and over a ridge, and Bogle says he decided against tramping there, as there was no track for his car, and he left a message for Ryan with Rowles. Supposing Rowles was even then burning bodies, and supposing Bogle had tramped to the bore and hadn't found either man there. He might have made a third victim."

"Ryan's truck. Where was it?"

"At the camp."

There came to Upfield and the others the final shock. The police had known that Snowy Rowles was working at Hill View Station, one hundred and forty miles up the fence from the camel station and Narndee, but it was some time before they gathered sufficient evidence to justify questioning him as the obvious suspect. Detective-Sergeant Manning and other police arrived at the hut occupied by Rowles, to find him absent, so they parked their car in the scrub and concealed themselves to await his return: They were taking no chances.

"Why!" exclaimed Manning, when he eventually appeared, "you are John Thomas Smith, wanted for theft and gaol-breaking at Dalwallinu. I'm arresting you, Smith."

So Snowy Rowles was a thief and a gaol-breaker, and was sentenced to a term of imprisonment, giving the investigators into the case of the missing men ample time to prepare their case of homicide against John Thomas Smith.

"It's funny that the police haven't dug you up for a statement," remarked the inspector.

"Look, take my advice and write out a statement," urged the licensee of the Burracoppin Hotel.

"If the police want a statement, let them come and get it," snorted Upfield.

They didn't 'dig him up'. The inspector found him next at the twenty-five-mile peg, south of Burracoppin. He watched Upfield open a parcel from London. He handled one of the six presentation copies of *The Sands of Windee*, and departed with a folder issued by the Crime Book Club, which had made this title their selection for the month. Nothing else happened. The police went to sleep, or appeared to do so. They were not interested in Upfield, or so it seemed. But down in Perth for a few days, Upfield called on the doyen of booksellers, Mr. Albert, who said, with a twinkle in his eye:

"The book is selling splendidly after that fine review of it by John Ewers in the *West Australian*. Even some of the detectives have been in and bought a copy."

Back again patrolling a section of the world's longest fence, Upfield wrote his statement.

Months passed, and in Perth one morning Sergeant Manning called at Upfield's apartment.

"Wondering if you'd come along to see the Crown Prosecutor. Wants to talk to you," Manning said.

"All right. What about a cup of tea and a biscuit while I change?"

"Thanks. You writing another book?"

"Yes. I've been thinking you had forgotten all about *The Sands of Windee*."

Detective-Sergeant Manning chuckled.

"Never forget that yarn. Best book I've ever read."

Even the Crown Prosecutor said he liked it. Upfield liked him, and enjoyed the interview.

That Detective-Sergeant Manning! What a man! Erase Napoleon Bonaparte's complexion, and there was Manning's twin. When

Manning read *The Sands of Windee*, he saw himself delving in those ashes into which Bony had delved.

2

In Bonaparte's investigation, on Windee Station in New South Wales, of the disappearance of a man named Marks, he had to contend with the operations of two men earning their living by shooting kangaroos for their skins. The one condition laid down by the squatter was that every carcass had to be destroyed by fire to prevent the increase of the blow- fly, that great enemy of sheep. Extraneous circumstances convinced Bonaparte that Marks, who, superficially, had wandered from his disabled car and perished of thirst, had met with foul play, and from this point he deduced from the characters of all the people in the locality that the body had been destroyed by fire and not buried. Thus he studied almost a hundred fire-sites within a radius of some two miles of the abandoned car, and finally chose three for close investigation.

On each of the mounds of ashes were the charred bones of kangaroos, proving that the hunters had complied with the squatter's condition. One of the three sites had a peculiarity not associated with the others. Elsewhere, the carcasses had all been tossed haphazardly on to tree branches for burning, but at this particular site there was evidence that the carcasses, had been placed on a thick bed of wood.

Bonaparte sieved the ashes of this fire. He found the melted remains of two bullets equalling in weight a .44, which was the size of the rifles used by the hunters. The area of the fire-site tallied with two carcasses having been burned there. The only other item of the slightest significance was one boot sprig. The position of the ,tiny nail in the bed of ash proved that at least an old boot had been burned in one fire, and above it another fire had consumed the carcasses of two kangaroos.

No Crown Prosecutor would accept the theory that a human body had been destroyed, on the production of one boot sprig, and it was an extraneous clue found many yards distant which enabled Bonaparte to prove that a man had been killed and his body entirely consumed by fire.

Thus the murderer of Marks had followed the simple formula set out by George Ritchie.

The Western Australian police had a far harder task at the beginning of their investigations, and later much easier, than had Napoleon Bonaparte. They had to cover thousands of square miles of country, but were assisted in eliminating much of it by the fact that it is so rugged and so scrubby that only on defined routes could a motor vehicle leave the tracks.

From the fire-sites about the camp of James Ryan, they sieved items which might bear scientific examination, sufficient only to fill a one- ounce cooking-essence bottle. But they found also in these ashes the metal ribs of an accordion. When the police learned that Ryan had bought a new accordion for Lloyd to play, the natural question was why a brand-new accordion should have been burned–and at the same time when, according to Mr. Bogle, the station owner, he had found Snowy Rowles 'cleaning up' about the camp. Actually there was no rule or condition attached to Ryan's contract that on completion he was to gather and burn all litter and part carcasses of kangaroos he had shot for meat.

At what point in their enquiries they first heard of Upfield's search for the perfect murder, and the solution provided by George Ritchie, the police never divulged. They must have deduced from the items collected into their essence bottle and the bones of the accordion found deep in the ash piles that Rowles had followed Ritchie's formula, and had chosen the camp-site because of the numerous carcasses of kangaroos shot by Ryan during his occupancy.

And when the police went into conference with the fence

inspector, during which he drew for them a plan of all the local tracks, water-holes, bores and open wells, he told them that at the one-hundred-and-seventy-three-mile bore a number of kangaroos had perished since the bore had been out of action. Doubtless he mentioned other places where these animals had died at water sources which had given out.

And, as the police must have hopefully anticipated, they found several mounds of ashes of fires lit in the close vicinity of the disused bore at the one-hundred-and-seventy-three-mile peg on the number one rabbit fence. And in those ashes, among other items, they found, under the bones of kangaroos, part of a human skull, human teeth, and a wedding-ring which miraculously had not been melted to a slug of gold.

The wedding-ring found in the ashes was a truly remarkable clue.

3

Louis Carron, in New Zealand, took his wife-to-be to a jeweller to buy a wedding-ring. From stock the jeweller hadn't a ring that fitted the lady's finger, and one had to be cut, the segment removed and the golden band re-joined. The jeweller cut the ring himself and gave it to an assistant to weld the two ends, and when the customers called the next day he noticed that the assistant had made a poor job of it, and he would have tossed it into the melting-pot and worked on a second ring, had not the Carrons insisted it wouldn't be noticed and that they were in a hurry.

Subsequently the Carrons parted, and, with the ring on his own finger, Louis Carron came to Western Australia. In Perth he fell in with a young man named Lemon, and these two tramped and hitch-hiked right up into the Murchison District, where Lemon gained work on Narndee, and Carron obtained a job on the neighbouring station named Widgee.

It appeared that Louis Carron wasn't happy with his job, and as the Wiluna gold mine had taken on another lease of life, he decided to go there and obtain work. With Rowles he turned up at Lemon's camp, Rowles still owning Ryan's utility, and inclined to 'give Wiluna a go' too. Having promised Lemon to write, and 'also to have some films developed and send him the prints, Carron departed with Snowy Rowles.

Time passed, and Carron neither wrote nor posted the prints, and Lemon eventually wrote to Rowles, who had turned up again in the district, seeking news of Carron. Lemon had to write more than once before receiving the reply that Carron had been unable to find work at Wiluna, and had gone across to Geraldton, since when Rowles hadn't heard of him.

Having struggled and starved and planned together, Lemon had been able to estimate Carron's character, and he was convinced that Carron would have done as promised by, at least, writing. Nothing if not tenacious, Lemon wrote to the police at Mount Magnet and was put off by the statement that doubtless Carron would write when he became settled. Police opinion was reasonable, in view of the eternal movement of Australia's floating population. It was when Mrs. Carron wrote from New Zealand, some time afterwards, that the Mount Magnet police began enquiring after her husband.

At the trial of John Thomas Smith for the murder of Louis Carron, the jeweller was cross-examined by Mr. Curren on the following lines:

Mr. Curren: "You have said that you identify this ring as the ring you sold to Mrs. Carron, at Auckland, New Zealand. This mark or brand, now. Is it the mark or brand of a wholesaler from whom you obtain your supply of wedding-rings?"

Witness: "Yes."

Mr. Curren: "I suggest that you purchase and sell a number of rings bearing this trademark, and that the wholesaler also supplies many other jewellers."

Witness: "That is so."

Mr. Curren: "Then how do you identify this particular ring of the many you sell every year, and the probable thousands which are manufactured by the wholesalers?"

Witness: "Well, it's quite a story. I clearly remember the day that Mrs. Carron and her husband entered my shop wishing to buy a wedding-ring. They were in a hurry and it was a busy period with me, and made slightly more difficult because my former assistant, who was a goldsmith, had left me, and the then assistant, who was a good jeweller, was not a tradesman goldsmith.

"The following day when the Carrons came into the shop for the ring, which I had cut and passed to the new assistant to weld, I found that his work was carelessly done, and I wanted to toss the ring into the melting-pot and cut another. I asked the Carrons to call again next day, but, as I said, they were in a hurry, and, much against the grain, I had to allow them to take the ring.

"What had happened is simple enough. My assistant, who was not an expert goldsmith, used a nine-carat solder on that eighteen carat ring. You will see the difference in the colour of the solder on the ring now exhibited."

The next witness was then called.

There was astounding evidence given by another jeweller, this time in Perth, where there could be two or three dozen jewellery establishments.

Carron owned a watch, which Lemon remembered. This watch was found in Smith's possession when arrested. When Carron arrived at Widgee Station, one of the first things he did was to post the watch to the Perth jeweller for cleaning. The watch was marked when received, and the mark, plus other details, was entered in a card index. When Rowles came into possession of this watch, it needed expert attention, and of all the jewellers in Perth, he posted it to the very same firm. And the details, including his alias, Rowles, and address, were also entered in the card index.

There were over fifty witnesses, and the trial occupied many days. Upfield, of course, was put on the stand, he having to repeat the evidence given at the Coroner's inquest, detailing the method of body destruction which he had incorporated in his book, *The Sands of Windee*, one of the exhibits.

The New Zealand dentist identified his work on the plate found in the ashes, as having been done for Louis Carron. Lemon identified a coat, a camera, and other articles found in Rowles's possession, as having once belonged to Louis Carron. An expert anthropologist gave it as his opinion that the piece of skull bone found in the ashes had once been part of a white man's skull, not that of an aborigine.

On the witness-stand Snowy Rowles conducted himself calmly and confidently. He was dressed well and he looked well. He might have walked to the stand as anyone of the witnesses, instead of having been for a year and more in gaol. He was naturally subdued, and yet the same debonair Snowy Rowles whom all the witnesses had known and liked. They would have rejoiced had Rowles been acquitted of the murder of Louis Carron, for there was no body produced, no identifiable portion of a body; would have rejoiced freely had they not known the circumstances surrounding the disappearance of Ryan and Lloyd.

Snowy Rowles, the magnificent horseman, the daring bike rider, the good fellow, was hanged on the morning of June 13th, 1932.

That he murdered two men for the utility owned by one, that he had put into effect the formula of body destruction set out in Upfield's *The Sands of Windee*, is reasonably certain. That he murdered Louis Carron for his station pay cheque of twenty-five pounds was surely proved by the evidence. While in the condemned cell Rowles admitted to his counsel that he had camped with Carron, and the next day had left Carron in camp while he went to Paynes Find with the cheque to purchase rations and a case of beer. On his return he had found Carron dead, having eaten poison baits in error. Possessed of a record, having broken gaol, he realised the position he was then in, and had taken the body to the disused bore, and there had burned it.

Time periods and distances from point to point pull the foundations from under this story. Mrs. Lloyd, in Adelaide, implored him to state what had happened to her husband, but, to the last, he said he had left Lloyd with Ryan to seek work farther to the north. That was all of twenty-three years ago, and neither Ryan nor Lloyd have ever been seen.

If you do such and such and such, how can you make a slip when destroying your enemy? That may appear to be the perfect murder formula, and yet there is a major flaw, and the flaw was revealed to Upfield in a moment of stress. Like the formula itself, the flaw is simple and clear, but Upfield won't divulge the flaw.

The question of Upfield's responsibility might be answered by General Leane, then Chief Commissioner of the South Australian Police Department, who, when asked by the *Adelaide Advertiser* did he think detective-crime stories encouraged criminals, replied: "Not as much as razors."

4

It was not a day swiftly to be forgotten, the thirteenth of June, 1932.

Arthur William Upfield sat on a granite boulder high on an escarpment of the Darling Ranges, high above the city of Perth, with Fremantle beyond the city, and the silvered sliver of the Indian Ocean marking the far-away horizon. The sky was clear, and the air cold and clean following the darkness of dreadful night.

Snowy Rowles had been hanged this beautiful morning down there amid that conglomeration of greys and reds and greens blotching the earth, and called a city, and but little more than a hundred years before this day an aborigine, carrying a spear, had sat on this same rock and gazed upon a carpet of dark-green trees on which was no scar made by the human herd.

Upfield had experienced a god-like aloofness, outside and beyond and above the herd whose habits and instincts somehow , had never touched him. And then without an awareness of the threat, he had been drawn into the herd, claimed by it, and now felt a little frightened and infinitely lonely.

All the people in that sprawling city knew of and about him. Three of the newspapers were running his books as serials. He felt no satisfaction, no triumph, because his work was being read by the herd not for its worth, but for the notoriety brought to it by Snowy Rowles. One of those newspapers had wanted him to report the inquest, and he had refused on the grounds of his closeness to the actors in the drama begun in the desert and ended in that city, and the idea of 'cashing in' on the trial, condemnation and death of a man with whom he had eaten was wholly abhorrent.

As General Leane had inferred, Upfield was no more responsible for the death of four men than the manufacturer of a razor is responsible for the death of a man found with his throat cut in a dark alley, but there was the difference that the man in the alley had not been known to the maker of the death instrument.

The judge and the jury, the police and the gaolers, and the general public knew John Thomas Smith as a human tiger, but Upfield and others had known Snowy Rowles the fearless, the happy-go-lucky, the good companion; and this morning when Upfield sat on the rock overlooking Perth, the memories of Snowy Rowles strove to triumph over the horrific memories of the recent few weeks, established by the revelations of the dual personality of John Thomas Smith.

He was the son of excellent parents. The world was his in accordance with the rules of the herd. He possessed good looks, could be gay and venturesome, easily command admiration and affection. What started him on petty crime was probably the youthful urge to show off, to become outstanding among his fellows, and, once started, he must go on to outdo his most recent exploit. With another young fellow, he had broken into a hut on a rifle range and stolen rifles and ammunition, and they escaped by car and headed north along the number one vermin fence, indulging in the 'sport' of shooting emus, and thoughtlessly endangering Upfield and his camels.

Where he had obtained the motor-cycle on which he had subsequently arrived at the Government station in time to ride unbroken mules, only the police might know, but on that day he could have wiped clean the slate of his crimes and lived free and adventurously had it not been for the 'Mr. Hyde' in his system. It was Mr. Hyde who urged him to be the big fellow, urged him to prove how good he was on a horse, on a motor-cycle. Mr. Hyde it was who spoke the words to Upfield, the sense of which Upfield could understand. He complained that his employer's wife addressed him in superior tones as 'Rowles'. He resented this, knowing he ought to have been in a much better position than he was. He resented being a hired hand, and resented owning, for he did own it, an old crock of a car. He wanted passionately to be someone, even among the far-scattered community of the east Murchison District, as he had wanted to be a figure among his youthful associates.

He had come to know all about James Ryan, that Ryan had almost completed a contract and with the money intended to go south to purchase a good utility, and even then he must have decided to do something about that promised vehicle, for he prepared minds to accept his ultimate possession of it. That he employed Ritchie's formula is indicated by the remarkable paucity of human remains and metal objects in the ashes of the fires with which Mr. Bogle had found him engaged, and had he stopped at that double murder he might well have got away with it.

But Mr. Hyde doesn't retire. Trapping foxes and hunting kangaroos requires effort, and Rowles disliked work save on the back of a stock horse.

When Louis Carron accompanied him, he had in Carron another member of the floating population, another in whom interest is slight and swiftly passing. He knew all about the bore at the one-hundred- and-seventy-three-mile peg, knew it hadn't been working for some time and that no stockmen ever went there. He knew that kangaroos had smelled water in the small tank which serviced an occupant of the hut, had lingered there until they died.

Kangaroo carcasses were an important item of the formula which Upfield and Ritchie and Upfield's friends all said was unbreakable.

The killing of Ryan and Lloyd had been so successful, so why be meticulous with the destruction of Louis Carron's body?

CHAPTER THIRTEEN

A LAMB IN THE JUNGLE

I

In 1931, when Arthur Upfield left the bush to try living by his pen, he entered the fringe of the 'jungle' in Perth, W.A., and he penetrated to the heart of the 'jungle' late the following year when he contracted to work for the *Herald* newspaper in Melbounie.

Upfield had for many years been one with people who were free personalities, people with whom to help and be helped was the first rule of life, people spiritually advanced because they were not handicapped by a struggle to survive. They were people who, from time to time, enter the 'jungle' for holiday experience, or for business reasons, and promptly leave it with thankfulness that they haven't to remain, and it was for reasons beyond ambition to earn fame and fortune that Upfield did finally immigrate to the cities.

His people, for Upfield claims to be one of them, occupy nine-tenths of a country comprising three million square miles, and representing something like one-fiftieth of the continent's population, which is about that of Greater London. Since the beginning of the century politician after politician has shouted: "We must populate or perish. We must fill our empty spaces." And ever since the coming of the petrol engine, the population occupying the nine-tenths has steadily decreased, and the one-tenth along the coasts has enormously increased.

Because living conditions in the interior are less luxurious than in the cities, and because it is so vitally essential to populate the interior in the face of the grossly over-populated countries of Asia, the ordinary person might be excused for asking why nothing has been done about it, excepting to yell slogans.

The sole objective of immigration to Australia is to fill those empty spaces, and immigrants are expected to go into the open spaces, stay there, and be damn grateful to be given the god-sent blessings of working for wages lower than those paid in the cities, plus a higher cost of living, and minus reasonable amenities. The immigrants are naturally not so stupid as to comply, and the spaces remain empty.

Under such circumstances what can be said of the seven Governments which tax a man for sinking a bore, for erecting a fence, for building a house, for compelling the Upfields, and all those mentioned in this record, to pay taxes? Instead of being placed at a great disadvantage compared to those in the cities and farming centres, they ought to be tax-free; in fact, granted a bonus to compensate for all the hardships and lack of amenities. People must be encouraged, not taxed, to populate empty spaces before the Asians do so.

To Upfield there was only one people worth tuppence, and one country worth sixpence, and as he had begun in the days of Wheeler's Well, so he determined to carry on–to tell the people outside Australia of the New Heaven within which they could throw off their economic chains and all the inhibitions born of the mania to 'keep up with the Joneses'.

This was in his mind when he arrived at the editorial offices of the Melbourne *Herald*, and was then instructed to write a racing serial!

A racing serial! Metaphorically, the 1932 Don Quixote was bucked from his donkey. He explained to Mr. Sidney Deamer that he knew nothing whatever about horse-racing, that during the rare occasions he had visited a race-course he had put a couple of shillings on a nag for its colour or the look in its eyes, and that wasn't sufficient know-how to write a racing serial. But then, editors of great newspapers are willful people, being accustomed to saying to a feature writer: "Go to the moon and give me a thousand words on the wife of the man living there," or "Give me a racing serial," to a man who didn't know a race-horse's form from a rooster's. As though asking Upfield to go out and borrow a match, Mr. Deamer continued:

"I want to begin it in three weeks. Bring in the Melbourne Cup. Don't worry about knowing nothing of racing. The racing experts on the next floor will put you right on the details."

Why not a serial on building a battleship? Why not a super-story on high life at Monte Carlo? Why not commission John Galsworthy to draw a comic strip? Mr. Deamer did not want a comic strip, nor a story of high life in Monte Carlo or anywhere else. He wanted a racing serial.So Upfield settled in and proceeded to pound a typewriter. Having to determine if the horses went round clockwise or its reverse, and matters equally important to a racing serial, and aware that he couldn't trick anyone of four-hundred-thousand racing fiends, he obtained press tickets to follow the horses on the Metropolitan courses. There he watched the races. He studied the totalisator, and lounged about close to the bookmakers' umbrellas in an effort to understand their language and the extraordinary working of their minds.

The story was born, grew, foundered, expired. It was reborn, nursed along by Desperation out of Sheer Fury. The sporting staff was sympathetic. It had taken them years and years to report a race well enough to print, and thank God they hadn't been ordered to write a racing serial to begin in three weeks. Mr. Laby, the editor of *Sporting Globe*, thought the story would turn out all right, and he suggested that Upfield write a boxing serial for him. And he wasn't being facetious, either.

Upfield grew to hate race-courses and horses and bookies and totes. No matter. The editor demanded a racing serial, and that meant seventy thousand words describing racing horses, triers, jockeys primed or innocent, tipsters, honest backers, thugs, and the hopeful punter. The Melbourne Cup race had to be in this serial. On a quiet day Upfield went out to Flemington, confessed to an official, and was permitted to study the course by walking its two full miles.

He described the running of the Melbourne Cup as from the back of one of the horses, and gave it to Cardigan to read. He described how, on coming round the turn into the straight for the last time, or something, one of the horses faltered and dropped dead, basely poisoned by the villain. When Cardigan said the description of the race might pass, he also pointed out that in a Melbourne Cup race told by Nat Gould the favourite had dropped dead through delayed-action dope.

"All right," Upfield said. "Then we'll have three horses drop dead in this one."

"That's a bit unlikely," objected Cardigan.

"Is it? Well, we'll compromise on two."

In course of labour, there was due to be born a new evening paper to be christened the *Star,* and it was tipped by the underground that the *Star* would start a racing serial with its first issue. The *Herald* had, of course, to be first, and Mr. Deamer began Upfield's racing serial on the three weeks' deadline, and when only half had been written. Upfield was appalled. What if he dropped dead before reaching the finishing post? He was tempted to argue, but then no one argues with an editor of the Melbourne *Herald.*

He had entitled his story 'The Melbourne Cup Mystery', but that was no good. It had to be 'The GREAT Melbourne Cup Mystery'. It was given more publicity than all of Nat Gould's works put together, beginning on a Saturday evening, and advertised on the display boards on every *Herald* delivery van. And the running description of the Cup, as seen through the jockey's eyes, including the dropping dead of two competitors, ran in the *Herald* on Cup Day.

For weeks Upfield refrained from looking people in the eye when he went up to the Herald restaurant for lunch. Nothing was said. 'The Great Melbourne Cup Mystery' was just another racing serial, just another job of work. No infuriated racing fan wrote a withering protest to the editor, and the all-powerful controller, Sir Keith Murdoch, didn't invite the author to dinner.

2

Beside Mr. Sidney Deamer, Upfield received encouragement from Mr. Ralph Simmonds, then assistant editor, and next he wrote special articles for the magazine section and for column four of the leading article page. He wrote of the aboriginal problems, and of the neglected opportunities of development of the interior, and when he came up with a series of articles on outback adventures, this series was announced on the contents bills and on the delivery vans. It was so successful that it was followed by a second series, and the serialised version of a Napoleon Bonaparte case.

At the end of six months he had had approximately two hundred thousand words in the Melbourne *Herald*. He was met one morning by a director who clapped him on the back and said: "We're making a good journalist out of you." Three days later, Upfield was sacked. The order had not been given by the editors, but someone higher, and the hidden reason was never unearthed by the victim. Thereafter his articles were accepted, but on the lineage rate of tuppence-farthing, and he was confronted by the necessity of living by free-lance work or returning to the bush.

Actually, Upfield wasn't equipped for the 'jungle', the heart of which can be found in a newspaper office or within the literary world hanging on the outskirts. To many self-important people in the newspaper world, Upfield had come up too fast, and, moreover, he wasn't university, and had no social background. He was merely an unshorn lamb that had wandered in from the back paddock.

However, at the end of his six months at the *Herald* office he had many friends on the staff, and his name was familiar to the people of Melbourne and the State of Victoria, but his six novels published in London could not be termed financially successful, and the seventh had been declined by the publishers. Altogether, his future appeared far from brilliant.

He had received a few letters from readers, either congratulating him or asking how to have a book published, and one day came a letter from a writer signing herself Florence March. She reminded Upfield that he had known her many years before and she longed to meet him again. He wouldn't know her married name, and would he consent to lunch with her at Menzies Hotel?

Inborn curiosity drove Upfield to accept this invitation, and he met the woman in the hotel lounge. She was well dressed, matronly, exceedingly pleasant to look upon, and faintly he was reminded of someone although sure he had never previously met her. She said:

"I would have easily recognised you in the street. Don't you really remember me?"

"I must be slipping," he excused himself. "I have prided myself on never forgetting a pretty woman."

"Just the same Arthur Upfield, quick with the blarney." She giggled, and that reminded Upfield again of someone whose mental picture he could not focus. She said:

"You did work on Koondee Station, didn't you?"

He nodded.

"You must remember Mrs. Early and her daughter-Florence?"

"Florence! You are Florence Early!"

She giggled, delightfully, and Upfield began to chuckle. Laughter swayed them, and the drink waiter glanced their way. The laughter went on in this very exclusive lounge, and neither could control it, or wanted to.

Florence Early! Mrs. Early had been housekeeper at the homestead of Koondee, a station property out from Bourke, and

Florence had assisted as housemaid.

In local terminology, Upfield had proceeded to try her out, and eventually she consented to take a walk with him beside the billabong.

She was decidedly good-looking, a brunette, and about twenty years old. And, in accordance with the technique of those times, he proceeded with caution.

The evening came when he decided to storm the citadel, and was repulsed. He attacked again some evenings later, and again was thrown back in confusion. Florence wasn't that kind of girl, and if Arthur didn't behave himself these walks in the gloaming would have to stop.

Arthur did behave. They continued 'walking out', going about a mile along the billabong to its junction with the river, where they sat on a fallen red-gum, and, of many subjects, talked of art, as Florence had a natural aptitude for drawing. Upfield lounged and smoked his pipe and afterwards they returned to the house, where Florence permitted a chaste kiss before going in.

Innocent little girl with a satyr! One evening Upfield suggested sitting on a different log, and one not far from the house. It was a little late–the opportunity to play a dirty trick. It seemed to happen that where Florence Early placed her feet that night there was a green-ants' nest. These ants are not large, and they are silent walkers on the flesh, and it wasn't long before Florence bounded up, emitted a stifled scream and raced for home and mother.

Meanwhile, Upfield, sure there were no silent walkers prospecting him, permitted half an hour to elapse before he entered the kitchen, where Mrs. Early told him her daughter was in a 'frightful state', having been bitten all over by green ants. Expressing concern, Upfield asked what she had done about it and Mrs. Early replied that she had dabbed the marks with ammonia. Poor Florence was then lying down in her room.

"Ammonia!" exclaimed Upfield. "That's no good for green-ant bites. There is only the one remedy for them."

He strode to the bedroom door, and Mrs. Early protested unheard. She followed Upfield into the girl's room, where he pulled the mouthpiece from his pipe, and, professionally, swept back the sheet, pulled up the nightdress, and dabbed the bites with nicotine, actually quite a good antidote. The girl wriggled but was held down with one hand. Again the mother's protest was ignored. Having attended to the patient, Doctor Upfield pulled down the nightdress, pulled up the sheet, tucked it about the patient, kissed her and gravely departed.

Now their eyes clashed again across the luncheon table, and they renewed the struggle to suppress their laughter. The lunch was wholly successful, and over coffee Florence said, again with suppressed giggles, she was a 'respectable' married woman, that her husband was an oil company executive, and that they had five children.

Her memory was more alive than Upfield's and, when waiting for a taxi, she asked: "Do you remember what you said the next time we went for a walk down by the billabong?"

"What did I say?"

"That Aristotle believed that fighting a virgin is work fit only for a coal-heaver. And then you said you might go to Newcastle to learn to be a coal-heaver."

"I did not."

"You did. A girl doesn't forget," and, still smiling, she said: "Good-bye."

Upfield watched her taxi weaving down Bourke Street, and when walking, with plenty of time to catch a train, he felt Wandering Millie tug at his heart and heard her whisper: "Give all this back to the jungle dwellers. Pack your traps, and come again with me."

The Temptress often nudged and whispered. She would come with the north wind. She would appear like Aladdin's genie in the smoke from burning gum leaves in the gardens, and beckon from the hot sunset in late autumn. Money was scarce with Upfield, and in Melbourne money is so necessary, and sometimes Wandering Millie would appear and say: "Let's go bush again where there's no such thing as money."

Money! Len Sayers oozed money. He wore a light-grey suit, and a light-grey Panama hat to match. He wore expensive shoes and a tie to make young men envious. When Upfield had last seen him, the seat was out of his trousers, although he did own a readymade suit. Now on his wrist was a valuable gold watch, and on his face the satisfied smile of the tycoon.

"Fancy meeting you on Collins Street," he said. "Come and have a drink. The wife! Oh, she's fine. You'll have to come out some time. She'll be glad to see you."

The saltbush plain, with Broken Hill just over the humped horizon- here Len Sayers had recently been granted fifty thousand acres by the Lands Board. Already his few pounds were sunk in cleaning out a dam and building a shack, and he was short of the necessary deposit on the purchase of sheep to stock the selection.

Two hundred pounds would buy a thousand ewes on terms. Upfield had the money, Len had the land and the small dam recently filled by a quick rain. They having reached agreement on percentages, the sheep were brought to graze on the selection. That summer was hot, as usual, and lucky thunderstorms maintained the water in the dam, to bring up green feed which the hot winds swiftly burned away.

The March rain failed to come, and so did the April rains, and the May and June rains. Len was a good shearer, and Upfield was the rest. Spring came again but no rain. Len's wife would look at the sunset and say:

"It'll rain soon." Or look up at the clouds which never blocked out the sun and say: "It'll rain soon."

She was always wrong. The sheep died, and Upfield and Len skinned them for skins, worth only a shilling or two. The flock slowly dwindled. The sheep came in long lines, staggering to the dam, and in longer lines staggered away to the poor feed where there was no surface water. The long walk, to water and back to feed, in their weakened condition, was the killer. They would fill themselves with water at the trough, lie down, and never get up again.

And Len's heroically optimistic wife: "Look, it's going to rain soon."

When of the thousand ewes there were but a hundred left, Upfield pulled out, packing a swag on his bike, and resigned to cutting his loss. It rained the following month. Two years after that Len repaid Upfield his money. And six years after that Len sold out for thirty-odd thousand pounds. That wasn't luck. It was faith. A woman's faith.

3

The local *literati* Upfield could not understand, and quickly they rejected him. He attended a few of their gatherings, and met personally several whose novels had been reviewed in the Also Ran columns of *The Times Literary Supplement*. He was presented to lofty people who wrote poetry, or had written paragraphs for the *Bulletin*, and those who had produced a short story or two which was awarded something or other by a literary society. They were nice people, but when they came to discuss Australian literature they were intolerable.

These people never wrote for money! Oh no! They referred to themselves and their fellows as creative writers. Charles Dickens was regarded as a commercial writer of sentimental slop, and the only really great writers owned Russian names. In the press they lauded the work of their fellows, and in return were lauded; for this was at the close of a short era when tenth-rate Australian novels had been praised as works of high literary merit, and the swindled public threatened to knock down a bookseller or librarian who offered one.

A brighter era began when a new kind of writer emerged to revive the interest of Australians in their own authors. Almost simultaneously, Angus & Robertson published two books which swept across the Continent. They were *Sheepmates* by William Hatfield, and *Lassiter's Last Ride* by Ion Idriess. And in Western Australia there was a woman, Katharine Susannah Prichard, writing exceedingly well of the north of that great State; and because these three writers influenced the Australian people to read them, the works of other able writers independent of the *claqueurs* came into favour.

Among these was Arthur Upfield. And the man behind this renaissance was the managing director of Angus & Robertson, Mr. Walter Cousins. He published eight of Upfield's Napoleon Bonaparte series before the beginning of the Second War.

Immediately Hitler went to market, there swung into action the nucleus of the war-time departments and organisations. And a man approached Upfield saying:

"We can use your criminal mind. Come hither."

After the American boys arrived in Australia, another man said: "Look! America is cabling for special articles and stories from Australia, as the people over there are keen to know all about us now their lads are here. Why don't you push some of your books across?"

Upfield wrote to Walter Cousins, who despatched six titles to his firm's agents in New York. They gained a contract from Doubleday & Company, under which these publishers would issue four titles and take an option on the other two.

The history of one of these books provides interest. It was the seventh book submitted to Upfield's London publishers, and one which they declined. It was published by Angus & Robertson, Sydney, in the mid 'thirties and sold steadily. It never appeared in Great Britain. It was the same book as chosen by Doubleday & Company to introduce a half-aborigine detective to the United States, and it sold 22,000 copies at the time when America was beginning to feel the paper shortage. And Upfield received the best press notices of his career up to that date. Despite the fact that paper became more and more restricted, Upfield's books continued to appear in America, and when the war ended, eight of his titles had been issued. Now came the crisis. When American servicemen returned to the States, when American interest had switched to Japan, what would happen to Napoleon Bonaparte?

Bonaparte had been properly launched in America. Would he hold the position gained now the peace had come?

Not only did he hold it, he increased it, and has maintained steady popularity ever since. His sales and his press notices clearly prove how right Upfield was in that early beginning, when he set out to tell of the real Australia. His faith was justified.

There were no spectacular heights of literary success, no enormous sales figures in the category of *The Robe*, no colossal film offers. From the beginning his fan mail has been steady, and the notepaper establishes that the great majority of writers are in the upper brackets of American life. A daughter of one of Doubleday's executives was a student at Harvard University when Ernest Rooton, Professor of Anthropology, urged his class to study Upfield's Napoleon Bonaparte, and commented for publication:

> "Mr. Upfield is a shrewd anthropological observer as well as a skilful novelist. 'Bony', his half-caste aboriginal detective, is an unique figure in this class of literature."

The war over, there arose a problem Upfield decided would have to be dealt with. The problem would still have arisen if, when he first came to Melbourne, he had doffed his hat and pulled his forelock to the literary *claqueurs* and sycophants. But why should he bow to those reasonably successful writers whose efforts were in no wise superior to his own, as proved by *The Times Literary Supplement*?

They knew of his success in America, knew of his position during the war years, and when peace came there was indubitable evidence, in the word or two dropped to Upfield, in the changed attitude of people he had known in the writing world, of a whispering campaign. There broke a widespread agitation, worked up by the *claqueurs,* to restrict English books from entering the country, on the ground that free imports almost wiped out local books. A Commission was set up to report on this matter, and there was, of course, almost universal protest by the press and by individuals at the proposal to curtail the entry of overseas literature.

Naturally the Commission declined to recommend restriction of imported books, to favour writers of any class or quality, but it did recommend the creation of a Literary Fund for the purpose of assisting authors of special books which normally would be difficult to publish because of the limited reader-interest. And the leaders of the *claqueurs* received appointments under the new scheme.

Upfield could afford to ignore this set-up of literary dictatorship, but other writers were dismayed, and none dared buck.

"You couldn't break a window," sneered the Leader of the Push.
"I'll pull your ruddy house down," yelled The Bastard from the Bush.

And he wrote *An Author Bites the Dust,* in which a literary *claqueur* was bumped off with coffin dust.

This book didn't topple a windmill when published enthusiastically by Walter Cousins, and it never earned a million dollars overseas, where it was published in the United States, and subsequently in Germany and Mexico, but it did make a windmill tremble, and it did begin a resistance movement which demolished "a house" in the Commonwealth Parliament on the afternoon of August 28th, 1952, and caused another to be built.

4

In the 'jungle' on the coasts of Australia, they talk sometimes of the great Australian novel to come, the magnificent play yet to be written, as though in such a jungle, where the tendency is to drag everyone down to the lowest level, there could emerge another Tolstoy, another Shakespeare.

Although for years now Upfield has lived close to the 'jungle' he has never been a part of it, and still quite often Wandering Millie makes an assault on him, sometimes coming within an ace of conquering him, as she did when literally she pushed Bill Saunders against him in Little Collins Street one afternoon.

They recognised each other instantly, although neither had seen the other for thirty years. Upfield had leaned his bike against the verandah post of a wayside hotel, and entered to meet Saunders, the licensee, and his wife. He had been staying there on a cheque spent in an orderly manner, when Mrs. Saunders, infected by the city fever, packed and left for Adelaide on the motor mail coach.

Times were quiet, trade was slow. Bill caught the fever from his wife and also cleared away to Adelaide. Upfield was left in charge of the pub and no change in the till, and three weeks elapsed before they returned together on the mail coach, broke wide open, more than a little anxious about the stock and the till. They found the bar full of customers, the till overflowing and more money under the mattress of their bed. They found Upfield still on his feet, and a ruffian called Paroo Charlie installed as cook, and the rum oozing from his ears.

Now in his early sixties, Arthur Upfield is remarkably virile mentally and physically; he has a fondness for good brandy, but after such indulgence is unable to write a line. He must have inherited a strong constitution, for even today he smokes five or six cigarettes and drinks five or six cups of tea before breakfast. Outwardly arrogant, he is inwardly humble; welcomes friends generously and dislikes meeting strangers, unless they have the stamp of the inland upon them. He takes his work seriously; himself never. He invariably refers to himself as 'the famous ruddy author', and his notepaper used for special occasions bears the headlines: 'All fame and no bloody money'. He admires the work of John Steinbeck, and fully appreciates classics such as the unexpurgated editions of *The Decameron* and *The Arabian Nights*.

Squirrel-like, Upfield enthusiastically builds provision for winter fires, from which he refuses to budge for anyone, especially resisting calls to the cities, which he loathes with a great loathing. Yet he is no squirrel with money. Money comes slowly, and departs at the millionaire rate. He has no patience with snobs, and by social climbers on the ladder of books he is disgusted.

A great writer? No. By the world's yard stick a great man? Of course not. A born story-teller? His critics have said so. What has he achieved against all his failures? Let him tell you.

"Only after years of varied experience did I come to understand that all the inland people had undergone a re-moulding in a common mould, and this indicated a Moulder. Who or what is the Moulder? I know the answer, and for thirty years have striven to express it, without success because only a Milton can create the image for men to see That Which Is.

"However, I do claim a measure of success in the portrayal of the re-moulded Man by stressing the attributes of Tracker Leon and adding those of the One Spur Dicks, the Larries and their Emilies, and all those others the readers of this work will have encountered. I have named this composite man Napoleon Bonaparte, and I have never submerged his duality of race. I have brought him from his native background, and prodded him over the colour bar to be welcomed by the people of the Americas, the United Kingdom and of Europe."

Upfield's friends can tell when his feet itch for the outback tracks, and the danger signs are clear when he is found gazing at a sunset, gazing intently at gathering clouds, or when he slips an unlighted cigarette to a neighbour's pet sheep. He is often aware of his limitations, often acutely conscious of his inability to see beyond the mirage and to tell of what he knows is beyond it. He would have returned to the inland once again to push a bike carrying a swag and a billy-can, and a pup or a cat in a sugar-bag, were it not for the reason which has trapped the feet of so many wanderers:

> 'Won't you stay and walk with me?
> Won't you write and work with me?
> Don't you like my red-gold hair,
> My eyes, my mouth, my heart–just me?'

www.ingramcontent.com/pod-product-compliance
Lightning Source LLC
Chambersburg PA
CBHW050336170426
43200CB00009BA/1623